ESTATE PLANNING
FOR *Small Business Owners*

BOND, SCHOENECK & KING, PLLC
ATTORNEYS AT LAW ▪ NEW YORK   FLORIDA   KANSAS

John, Enjoy! I worked with George on a few matters — He was very effective — Bob.

PRENTICE HALL
Englewood Cliffs, New Jersey 07632

Prentice-Hall International (UK) Limited, *London*
Prentice-Hall of Australia Pty. Limited, *Sydney*
Prentice-Hall Canada, Inc., *Toronto*
Prentice-Hall Hispanoamericana, S.A., *Mexico*
Prentice-Hall of India Private Limited, *New Delhi*
Prentice-Hall of Japan, Inc., *Tokyo*
Simon & Schuster Asia Pte. Ltd., *Singapore*
Editora Prentice-Hall do Brasil, Ltda., *Rio de Janeiro*

© 1993 by

George C. Shattuck

10 9 8 7 6 5 4 3 2 1

Library of Congress Cataloging-in-Publication Data

Shattuck, George C.
  Estate Planning for Small Business Owners/George C. Shattuck.
    p.   cm.
  Includes index.
  ISBN 0-13-285461-9

  1. Estate planning—United States. 2. Inheritance and transfer
tax—Law and legislation —United States. 3. Small business—
Taxation—Law and legislation—United States. I. Title.
KF750.S46 1993
343.7305'3—dc20   93-16846
[347.30353]   CIP

ISBN 0-13-285461-9

PRENTICE HALL
Career and Personal Development
Englewood Cliffs, NJ 07632
Simon & Schuster, A Paramount Communications Company

Printed in the United States of America

FOR CARLA AND MORGAN

THE AUTHOR

George C. Shattuck is a graduate of the Syracuse University College of Law and has over 39 years of experience in all matters associated with federal and state tax laws. His law practice has emphasized estate planning related to closely held corporations, but he also has years of experience in the tax issues of business sale and acquisition transactions, tax assessment disputes and tax litigation. Unlike many persons who write about estate planning, Mr. Shattuck worked with families in the probate, administration and audit of estates, where he did the predeath drafting and planning. This is not just numbers, it is working with people to implement the plans he has conceived. Mr. Shattuck has been recognized by a listing in *The Best Lawyers In America*.

In addition to tax law, Shattuck achieved great success in representing the Oneida Indian Nation in land claims against New York State. His 1974 victory in the United States Supreme Court overturned 200 years of precedent against such Indian claims.

George Shattuck has always enjoyed a good challenge. So when he read early in his career that it was impossible to create a slide rule to calculate income and estate taxes, he simply invented one. "Keep in mind that this was before the age of calculators," Shattuck explains. "My slide rule proved to be a fast and quite accurate substitute for the high-tech electronic devices we have access to today. As a matter of fact, I still find myself using one to do quick estate tax computations."

This "can do" approach is demonstrated in his book.

INTRODUCTION

Business Succession Problems—
This Book Solves Them

Your successful business has an inherent problem of management and ownership succession in the event you, the business owner, die, retire, or become disabled. This book is written to help you recognize and think through the succession issues. It is directly addressed to you, the owner. Your professional advisers (lawyer, accountant, insurance expert, trust officer, and financial adviser) may also read it with benefit, but it is not directed to them.

As time goes on, values that you have built up by your creativity and years of hard work are subject to two increasing risks:

- a lack of management ready to take your place at any time when you, the owner, cannot function; and
- the ruinous burden of estate taxes.

Both risks can be reduced significantly if you plan carefully for ownership succession and tax reduction. This book explains in concrete detail the way you can best approach and solve these worrisome problems.

Estate Planning for Small Business Owners focuses on the tax and financial problems involved in transferring business ownership to the next generation. It presents a serious, practical tool to enable the reader to extract useful information.

The initial thrust of this book is how to minimize, defer, and fund estate taxes. *With estate tax rates in excess of 50 percent, few businesses can survive if the full tax must be paid out of the business at the owner's death.* But, there are ways to surmount this problem. This book explains the estate tax problems and then offers practical and effective solutions. There are tried-and-true techniques which you can explore here, understand, and then implement with counsel from your professional advisors.

Taxes are a cost which must be met and can be met. However, providing for taxes is only part of the picture. In a family business situation, the death, retirement, or disability of the managing owner can be a greater disaster than the tax bill. As you progress through the book, you will learn how to attract and keep valuable key employees. You will understand the very difficult task of dividing your estate in an equitable way among the children who manage the business and are responsible for its continuance, and your other children who may view the business as a source of wealth apart from their own labors.

Can one short book do all this? Yes. This book will not make you a tax expert. On the contrary, you should leave the details of implementation to your professional advisors. What the book will do is alert you to the problems, explain alternate solutions, and give you access to practical answers expressed in plain language. This book contains no Internal Revenue Code sections, no case citations, no footnotes. It reads like a business letter and not like a law review article.

The tax law is a changing and evolving thing. What is written today may be incomplete, or even incorrect a year from now. However, the statement of concepts will remain accurate. You should consult your professional advisors at all times to remain current on the application of the concepts.

You will not have to flip back and forth to obtain information on a given point. This book is arranged topically with information presented by subject matter, broadly by parts which are subdivided into more focused chapters and sections. However, the topical format presents a challenge: make the text readable to the business-oriented person who has little or no information on the subject. We believe this challenge is met.

The structure of the book is designed to present first a topical, subject-by-subject discussion of estate planning for the owner of a business. This will enable the reader to extract useful, practical information and to learn the basic concepts. Then the information is pulled together in a case study about the success of two fictional business owners and their electronics business. Their reaction to the estate planning process will help you understand that this is a very human process, based ultimately on the wishes of the business owners rather than the dictates of the IRS rules.

George C. Shattuck

ACKNOWLEDGMENTS

Thanks to Ms. Jan Jinske for her expert and willing work in typing and correcting the drafts, and assembling the various components, of what we now call a book. That is the kind of basic construction that keeps the tip of the iceberg above the water.

Thanks to Ms. Stephanie Laris for her creative work on the illustrations, and to Ann Schneid, CPA, Mary Meyer, CPA, and Marsha Ashman, CPA, for their indispensable work on the computer printouts that, unseen, underpin much of the text. My thanks to Barbara Baker, who typed the early drafts of the Case Study.

J. Warren Young, CLU, Ch.F.P., (the Joe Warren of the Case Study), was most helpful in furnishing the insurance information and in helping me understand the various options of insurance investment.

The efforts of Ms. Bonita K. Nelson, Literary Agent, and Ms. Ruth Mills, Editor, have helped turn a set of ideas into a publishable book.

Finally, thanks to the lawyers of Bond, Schoeneck & King, Law Firm, who helped me complete this book. Arthur E. Bongiovanni, Esq. contributed significantly to Part One. Jack Capron, CPA, Esq., Daniel Gallagher, Esq. and Martin Schwab, CPA, Esq. contributed significantly to Part Two. William Burke, Esq. and Stephen J. Ford, Esq. contributed significantly to Part Three. Stephen C. Daley, Esq. contributed significantly to Part Four. Gary R. Germain CPA, Esq. and James E. Mackin, Esq. contributed significantly to Part Five.

CONTENTS

Introduction: Business Succession Problems—This Book Solves Them . .v

Part One: How to Reduce and Defer Estate Taxes 1

    Chapter 1:   The Impact of Estate Taxes: Your Silent
                  Parnter Is Uncle Sam (3)
    Chapter 2:   Using the Unlimited Marital Deduction
                  to Defer Estate Taxes (9)
    Chapter 3:   Using Gifts to Reduce Estate Taxes (21)
    Chapter 4:   Managers or Owners? How to Divide
                  a Business Among the Family (35)

Part Two: How to Prepare for the Estate Tax Burden 41

    Chapter 5:   How to Fund Taxes with Tax-Free Life
                  Insurance (43)
    Chapter 6:   How to Defer Tax Payments to the IRS (53)
    Chapter 7:   Using the Business as a Source of Tax
                  Funds (65)

Part Three: How to Freeze Your Estate 71

    Chapter 8:   Determining the Value of Your Business
                  for Estate Tax Purposes (73)
    Chapter 9:   How to Give Away Future Company
                  Growth, but Keep Control and Security (89)
    Chapter 10:   Using the Preferred Stock Freeze to Save
                  Taxes (99)
    Chapter 11:   Sale of Stock to Children (111)
    Chapter 12:   Using the Partnership Freeze to Save
                  Taxes (117)
    Chapter 13:   Will a Freeze Save Your Family Business
                  or Impair it? (123)

Part Four: How to Keep Your Key Employees .151

      Chapter 14:   Offering Stock Options, Restricted Stock,
                      and Phantom Stock as Incentives to Key
                      Employees (153)
      Chapter 15:   How Key Employees Can Aquire Stock
                      Painlessly—Use the Bonus-Out (167)
      Chapter 16:   The ESOP and the Stock Bonus Plan (179)
      Chapter 17:   Comparing Stock-Based Incentive Plans (187)

Part Five: How to Achieve a Smooth Management Transition 191

      Chapter 18:   Buy, Sell, and Redemption Agreements: Sale
                      of Stock to Others (193)
      Chapter 19:   Succession Planning for a Smooth Transition
                      (207)

**Part Six: Case Study: Estate Planning for KayJim Electronic
    Devices, Inc.** 215

      Chapter 20:   Building a Successful Business (217)
      Chapter 21:   The Business as "Star Performer": 10 Years
                      Later (239)
      Chapter 22:   The "Colossus": Estate Planning for the
                      $25-30 Million Business (259)

Epilogue 285

Glossary 287

Index 289

Part One

HOW TO REDUCE AND DEFER ESTATE TAXES

CHAPTER 1. The Impact of Estate Taxes: Your Silent Partner Is Uncle Sam

CHAPTER 2. Using the Unlimited Marital Deduction to Defer Estate Taxes

CHAPTER 3. Using Gifts to Reduce Estate Taxes

CHAPTER 4. Managers or Owners? How to Divide a Business Among the Family

Part One explains the estate tax and describes the basic structure of estate planning for business interests. This basic plan relies on two features.

First, an estate gets an unlimited deduction for property passing to a surviving spouse. All property left to a spouse (one dollar, ten million dollars, or whatever) goes tax free. This permits deferring the entire federal tax till the spouse dies. The gift to the spouse can be outright, or in a trust from which the spouse receives all the income for life.

Second, up to $600,000 of each spouse's property is also exempt from tax no matter who it goes to, so that $1,200,000 of both spouses' property can go to the children and be sheltered from all estate taxes.

Thus, we plan both to use the two $600,000 exemptions as a shelter, and to defer all tax on the remaining property until the spouse dies. In addition, a consistent gift policy can shelter large amounts of property from both estates.

1

The Impact of Estate Taxes: Your Silent Partner Is Uncle Sam

Estate taxes are a cost of doing business. If you own your own business and you want to pass it on to the next generation, an ultimate estate tax of 37 to 55 percent of the business value must be paid. Some states add several percentage points to those rates. These estate tax rates are based on values attained after years of paying income taxes on business profits. If you have a business at a given value now, and it grows at 10 percent, the eventual estate tax bite—Uncle Sam's share—will look like Figure 1.1.

The Tax Burden on Growth

That 10 percent growth looks steep on paper, but it is not unrealistic. Take an historic cost of dollar inflation, say 5 percent, and another few percentage points for real growth of your business and you easily have an 8 percent or 10 percent overall dollar growth. So, starting from now when your business is worth $2 million, you eventually pay an estate tax based on the $2 million plus a further tax on any growth your work imparts to the $2 million. Whatever your business is worth now, future growth is subject to tax at rates of 37 to 55 percent or more.

Our politicians profess fondness for small business, the family business, emerging growth companies, and the family farm. That is good politics perhaps, but the fact is that the estate tax is poised to extract the vital capital of a business at the very time it has lost its founder, or its driving force. This book is based on the premise that the federal estate tax is a moving, growing cost, sure to take its toll on future value increases, but also as sudden and capricious as death. To convey this sweep of time from now to the future you

3

Figure 1.1. Uncle Sam's 50 Percent Share of Future Business Growth

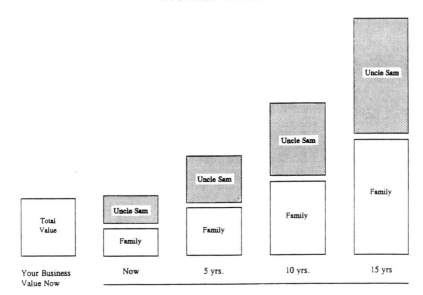

will find here many graphs and tables, all showing the relation of growth to increased tax. This leads to the conclusion that the most efficient way to escape the tax burden is to let part or all of the future growth be owned by someone else, such as the next generation. You will learn how to accomplish that without loss of control of your future security.

How the Estate Tax Works

The estate tax is imposed on the value of property transferred at death of the property's owner. Virtually all property is included in the "Gross Estate," house, stocks and bonds, cash, realty, personal property, life insurance owned by the decedent, and about everything else you can think of. From the Gross Estate you are allowed certain deductions, for example, debts, mortgages, and administration expenses. There is also allowed an unlimited marital deduction for property which passes to a surviving spouse.

Finally, there is a tax credit allowed that has the effect of a further $600,000 deduction from the lowest tax brackets. To keep things simple, this $600,000 is referred to here as the $600,000 exemption and illustrated as a deduction from the estate to arrive at the tax.

After all the deductions have been subtracted from the Gross Estate, the balance (i.e., the taxable estate) is multiplied by the progressive tax rates, which range from 37 to 55 percent, federal, plus additional tax in some states. (In New York State, the total federal and state tax on large estates can

Figure 1.2. Tax Structure of a $2.25 Million Estate

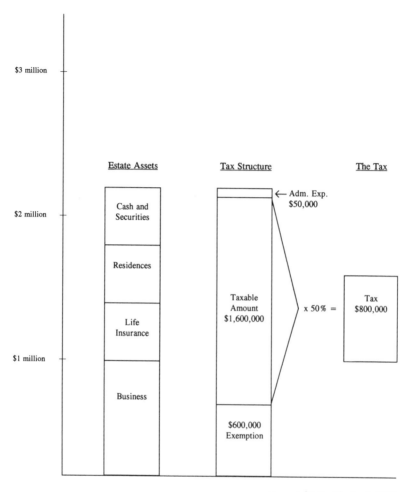

range to over 60 percent.) In graphic form, the tax structure looks like Figure 1.2, which shows how deductions are applied to a $2.25 million estate to arrive at a tax.

Tax Payment

The federal estate tax is due and payable nine months after death. A credit is allowable for state taxes paid. Under certain conditions described later in this book, payment of the federal tax may be deferred for up to 14 years. Interest is charged on any such deferral.

The Gift Tax

For many years there were separate estate and gift taxes, each with its own brackets and rates. In lifetime, you would start with low gift tax rates and go up the scale of brackets. Then, on death, the estate tax rates started again at low brackets. As might be expected, Congress eventually lumped the taxes together into one unified tax. So the estate tax rates now start where the gift tax rates left off, and the overall tax burden is increased. To achieve this, law requires that all prior taxable gifts must be reported in one's estate tax return. (A gift under $10,000 is not considered a taxable gift for this purpose.)

The $600,000 exemption also applies to gift taxes. You can give away $600,000 during your lifetime, paying no federal gift tax. However, once $600,000 has been used up by gifts, it is no longer available to reduce estate taxes when you die. The 37 percent bracket starts right after the $600,000 exemption; a $610,000 gift costs $3,700 in gift taxes.

In addition to the $600,000 exemption, you also can give up to $10,000 to any number of persons once a year. This is known as the "$10,000 annual exclusion." Such gifts are not taxable and do not serve to reduce the $600,000 exemption. There is no three-year "contemplation of death" rule anymore (except for life insurance).

No return is required on gifts of $10,000 or less. But you do have to file a return and pay a tax if one is due, on any gift over $10,000. The gift tax return is due April 15 of the year following the year of the gift.

Gift Splitting with Spouse

With your spouse's consent you can use his or her $10,000 annual exclusion and $600,000 exemption. If you have five children or other persons you want to make gifts to, you could give away $1,300,000 with no federal tax. For example,

Two $600,000 exemptions	$1,200,000
Five $20,000 annual exclusions	100,000
Total gifts free of federal tax	$1,300,000

Note: Not all states have this mix of exemption and exclusions for purposes of state gift taxes. On a gift of $1,300,000 you would have a tax in some states.

As stated before, the $600,000 exemption is available only one time, whether applied during life or in the estate. You can't elect to use the $600,000 or not on a given gift. If a gift exceeds the allowable annual exclusions, the excess is immediately applied to reduce the $600,000. This is not bad, it's good because the earlier the $600,000 is used the better, taxwise. (See Chapter 3.)

Table 1.1. Use of $600,000 Exemption

	No Prior Taxable Gifts	$600,000 of Prior Gifts
Gross estate, now	$2,250,000	$1,650,000
Plus prior taxable gifts	0	600,000
Total, gifts added back	$2,250,000	$2,250,000
Deduction for administration expenses	(50,000)	(50,000)
Balance	$2,200,000	$2,200,000
Exemption	(600,000)	(600,000)
Taxable	$1,600,000	$1,600,000
Tax @ 50%	$ 800,000	$ 800,000

Table 1.1 shows how the interplay of gifts and of estate taxes works in practice.

This table seems to indicate that there is no point in making such gifts during life. What Table 1.1 does not show is that the *growth* on the $600,000 lifetime gift is excluded from the estate—only the $600,000 gift amount is added back in the right hand column and to the value at date of death.

Summary

The point of this chapter is the huge burden that estate taxes lay on your business. Success is not rewarded, it is taxed. A partnership has been imposed on you, and Uncle Sam is your partner, your senior partner.

The federal estate tax rates vary from 37 to 55 percent, and some states taxes add several percentage points to that. However, to keep things simple, we will use a 50 percent rate in examples throughout this book.

If you follow the legal rules carefully, *you can defer and significantly reduce this tax*. You can make Uncle Sam a junior partner. The following chapter discusses a very important device to defer and reduce taxes.

2

Using the Unlimited Marital Deduction to Defer Estate Taxes

If you can't legally avoid a tax, the next best thing is to defer it. The tax law permits an unlimited deduction for property passing, by gift or through an estate, to a surviving spouse. It is then taxed in the spouse's estate at his or her death. The effect of this is that payment of the tax may be deferred for as long as the spouse lives. This is very important to the economic well-being of a family, even though the value may appreciate to the time of death of the second spouse. Remember, the spouse if he or she lives long enough may be able significantly to reduce the tax through a program of gifts.

How the Marital Deduction Works

Chapter 1 omits a very significant deduction, the unlimited marital deduction for property which passes to the surviving spouse either outright or in a qualifying trust. Even a $100 million estate would escape federal tax if the property were all left to the surviving spouse. The marital deduction also applies to gifts to your spouse during lifetime. One spouse can give the other an unlimited amount without gift tax if the gift is outright or in a trust which qualifies for the marital deduction.

Table 2.1 shows how the marital deduction works to reduce an estate with a large potential tax to one with zero tax.

Figure 2.1 corresponds to the numbers in this table and shows how the marital deduction fits in the basic structure of the federal estate tax system: start with all the assets of the decedent, subtract available deductions and then compute the tax on the balance; in this case zero. (Compare this with Figure 1.2, which uses the same assets but no marital deduction.) In Figure

Table 2.1. The Marital Deduction

Estate Assets, First Spouse to Die

Total Estate	$2,250,000
Administration Expenses	(50,000)
Balance	2,200,000
Marital Deduction = Bequest to Spouse	(2,200,000)
Balance	0
Exemption	(600,000)
Taxable	0
Tax @ 50%	0

Figure 2.1. The Marital Deduction Structure Two Estates

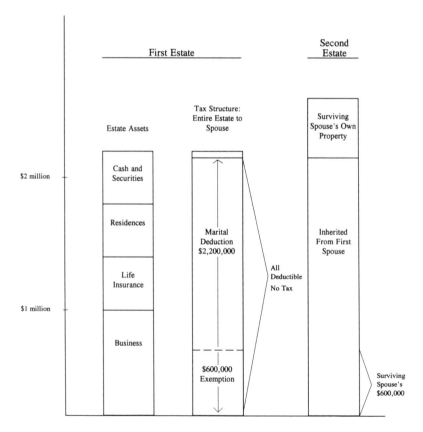

Copyright G. Shattuck 1992

2.1 the surviving spouse's estate consists of his or her own assets plus the net assets inherited from the first spouse. This total is taxable after taking into account that spouse's own $600,000 exemption.

As you can see from Table 2.1 and Figure 2.1, the first spouse's $600,000 exemption is "wasted" because it overlaps with the marital deduction. This does not matter in the first estate, but it does matter in the surviving spouse's estate. On the facts used above, the surviving spouse's estate would be taxed as follows:

Table 2.2. The Surviving Spouse's Estate

Assets inherited from spouse	$2,200,000
Survivor's own assets, assume	500,000
Survivor's estate	$2,700,000
Administration expenses	(50,000)
Balance	$2,650,000
Marital deduction (not applicable)	0
Balance	$2,650,000
Exemption	(600,000)
Taxable	$2,050,000
Tax @ 50%	$1,025,000

In Table 2.2 the surviving spouse inherited the whole $2,200,000 from the first spouse, all of which was included in the survivor's estate. If the first spouse had used the $600,000 exemption, and not given that $600,000 to the spouse, the survivor's estate would have been reduced by that amount.

Don't Waste That $600,000 Exemption

In Table 2.2 the whole $2,200,000 left to the spouse is deductible in the first estate. This marital deduction is unlimited. The catch is that the entire amount, and the entire growth from it, will be taxed in the surviving spouse's estate.

Another catch is that the initial $600,000 exemption is wasted because it overlaps the marital deduction. It was used on property that was already tax free. Is there a way to utilize the $600,000 exemption in the first estate and leave that property out of the second estate? Yes. You could leave the entire $600,000 to the children, skipping the surviving spouse's estate. This does not increase tax in the first estate, but saves $300,000 of tax at 50 percent in the surviving spouse's estate because the $600,000 is never in the second estate. If the $600,000 is invested and appreciates to $800,000 by the time the surviving spouse dies, you would have saved the children $400,000 in taxes in the second estate.

Suppose, however, that you do not want to exclude your spouse from that $600,000 because it may be needed for support. Set up a trust for the spouse under which the spouse gets income for life, and trust principal if needed. Only after the spouse's death does the trust go to the children. Such a trust may be excluded from the surviving spouse's estate by electing not to

Table 2.3. The Bypass Trust

	Case A	Case B	Case C
	Entire estate to spouse*	$600,000 to the children	$600,000 to a bypass trust for spouse
First spouse's estate	$2,250,000	$2,250,000	$2,250,000
Funeral & administrative expenses	(50,000)	(50,000)	(50,000)
Balance	$2,200,000	$2,200,000	$2,200,000
Marital deduction	(2,200,000)	(1,600,000)	(1,600,000)
Balance	$ 0	$ 600,000	$ 600,000
Exemption (not used)	(600,000)	NA	NA
Exemption for gift to children	NA	(600,000)	NA
Exemption for gift to bypass trust for spouse	NA	NA	(600,000)
Taxable	0	0	0
Tax in first estate	0	0	0
Second spouse's estate			
Spouse's own property	$ 500,000	$ 500,000	$ 500,000
Inherited from first spouse (marital ded.)	2,200,000	1,600,000	1,600,000
Total estate	2,700,000	2,100,000	2,100,000
Funeral and administration expenses	(50,000)	(40,000)	(40,000)
Balance	$2,650,000	$2,060,000	$2,060,000
Exemption	(600,000)	(600,000)	(600,000)
Taxable amount	$2,050,000	$1,460,000	$1,460,000
Tax @ 50%	1,025,000	730,000	730,000
Tax differential, saved in second estate	$ 0	$ 295,000	$ 295,000

* See Tables 2.1 and 2.2, above. This table assumes no growth of assets to the time of death of the surviving spouse.

use the marital deduction in the first spouse's estate. Because the trust by-passes the surviving spouse's estate, it is sometimes called a *bypass trust*.

Table 2.3 and Figure 2.2 show how the tax-free bypass trust for the spouse works. Table 2.3 compares a bypass trust for the spouse, with a gift to the children, with a gift of the whole estate to the spouse. The saving at the second death is dramatic. Table 2.3 does not allow for the tax on growth in value to the time of the surviving spouse's death. Figure 2.2 shows how growth in the bypass trust is eliminated from the second estate to save even more tax.

Figure 2.2. Long Term Impact of Marital Deduction Will and Bypass Trust—Defers and Saves Estate Taxes Through Two Estates

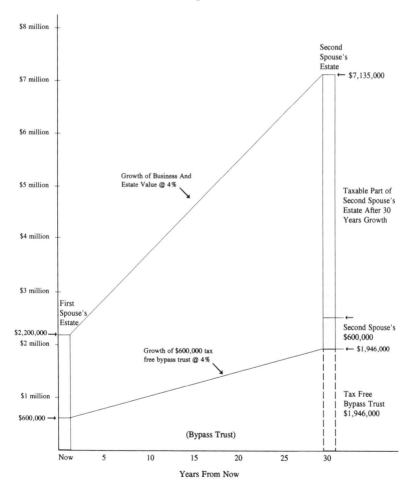

Using the Bypass Trust Effectively

We have learned that there are three very important points regarding estate planning for business owners:

- The estate tax, at 50 percent of net assets, is a huge burden to a business.
- That tax can be deferred in its entirety to the death of the second spouse, giving the family time to reduce taxes by gifts, to develop management skills, to sell the business, or whatever.
- Proper use of the owner's $600,000 exemption can save a significant sum in the second estate. It should be used in a bypass trust for the spouse which, together with growth in value, escapes tax in both estates.

In Table 2.3, the saving from the bypass trust was $295,000. However, this assumed that, during the life of the surviving spouse, the $600,000 trust was invested so that there was no growth. But, what if the $600,000 trust is invested in equities that have a long-term growth rate of only 6 percent? The $600,000 will double in the first 12 years and double again in the next 12. So if the spouse lives 24 years, the trust principal has grown to $2.4 million, saving about $1.2 million in tax in the second spouse's estate and the spouse will have had the income from the trust over all that time. The dramatic tax savings shown in Figure 2.3 are based on a growth rate of only 4 percent.

If you plan long term, you have to keep growth in mind. If you don't, the tax collector is a silent partner in 50 percent of all your hard work and future success.

How does one accomplish this combined tax deferral and tax savings? Each spouse should have a will that leaves the other spouse the excess over the $600,000. The $600,000 is given to a bypass trust for the spouse, and the balance over $600,000 is given to the spouse either outright or in a trust which qualifies for the marital deduction. Such a will is standard "boilerplate" in every lawyer's office; Exhibit 2.1 provides an example using a fictional family that will be used for illustration throughout the book and in the detailed case study in Part 6.

Exhibit 2.1. Excerpt from a Sample Marital Deduction Will

I, JAMES WOLCZK, declare this to be my will and I revoke all prior wills and codicils.

ONE.   Personal Information. I am married to CATHERINE RYAN WOLCZK ("Kate"). We have three children: Molly, James, and Maureen.

TWO.   Tangible Property. If Kate is living at my death, I give her all of my tangible personal property wherever located. If Kate dies before me, I give all of my tangible personal property to my children who are living at my death, to be divided among them as they may agree. To the extent they cannot agree on a division, my Executor may, in his sole discretion, make the division.

THREE.   Gift to Kate's Trust. (the $600,000 bypass trust)

(a) If Kate is living at my death I give to her as my Trustee $600,000 less (i) the total of my prior taxable gifts, and (ii) the total value of other taxable transfers of mine, whether or not under this will, which do not qualify for the estate tax marital deduction. This shall be known as "Kate's Trust." Kate may select the assets for this trust. It shall be made income producing at Kate's option.

(b) The Trustee shall distribute to or for the benefit of Kate for her lifetime the entire net income of the trust. A Trustee other than Kate may distribute to Kate, in such other Trustee's sole discretion, so much or all of the principal as is necessary or desirable for Kate's support, general welfare and comfort.

(c) At Kate's death, the trust shall go in accordance with Four (c).

FOUR.   Residuary Provisions for Kate (the $1,600,000 marital gift to Kate)

(a) I dispose of the rest of my property, of whatever nature and wherever located, (which if Kate dies before me shall also include the property that otherwise would have composed Kate's trust) in the following manner.

(b) If Kate is living at my death, I give her my residuary estate outright.

(c) If Kate dies before me, I give my residuary estate to my issue living at my death, children of a deceased child or grandchild to take the parent's share.

FIVE.   Fiduciaries

(a) I appoint Kate as Executor of this will. If for any reason she fails to qualify or ceases to act, I appoint Kate's brother, MICHAEL RYAN CPA, as Executor in her place.

(b) I appoint Kate as Trustee of the trust created by this will. If for any reason Kate ceases to act or fails to qualify, I appoint MICHAEL RYAN as Trustee. I empower Kate to appoint (but not remove) Michael Ryan, or another adult person, to act with her as Co-Trustee.

NOTE: This form is for illustration and should not be used as the basis of a legal instrument without advice of counsel in your state.

In the sample will, Exhibit 2.1, Jim gives to Kate outright the balance of his estate over $600,000. Alternatively, he could leave her the use of his assets in excess of $600,000 in a trust, partly or wholly, if that was desired by them. The essential point to the business owner is that the surviving spouse, as a practical matter, has the life use and control of the entire estate because she is trustee of all the assets held in trust for her and is the outright owner of the other property.

Thus, *a marital deduction will to defer and reduce estate taxes on your business is easily attainable.* Lifetime gifts to a spouse, either outright gifts or in trust, also qualify for the marital deduction. A person could give $100,000,000 to his or her spouse without any gift tax. The "catch" as pointed out before is that the same property is then taxed in the spouse's estate when he or she dies.

Where one spouse has many more assets than the other spouse, it is a good idea to transfer assets between the spouses (tax-free) to make sure that the other spouse has at least $600,000. This allows the combined $1,200,000 exemption to be used no matter which spouse dies first. In the illustrations above, if the spouse with $500,000 of assets died first, he or she could not use all of the $600,000 exemption since he or she owned only $500,000 of property. A $100,000 tax-free gift from the other spouse would let an additional $100,000 plus growth pass tax-free through both estates and hence save at least $50,000 in estate taxes.

The correct use of the estate tax marital deduction is very important for the business owner. It permits deferral of all tax in the first estate, a tax that might have to be borne by the business. The accompanying $600,000 bypass trust permits significant tax savings through both estates, in addition to the deferral. Correctly prepared wills are very important. The wrong trust wording may not qualify for the marital deduction: a disaster for the business.

Using Disclaimers to Adjust Taxes

The amount and timing of taxes can be adjusted, even after death. It is possible, by use of disclaimers, to adjust the estate taxes between two estates. This is especially valuable where one spouse dies soon after the other. Disclaimer is a legal term meaning that a person formally refuses to accept an asset which would otherwise pass to him or her under a will.

For example, suppose you have a business valued at several million dollars and you are concerned about the huge tax burden your children will have to bear when eventually they inherit. Your mother has just died leaving an estate of over $1 million as follows:

> "I give to my daughter, [you], if she survives me, my entire estate. If she predeceases me, I give my estate to her children to be held in trust for them until age 35."

If you inherit the $1 million, it goes on top of your already large estate and will be taxed at the highest tax rate at your death. What to do? Within nine months after mother dies, file a "disclaimer" which renounces her legacy to you. Legally this is treated as though you had died before your mother and the property skips your estate and goes to your children at age 35. You have not made a gift for gift tax purposes and the children's education can be funded out of their trusts. Obviously, one does not lightly turn away a large bequest. But once all the facts have been carefully reviewed, *the disclaimer can be a very effective tax planning device.*

A Disclaimer by Spouse May Reduce Taxes

Given the marital deduction, would a spouse ever disclaim? Yes. Sometimes. Suppose the spouses have a combined estate of about $800,000 and really do not want to bother with a trust, the trust that utilizes the $600,000 exemption and removes property from the surviving spouse's estate. With only $200,000 above the $600,000, they figure the surviving spouse would consume the $200,000 or give it to the children prior to death. Who wants to bother with a trust—however beneficial tax wise—if you don't have to?

But are we sure about the numbers? What if their estates increase to well over $800,000 before a new will is prepared? Is there a way the surviving spouse can take a second look, after the first spouse has died? Yes. Use a disclaimer will as shown by Exhibit 2.2.

In this will Mary Ryan gives her entire estate to her husband, Robert, in paragraph Two. Then in Three (a) she sets up a bypass trust for Robert as to any part of the gift in Two which he disclaims. Thus Robert, based on the facts at the time, has the power to control how much if any of Mary's estate goes to a tax-free bypass trust.

Exhibit 2.2. Sample Disclaimer Will

I, MARY RYAN, declare this to be my will and I revoke all prior wills and codicils.

ONE.   Personal Information. I am married to ROBERT RYAN ("Robert"). We have three adult children: CATHERINE, ROBERT JR. and MAUREEN.

TWO.   Disposition of Estate. I give my property, of whatever nature and wherever located to Robert if he is living at my death. If Robert is not living at my death, I dispose of my estate in accordance with Article Three (b).

THREE.   Trust in the Event of Disclaimer

(a) If Robert disclaims any or all of such gift of my estate, I give the disclaimed property to my Trustee, IN TRUST ("the residuary trust") and I direct my Trustee to distribute to Robert for his lifetime the entire net income and so much or all of the principal of the trust as in my Trustee's sole discretion is necessary or desirable for his reasonable support and comfort.

(b) Upon Robert's death, I give the remaining principal and undistributed income of the trust to my then living children in equal shares, or to the issue of any child who predeceases. If any of my children dies without issue, that child's share shall be divided between my living children, the issue of a deceased child taking the parent's share.

NOTE: This form is for illustration and should not be used as the basis of a legal instrument without advice of counsel in your state.

The key parts of the disclaimer will shown in Exhibit 2.2 are in paragraph Two where the entire estate goes to the spouse, Robert, outright, *but*, if Robert disclaims all or part of the estate, paragraph Three (a) operates to create a tax-free trust for Robert for the disclaimed amount. Thus, the survivor, within nine months of death, can decide how much of the estate would either pass tax-free to the survivor outright, because of the marital deduction and then be taxable in the survivor's estate *or* pass to a trust for the survivor which would be tax-free in the survivor's estate but taxable (after the first $600,000) in the first estate.

Exhibit 2.2 is only an illustrative form. There are other ways of accomplishing the same "post-death planning" result; your own tax advisor will tell you what way is best for you. The disclaimer concept is perfectly legal and is built into the Internal Revenue Code.

Thus, the surviving spouse may plan the decedent's estate based on known facts after death rather than projected facts as of the time of preparation of the will. Think of it as the ability to drain wealth from one tank (marital deduction) to another tank (no marital deduction). Figure 2.3 illustrates this approach. The upper tank in Figure 2.3 is the marital deduction tank which can be drained off into the lower tank, adjusting the tax impact of the first estate on the surviving spouse's estate.

The disclaimer may also serve to preserve the surviving spouse's estate from being totally consumed by health costs under the Medicaid rules. Suppose, for instance, that the spouses are elderly and concerned that the hospital and nursing home costs could eat up the entire estate and leave nothing for the children. If the first spouse leaves everything to the second outright, then all is at risk under the Medicaid rules. If the second spouse is in poor health at the time of the other's death, he or she could disclaim the outright gift, which is subject to Medicaid claims, and let it go to the trust whose principal will remain intact. (This, of course, is subject to the current federal and state application of the Medicaid rules.)

How does this information help the owner of a family business? It helps because the disclaimer allows the surviving spouse to fine tune the estate tax plan, after the other spouse is deceased. This tuning might eventually save the family—and the business—a large amount of money.

Figure 2.3. How a Disclaimer Can Plan an Estate After Death

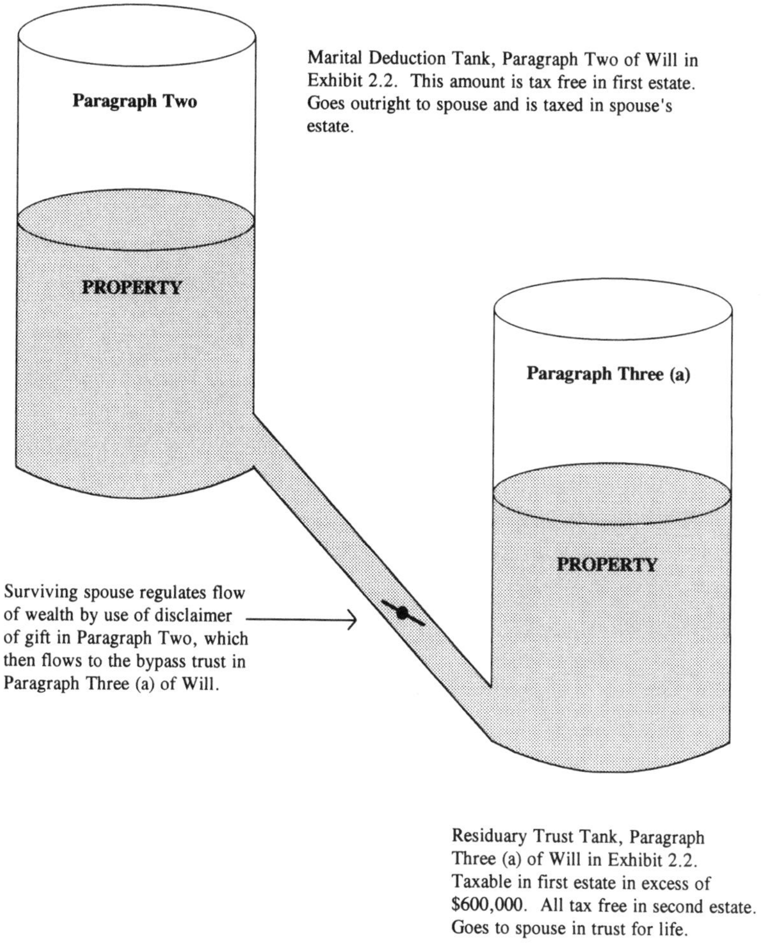

Marital Deduction Tank, Paragraph Two of Will in Exhibit 2.2. This amount is tax free in first estate. Goes outright to spouse and is taxed in spouse's estate.

Paragraph Two

PROPERTY

Paragraph Three (a)

PROPERTY

Surviving spouse regulates flow of wealth by use of disclaimer of gift in Paragraph Two, which then flows to the bypass trust in Paragraph Three (a) of Will.

Residuary Trust Tank, Paragraph Three (a) of Will in Exhibit 2.2. Taxable in first estate in excess of $600,000. All tax free in second estate. Goes to spouse in trust for life.

Copyright G. Shattuck 1992

Summary

The marital deduction will with bypass trust is the basic building block of planning to defer and reduce the impact of estate taxes on a business.

The business owner should also be aware of the disclaimer which will enable his or her spouse or heirs to fine tune the estate plan after death. At the time a will and other testamentary devices are prepared, they are of necessity based on projecting today's facts into the unknown future. To give more flexibility, consider building into your plan as many options as possible, including the use of a disclaimer.

The business owner who is not married cannot use the marital deduction to defer taxes and thus must give greater attention to the other deferral and tax reduction concepts discussed in Chapters 5, 6, 7, and Part Three.

3

Using Gifts to
Reduce Estate Taxes

The estate tax is a cost of business. Business is concerned with costs. Employee compensation is a current cost of doing business. Corporate income and franchise taxes, paid annually, are viewed as current costs. For some reason, the estate tax is not usually viewed as a current cost or even a business expense—in spite of the fact that the estate tax is a true cost of having a family own a business over a period of time. If a business owner sets up a reserve fund to pay estate taxes in the same manner as account rules require a reserve for pensions or deferred compensation or depreciation, the result would be a large reduction of accounting earnings and a reduction of balance sheet equity to account for the eventual cost.

After decades of experience and loophole-plugging, the federal estate tax is now effective. A smaller business may escape its impact by using will and trust planning as described in Chapter 2, but the expanding business worth, say $1 million or more, cannot escape it over the long run. An expanding and growing business creates so much value that a tax eventually is paid.

At this point, the name of the game is *eliminate value growth from your estate. Don't own the property when you die.* One effective way of not owning the property at death is to give it away now so it won't be taxed later.

Understanding the Gift Tax Structure

The tax law recognizes the desire to spread and conserve wealth by gifts to family or others. It allows two kinds of tax-free gifts:

- You may give $10,000 each year per person. For example, if you have three children, you can give them a total of $30,000 per year, or, if you

21

had six brothers and sisters, each of whom has five children (36 people in all) you could give away a total of $360,000 per year without filing returns or paying a tax.

- To the extent you exceed the $10,000 in any given year, you can use up part of your $600,000 estate tax exemption which was described in Chapter 1.

If you give your child $15,000 in one year (other than for support, tuition, or medical costs) you have made a "taxable" gift of $5,000: the excess over the $10,000 exclusion. The $5,000 must be reported on a gift tax return but no tax is payable because the $5,000 can be offset against your $600,000 lifetime exemption. If, however, you had used up your $600,000 exemption through prior gifts, the $5,000 would be taxed at a 37 percent federal rate, resulting in a tax of $1,850 for the year of the $15,000 gift. (Some states have similar gift taxes, but with lower rates.)

One way to think of this is to picture two bank accounts. One account is replenished at the rate of $10,000 per donee per year, for you to use or not on a noncumulative basis. The other is a one shot $600,000 account which you can draw down any time during your life, and your estate has the benefit of any remaining balance.

The benefit of these two concepts is shown by Figures 3.1 and 3.2, which assume a business growing at 10 percent per year. In Figures 3.1 and 3.2 the shaded area is the total value sheltered from eventual estate tax at

Figure 3.1. Effect of Gift of $10,000 Each Year of Stock That Grows at 10% Per Year

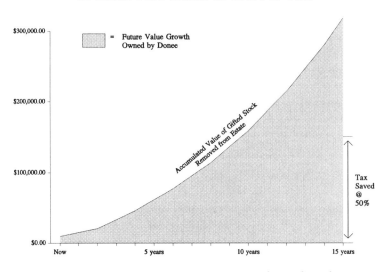

Copyright G. Shattuck 1992

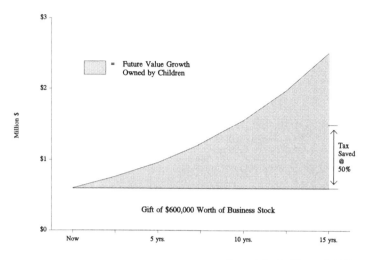

**Figure 3.2. Effect of Gift of One-Time Gift of
$600,000 Worth of Stock That Grows in Value
at 10% per Year**

your generation. The effect of the $10,000 annual gifts, shown in Figure 3.1, is twofold: first, each $10,000 itself is removed from the estate saving at least $3,700 in taxes, then the future value increase of the $10,000 is also removed from the estate. As explained in Chapter 1, the use of the $600,000 by gift, shown in Figure 3.2, does not save a tax on that $600,000 because the same exemption would have been available to the estate if not used by gift; the saving in Figure 3.2 is removing the gift's value increase from the estate— particularly important where a business interest is given.

Married Couples Can Make Joint Gifts

Just as a married couple can file a joint income tax return which pools income, deductions, and exemptions, a married couple can also file "joint" gift tax returns. This allows one spouse to "use" the $10,000 annual exclusions and the $600,000 exemption of the other spouse. For example, one spouse owns a valuable security which is appreciating rapidly in value. They want to eliminate this from their estates by making gifts to their three children. The spouse owning the security gives $60,000 ($20,000 to each child) exceeding the $10,000 annual limit. This gift must be reported on the donor's gift tax return on April 15 of the following year. The other spouse also files a gift tax return agreeing to let the first spouse have the benefit of his or her $10,000 exclusion. Thus, while the $20,000 gifts must be reported on returns, there is no tax and no draw down of the $600,000 exemption.

Suppose the couple wants to give each of the children $50,000 worth of a stock that year, total $150,000. Here the permissible $20,000 has been exceeded by $30,000 for each child; the total excess is $90,000. By filing the "joint" gift tax returns the couple has also agreed that the $600,000 exemption of each spouse will be reduced by the taxable part. Thus, each spouse's exemption will be reduced by $45,000: from $600,000 to $555,000. (See Table 3.1.)

How much do you save by using the joint gifts concept shown in Table 3.1? If Spouse A gave the same $150,000 with no use of the joint gift option, the result would be as shown on Table 3.2 below.

In this case, another effect would be that the three $10,000 exclusions of Spouse B would be unused for that year. Comparing Tables 3.1 and 3.2, the use of the joint gift preserved an extra $30,000 of this overall $1.2 million of exemptions. This represents a tax saving of $15,000.

Table 3.1. Effect of Joint Gifts*

	Spouse A	Spouse B
Total gift to the three children for that year	$150,000	0
Amount attributed to other spouse by "joint" gift tax returns	(75,000)	$ 75,000
Balance, gift attributed to each	$ 75,000	$ 75,000
Less 3 exclusions for each parent	(30,000)	(30,000)
Balance	$ 45,000	$ 45,000
Use of part of $600,000 exemption	(45,000)	(45,000)
Balance, taxable	0	0
Remaining exemptions	$555,000	$555,000

*NOTE: This is how the federal tax works, but various states have different structures.

Table 3.2. No Joint Gift

	Spouse A	Spouse B
Total gift to the three children	$150,000	0
Less 3 exclusions A.	(30,000)	0
Balance	$120,000	0
Use of part of $600,000 exemption	(120,000)	0
Balance = Taxable Gift	0	0
Remaining exemptions	$480,000	$600,000

Impact of a Sustained Giving Program

Annual gifts to children of nonvoting interests in the business can be a very effective shelter against estate taxes. Table 3.3 shows the results of such a sustained giving program. It assumes that the parents give $60,000 worth of stock each year to their three children. As the business grows in value, the number of shares given each year declines because the overall value of the gifts remains constant at $60,000 per year. You can see that a consistent gift

Table 3.3. Accumulation of Stock Gifts of $20,000 per Year to Each of Three Children, Assuming the Company Grows at 8% per Year

ASSUMPTIONS:

STARTING VALUE	$1,000,000
GROWTH RATE	8%
STARTING SHARES	$1,000,000
ANNUAL EXEMPT GIFTS	$ 60,000

Year	Company Value	Value per Share	Number of Shares Gifted	% of Company Gifted	Cumulative % of Co. Gifted
1	1,000,000	1.000	60,000	6.00%	6.00%
2	1,080,000	1.080	55,556	5.56%	11.56%
3	1,166,400	1.166	51,440	5.14%	16.70%
4	1,259,712	1.260	47,630	4.76%	21.46%
5	1,360,489	1.360	44,102	4.41%	25.87%
6	1,469,328	1.469	40,835	4.08%	29.96%
7	1,586,874	1.587	37,810	3.78%	33.74%
8	1,713,824	1.714	35,009	3.50%	37.24%
9	1,850,930	1.851	32,416	3.24%	40.48%
10	1,999,005	1.999	30,015	3.00%	43.48%
11	2,158,925	2.159	27,792	2.78%	46.26%
12	2,331,639	2.332	25,733	2.57%	48.83%
13	2,518,170	2.518	23,827	2.38%	51.22%
14	2,719,624	2.720	22,062	2.21%	53.42%
15	2,937,194	2.937	20,428	2.04%	55.47%
16	3,172,169	3.172	18,915	1.89%	57.36%
17	3,425,943	3.426	17,513	1.75%	59.11%
18	3,700,018	3.700	16,216	1.62%	60.73%
19	3,996,019	3.996	15,015	1.50%	62.23%
20	4,315,701	4.316	13,903	1.39%	63.62%

policy, over time, removes a very significant amount from your estate, especially if you start early enough when values are low. Table 3.3 shows that *by the 15th year you can give away 55 percent of a company that starts at $1 million and grows at 8 percent per year.*

Table 3.4 shows the effect where there is 10 percent growth. The amount given away after the 15th year is less, but the tax impact may be even greater because of the higher growth rate.

Table 3.4. Accumulation of Stock Gifts of $20,000 per Year to Each of Three Children, Assuming the Company Grows at 10% per Year

ASSUMPTIONS:

STARTING VALUE	$1,000,000
GROWTH RATE	10%
STARTING SHARES	$1,000,000
ANNUAL EXEMPT GIFTS	$ 60,000

Year	Company Value	Value per Share	Number of Shares Gifted	% of Company Gifted	Cumulative % of Co. Gifted
1	1,000,000	1.000	60,000	6.00%	6.00%
2	1,100,000	1.100	54,545	5.45%	11.45%
3	1,210,000	1.210	49,587	4.96%	16.41%
4	1,331,000	1.331	45,079	4.51%	20.92%
5	1,464,100	1.464	40,981	4.10%	25.02%
6	1,610,510	1.611	37,255	3.73%	28.74%
7	1,771,561	1.772	33,868	3.39%	32.13%
8	1,948,717	1.949	30,789	3.08%	35.21%
9	2,143,589	2.144	27,990	2.80%	38.01%
10	2,357,948	2.358	25,446	2.54%	40.55%
11	2,593,742	2.594	23,133	2.31%	42.87%
12	2,853,117	2.853	21,030	2.10%	44.97%
13	3,138,428	3.138	19,118	1.91%	46.88%
14	3,452,271	3.452	17,380	1.74%	48.62%
15	3,797,498	3.797	15,800	1.58%	50.20%
16	4,177,248	4.177	14,364	1.44%	51.64%
17	4,594,973	4.595	13,058	1.31%	52.94%
18	5,054,470	5.054	11,871	1.19%	54.13%
19	5,559,917	5.560	10,792	1.08%	55.21%
20	6,115,909	6.116	9,810	0.98%	56.19%

The impact of annual gifts is dramatic if you start from a value base of say $1.0 million as in Tables 3.3 and 3.4.

If you start from a higher value base, the $20,000 per year and the one-shot $600,000 exemption count for less as a percentage of your total estate. Suppose, instead of a $1 million value at the start, the business is worth $10 million at the start of the gift program. Compare:

	% Given Away in 10 years	% Given Away in 15 years	
(a) $60,000 per year of stock given when you start at $1 million value,	41%	50%	See Table 3.4
(b) —when you start at $10 million value,	4%	5%	See Table 3.5

Table 3.5 on page 28 illustrates how the $60,000 per year counts for relatively much less when the initial company value is higher; here, the example is $10 million rather than $1 million. Where the objective is to give away growth, the conclusion is to start the gift program early, while value is low.

Exclusions and Exemptions Are There to Be Used

The $10,000 annual exclusions and the $600,000 lifetime exemption are tax benefits—call them loopholes if you want—that each taxpayer possesses. Both waste away if not used.

The $10,000 annual exclusion is not cumulative. If you don't use it this year, it is gone forever. Moreover, the $10,000 amount, effective in 1982, degrades each year through inflation. The $10,000 of 1982, after cost of living adjustment, was really only $7,125 in January 1992.

The $600,000 exemption remains for your estate if you don't use it for gifts. It also degrades by inflation, or by growth in the asset potentially given away at this time. The $600,000 first became effective on January 1, 1987. Allowing for cost of living increases, the $600,000 amount of 1987 is worth only $496,000 in January 1992 dollars.

Let us carry the wasting asset concept into the future. Suppose you now have a $600,000 exemption, an amount you can use now to make gifts to reduce estate taxes, but you don't use it. If you die years from now, after dollar inflation of just 5 percent per year, Table 3.6 shows your wasting asset.

The same information is shown graphically in Figure 3.2., which shows the inflation shrinkage of the $600,000 you could use today. Figure 3.3 and Figure 3.2 picture the same concept in two different ways. Figure 3.2 shows the future growth you could have given away; Figure 3.3 shows the decline in value of your $600,000.

Many people feel they should "save" this $600,000 exemption, like money in the bank. Actually, in this case, as shown by Figures 3.2 and 3.3, you are better off to "spend" the $600,000 right now. Or "spend" the whole $1.2 million available to yourself and your spouse.

Table 3.5. Accumulation of Stock Gifts of $20,000 per Year to Each of Three Children, Assuming the Company Grows at 10% per Year

ASSUMPTIONS:

STARTING VALUE	$10,000,000
GROWTH RATE	10%
STARTING SHARES	$ 1,000,000
ANNUAL EXEMPT GIFTS	$ 60,000

Year	Company Value	Value per Share	Number of Shares Gifted	% of Company Gifted	Cumulative % of Co. Gifted
1	10,000,000	10.000	6,000	0.60%	0.60%
2	11,000,000	11.000	5,455	0.55%	1.15%
3	12,100,000	12.100	4,959	0.50%	1.64%
4	13,310,000	13.310	4,508	0.45%	2.09%
5	14,641,000	14.641	4,098	0.41%	2.50%
6	16,105,100	16.105	3,726	0.37%	2.87%
7	17,715,610	17.716	3,387	0.34%	3.21%
8	19,487,171	19.487	3,079	0.31%	3.52%
9	21,435,888	21.436	2,799	0.28%	3.80%
10	23,579,477	23.579	2,545	0.25%	4.06%
11	25,937,425	25.937	2,313	0.23%	4.29%
12	28,531,167	28.531	2,103	0.21%	4.50%
13	31,384,284	31.384	1,912	0.19%	4.69%
14	34,522,712	34.523	1,738	0.17%	4.86%
15	37,974,983	37.975	1,580	0.16%	5.02%
16	41,772,482	41.772	1,436	0.14%	5.16%
17	45,949,730	45.950	1,306	0.13%	5.29%
18	50,544,703	50.545	1,187	0.12%	5.41%
19	55,599,173	55.599	1,079	0.11%	5.52%
20	61,159,090	61.159	981	0.10%	5.62%

Table 3.6. Effect of Inflation on $600,000 Exemption

Time	"Real Dollar" Value After Inflation
Now	$600,000
1 year	570,000
2 years	542,000
3 years	514,000
4 years	489,000
5 years	464,000
10 years	359,000
15 years	278,000

Figure 3.3. Effect of 5% Inflation on your $600,000 Exemption

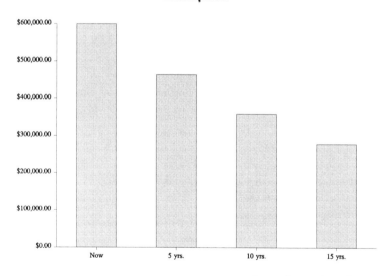

Copyright G. Shattuck 1992

But Don't Give Away the Store

Reducing the estate tax burden on business should have a high priority. But the highest, your absolute top priority, is the personal well being and financial security of you, the present owner, and your spouse. Property given to children and grandchildren is gone. You will never get it back as a practical matter. That is acceptable as long as there is enough left for you and for your spouse and as long as you remain in control as long as you want. Give away growth to save taxes, but don't give away the store.

There are many tax-approved ways of giving away future growth while still keeping control,

1. Corporation issues 100 shares of voting common stock and 900 shares of nonvoting common stock. The nonvoting is then given to the children and/or grandchildren. Value and future growth of gifted stock are eliminated from the parents' estates, but the owner still keeps control by way of the retained voting stock.

2. Corporation recapitalizes so that 80 percent of its value is represented by voting cumulative preferred stock, 20 percent of the value is represented by nonvoting common stock. The common, growth stock, is given to the children. The voting preferred, nongrowth stock, is retained by the parents. (This transaction has other ramifications, which are discussed in Chapter 10.)

3. A business partnership or real estate partnership recapitalizes into a managing preferred interest and a growth interest, analogous to the voting preferred stock and nonvoting common stock approach in item 2. The partnership growth interest goes to the children and the parents retain management and security via the preferred interest. (See Chapter 12.)

4. Parents give stock or partnership interests to trusts for the children and grandchildren. Well-selected independent trustees ensure that the donees will not act adversely to the interests of the business. The children get the economic benefits of the trusts for as long as the parents direct in the trust instruments.

5. Parents start new spinoff business entities in the children's names, but keep management powers (through one of the means described above) until the children are mature enough to run things themselves.

The simplest way by far to make such gifts is the voting/nonvoting stock approach described in item 1 above. What if a child or grandchild subsequently wants to sell the stock or gets into marital or financial trouble? One way to handle this is to have the donee sign a restrictive agreement to inhibit transfers. Exhibit 3.1 provides a sample of such an agreement. This form can be adapted for a partnership business, or the restrictions can be built right into the partnership agreement. NOTE: State laws vary, and no form herein should be used without advice of legal counsel.

Exhibit 3.1. Sample Agreement Restricting Stock Transfers

KAYJIM ELECTRONIC DEVICES, INC.
STOCK RESTRICTIVE AGREEMENT

The undersigned Stockholder of KAYJIM ELECTRONIC DE-VICES, INC., in consideration of past and future gifts of stock by James and Catherine Wolczk and for other valuable past consideration received, agrees with James and Catherine Wolczk and the Corporation as follows:

(1) No stock of the Corporation, whether now owned or in the future acquired by the stockholder, shall be sold, exchanged, given, pledged, bequeathed or transferred to heirs, or otherwise transferred or disposed of, voluntarily or nonvoluntarily, (all "transfer") except pursuant to the terms of this Agreement.

(2) In case of any proposed transfer to a non-Stockholder, the Stockholder shall first give to the Corporation a written irrevocable 90-day option to purchase all or any part of the Stockholder's stock of the Corporation of all classes at the lower of:

(a) the price at which the Stockholder has agreed to sell or pledge to another party, or

(b) the book value per share of the stock as of the end of the last prior year.

In case of a transfer which is not an arm's length sale, the price shall be determined by (b).

(3) To the extent the Corporation does not purchase the offered stock, the Stockholder shall give the other Stockholders of the same class of stock, pro rata, a written 90-day option to purchase the balance of the undersigned's stock of the Corporation at the price provided in (2). Any stock not purchased by the other Stockholders may be transferred to a non-Stockholder who shall similarly be bound by this Agreement.

(4) The purchasing Corporation or other Stockholders may elect to pay in cash, or over 15 years in level annual principal installments plus 6 percent interest.

(5) The undersigned may bequeath stock to his or her issue or spouse, or to a trustee for issue or spouse, provided that any such transferee must execute an Agreement similar to this before the stock is registered in his/her/its name. No trustee shall distribute stock to a beneficiary unless the beneficiary has previously executed an Agreement in this form.

(6) Any seizure or order for sale of or direction to transfer the undersigned's stock by judgment, or decree in a divorce or separation action, and any insolvency proceeding of Stockholder, shall be deemed an offer pursuant to (2) and (3).

(7) A legend giving notice of this Agreement shall be typed on the face of each stock certificate of the Corporation. The Corporation shall not

register a transfer nor issue new stock certificates unless the transfer complies with this agreement.

(8) This Agreement may be amended or terminated only by consent of the holders of 75 percent of the voting common stock of the Corporation and all other parties who each own over 10 percent of the outstanding stock.

(9) The undersigned Stockholder agrees to vote his/her shares (a) in favor of an election to be taxed under Subchapter S of the Internal Revenue Code and similar state law if requested by the Directors of the Corporation and (b) in favor of any sale or merger of the Corporation or sale of its assets which is requested by the Directors.

(10) This Agreement shall bind all the heirs, executors, transferees, and assigns of the undersigned and any permitted Transferee hereunder, including a purchaser, shall execute this Agreement before certificates of shares are issued. Any attempt to transfer in violation of this Agreement shall be deemed to be an offer under (2) and (3).

(11) If this Agreement is executed by a guardian/custodian for a minor child, it is understood that any gift of stock of the Corporation is made subject to the terms and restrictions of this Agreement and no certificate shall be registered in the name of the child on attaining age 18 until he or she executes a copy of this Agreement.

Dated: _____
                              "Stockholder", Molly Wolczk

                          _____
                                   James Wolczk

                          _____
                                 Catherine Wolczk

KAYJIM ELECTRONIC DEVICES, INC.

By: _____

    NOTE: Exhibit 3.1 should not be used without advice of legal counsel.

If the children or grandchildren of the business owners are minors and are too young to sign a restrictive agreement like the sample in Exhibit 3.1, another alternative is to adopt a corporate bylaw which restricts transfer. A bylaw binds all shareholders and may effectively be used to restrict transfer. The Corporation should formally adopt the bylaw before stock transfers are made, and a notice of the bylaw restriction should be printed on all stock certificates. It is also possible to put such a restriction in the Corporation's charter or certificate of incorporation; depending on your state law, this may be advisable in place of a bylaw or agreement.

Exhibit 3.2 is a sample bylaw which can be tailored by legal counsel to suit the situation and the laws of the owner's state. Any restrictive agreement, or bylaw, or charter provision, should be reviewed in the light of the "two class of stock" rule governing corporations electing to be taxed under Subchapter S, IRC.

Exhibit 3.2. Sample By-Law to Restrict Stock Transfer—XVII Stock Transfer Restriction

1. No stock of this corporation shall be sold exchanged, given, pledged, bequeathed, or transferred to heirs, or otherwise transferred or disposed of, voluntarily or involuntarily, (all "transfer") unless the stockholder has previously given the corporation, and then the other stockholders pro rata by class, successive 90-day written, irrevocable options to purchase all of the transferor's shares of all classes.

2. The price shall be the lower of (a) the cash price at which the offering shareholder has agreed to transfer, or (b) the per share book value as of the end of the last prior year. In the case of a transfer not at arms' length, the price shall be determined by (b).

NOTE: Exhibit 3.2 should not be used without advice of legal counsel.

Summary

Gifts of an interest in the business are a very effective way to:

• eliminate property from your estate,
• eliminate value growth from your estate.

If used effectively, the current tax rules can permit very significant tax reduction for the owner of a family business. However, you don't want to give away the store. Your legal counsel should make sure, by way of voting and nonvoting stock, by restrictive agreement, or otherwise, that you maintain control as long as you want and that the donees won't transfer the stock out of the family.

No gifting of a business interest should be done without a written opinion from your CPA or other tax advisor that the business value is within the dollar limits discussed above. Chapter 8 discusses valuation of a family business.

4

Managers or Owners?
How to Divide a Business
Among the Family

The owner of a successful business often wants to pass ownership to the children. This brings out two crucial questions: When? Which children?

The When? question comes up because of the compelling need to postpone estate taxes by giving the business interest to the spouse, outright or in a lifetime trust. Using the marital deduction postpones the tax, but the children then have to wait until the surviving parent dies to enjoy the rewards of ownership. Gifts in the interim will help, but the amount of gifts is subject to the limitations described above in Chapter 3.

When the business eventually does pass to the next generation, the question arises "Which children?" Typically, some children are not involved in the business and others are. Does the owner want the noninvolved to share in the business as passive owners? Or to make provision for them with other nonbusiness assets? Are there enough nonbusiness assets to go around?

Let us take a look at a case that deals with these issues.

Illustrative Case

Jim and Kate Wolczk, at middle age, own and run a very successful electronics business. Its value is around $4 million and growing. They have invested their lives and wealth in the business and own few other assets except a residence, a vacation home, and $500,000 of insurance on Jim's life. They also have three children. Molly, the oldest, works in the business at a lower management level and aspires, some day, to take over the helm. Jim

Jr. is a medical intern. Maureen, the youngest, has just married and lives out-of-state.

Jim and Kate are planning their estate so that each leaves everything to the other. They will take advantage of the marital deduction and bypass trust to defer all estate taxes to the death of the survivor. But then what? The Wolczks could easily sell the business, but they won't. Their estates could sell the business, but they do not want that. They want it to stay in the family and believe that Molly eventually will be qualified to be CEO. They are also aware that the business is growing rapidly. When the business eventually is divided—after Jim and Kate both die—it may be worth several times what it is now, as shown in Table 4.1.

Table 4.1. Assumed Business Growth

	Now	Survivor Dies 10 Years*	Survivor Dies 20 Years*
Value of voting stock (10%)	$ 400,000	$ 860,000	$ 1,860,000
Value of nonvoting stock (90%)	3,600,000	7,740,000	16,740,000
Value of business as whole	$ 4,000,000	$ 8,600,000	$18,600,000
Estate tax @ 50% on whole	$ 2,000,000	$ 4,300,000	$ 9,300,000
Value of business after tax	$ 2,000,000	$ 4,300,000	$ 9,300,000
Number of children	3	3	3
Each child's share, after tax	$ 667,000	$ 1,433,000	$ 3,100,000

* Growth at 8% per annum.

Elements of the Problem

Jim and Kate need to resolve the fact that they have contradictory goals, namely:

- *Defer estate taxes* until the death of the survivor of Jim and Kate; this implies that division of the bulk of their estate must likewise be deferred;
- *Achieve equality* among the three children in terms of what wealth is left to them;
- *Achieve equity* in the sense of currently recognizing Molly's extra contribution to the business and giving her voting control;
- *Reduce* estate taxes to a minimum and *have the business pay the estate taxes* which remain—there are no other assets sufficient to do this.

Jim and Kate also realize that they are doing Jim Jr. and Maureen no big favor by leaving them a share of a closely-held business. The other side of this coin is that they would prefer not to saddle Molly and the company with the responsibility of paying dividends to the other two owners, particularly after the business has already been saddled with the payment of large estate taxes. As a practical matter, on these facts, the business will have been saddled with the tax obligation shown on Table 4.1 that Jim Jr. and Maureen won't see anything out of it for years to come. Molly may draw a reasonable salary for her work as CEO.

These factors, then, are what we have to deal with. How do Jim and Kate handle the estate tax burden, keep the business in the family under Molly's management, and still divide into thirds for their children?

Insurance Funding, Its Limits

In the above example, Table 4.1, each child would wind up with one-third of the net value and Molly's share would be comprised of all the voting stock plus some nonvoting stock. Jim Jr. and Maureen would each own nonvoting stock and the business would be saddled with a tax of half its value. Suppose Kate and Jim set up a life insurance trust to provide funds to pay estate taxes. (See Chapter 5, below.)

Table 4.2 shows how tax-free insurance proceeds have saved the business a huge tax burden and passed a viable legacy on to the children. But, Jim Jr. and Maureen still wind up with nonvoting stock and are largely dependent on Molly to declare dividends because she is the sole owner of voting stock. If the expanding business needs all the cash it can get, the other two children may have little economic advantage from their share.

Can we get still more tax free insurance to "buy out" Jim Jr. and Maureen, so they will have cash to invest and Molly gets all or a larger share of the business?

Table 4.2. Assume Tax Free Insurance Trust
to Fund Taxes

	Now	Survivor Dies 10 Years*	Survivor Dies 20 Years*
Value of business, Table 4.1	$ 4,000,000	$ 8,600,000	$18,600,000
Less taxes @ 50%	(2,000,000)	(4,300,000)	(9,300,000)
Plus insurance (tax free)	2,000,000	4,300,000	9,300,000
Value of business after tax	$ 4,000,000	$ 8,600,000	$18,600,000
Number of children	3	3	3
Each child's share, after tax and insurance payment	$ 1,333,000	$ 2,867,000	$ 6,200,000

* Growth at 8% per annum.

Table 4.3 demonstrates that, as the business grows in size, funding a complete buy-out of the children not in the business requires more and more insurance. If you add the insurance needed to fund taxes the total insurance need is even larger. The number of children to buy-out also dramatically affects the overall amount of insurance. Still, if all were orderly and predictable, a nice even 8 percent growth rate and plenty of cash flow, it might be possible to work out a plan as shown in Table 4.3. However, things do not work out that way. No one who owns a business worth $4 million today is going to purchase tens of millions of insurance, at huge cost, to provide for a value increase that may never occur. Insurance is a good answer but usually only a partial answer to the division problem.

The Solution?

Is there a solution to the problem of division among the family? Tables 4.2 and 4.3 show that with a fairly small business value it may be possible to acquire enough other assets, or purchase enough insurance, to treat the children equally—some receiving cash and other assets, and with the business going to those who work in it. As the business gets larger the funding of a complete buy-out becomes improbable; then it becomes impossible. The owner of such an expanding business will have to abandon the funded buy out concept and consider

- treating the children unequally,
- selling the business out of the family to achieve division,
- working out a form of LBO with the child or children in the business, or

Table 4.3. Assume Tax Free Insurance Trust #2
Funds Amount for Division Among Children

	Now	Survivor Dies 10 Years*	Survivor Dies 20 Years*
Value of business after tax, from Table 4.2	$ 4,000,000	$ 8,600,000	$18,600,000
Molly's share, stock	$ 4,000,000	$ 8,600,000	$18,600,000
Jim's share, insurance	$ 4,000,000	$ 8,600,000	$18,600,000
Maureen's share, insurance	$ 4,000,000	$ 8,600,000	$18,600,000
Total additional insurance needed for buy-out	$ 8,000,000	$17,200,000	$37,200,000

* Growth at 8% per annum.

- embarking on a program to give stock to all the children, with the assumption that they will just have to get along together as shareholders,
- giving stock equally by value, but using voting stock to give the children in management effective control of the business.

In terms of Jim and Kate Wolczk and their three children, there are many possible options. They could, for example, decide that Molly is working for the business and helping make it grow. The other two children have other life careers and Jim and Kate could take out a tax-free insurance policy for them (See Chapter 5), say $1 million each, and then leave the business to Molly, whatever its then value. This would not be equal, but it might be equitable in the Wolczk's view. They could also work out a leveraged buy out (LBO), either now or pursuant to their wills, so that Molly would have a chance to buy the whole business. Or, depending on the size of the business, they could start a gifting program now of $20,000 per year per child: Molly would receive her $20,000 in stock of the business and Jim, Jr. and Maureen would receive cash or other assets. If the other assets were not sufficient, Molly would receive voting shares equivalent to the others' nonvoting shares.

Summary

Passing the business on to the family is a fine goal, but one whose accomplishment is fraught with difficulty. To accomplish this, the owner must first surmount the estate tax problem. Then the differing contributions of the children must be considered. Then the question of how or whether to divide an essentially nondivisible asset among them. In the chapters that follow, answers to these troublesome issues will be presented.

Part Two

HOW TO PREPARE FOR
THE ESTATE TAX BURDEN

CHAPTER 5. **How to Fund Taxes with Tax-Free Life Insurance**

CHAPTER 6. **How to Defer Tax Payments to the IRS**

CHAPTER 7. **Using the Business as a Source of Tax Funds**

Chapters 1, 2, and 3 show how to defer or reduce taxes by using correct wills and a policy of giving assets to reduce the taxable estate. Chapter 4 outlines some human aspects of estate division and the impact of taxes.

At some point, unforgiving, the estate tax will come due. Even if careful planning has removed a part of the business value from the estate, a tax of about 50 percent on the then remaining value will be payable. Assume you start your planning process at a point where your business is worth $1 million. The surviving spouse dies after 20 years of business growth at 9 percent and the business is worth $6 million, of which assume one-third has already been removed by gifts and good planning. This still leaves a $4 million value to be taxed.

The tax on the $4 million will be at least $2 million, assuming a 50 percent tax rate. How can a business worth $6 million raise $2 million, payable in nine months after death, for a purely nonproductive use? That is the situation addressed in Part Two.

5

How to Fund Taxes
with Tax-Free
Life Insurance

The introduction to Part Two raises the question: Where does the estate tax cash come from? Let us consider some possible ways to obtain the needed cash.

- Use other estate assets, such as the owner's residence or liquid investments. The typical business owner, however, does not accumulate a large liquid estate; all the cash flow has been reinvested in the growth of the business. In any event, 50 percent of the nonbusiness assets will be used to pay the tax just on those assets, and, in most situations, nonbusiness assets must be used for debts, administration expenses, and cash bequests.

- Use life insurance on the business owner. That is also a good source of liquid funds but, again, the insurance itself is taxed at 50 percent. Only the after-tax balance is available to pay taxes on the business. Insurance used this way is only 50-percent efficient in terms of ability to pay the tax on the business assets, taking $2 million of insurance to furnish $1 million to fund taxes on the business. This approach is discussed in more detail in the next section of this chapter.

- Accumulate a tax fund in the corporation. This is easier said than done: the capital demands of an expanding business are incessant. The time of death is unknown. Moreover, unless the corporation has elected to be taxed under Subchapter S, there is a risk of imposition of the accumulated earnings tax. (Incredibly, in our era of supposed support for the family business, the funding of eventual estate taxes is not accepted by the IRS as a valid reason to accumulate income.)

- Sell the business, or part of it. This is possible, of course, but typically a forced sale, i.e., a tax sale, produces less than actual value.
- Borrow. This is also a possibility—but the loan must be paid back. If the business can do it, borrowing may be a good answer, but if the business cannot readily borrow up to half its total value, borrowing is not the answer.

Using Tax-Free Life Insurance for Leverage

As noted in the previous section, the use of life insurance is one way to fund estate taxes. If you have a business interest worth $4 million and a projected estate tax of $2 million, why not take out a $2 million life insurance policy to provide the taxes? Good idea, but if you own the policy the $2 million of insurance will also be taxed at a 50 percent. Assuming that, you will need a $4 million policy to provide the $2 million tax on the business.

Thus, the question arises, "Can I keep the $2 million of insurance out of my taxable estate?" Yes. The following paragraphs describe possible ways.

If you are married, have your spouse own the policy. This is not a good idea in most cases. If you die first, the proceeds go tax free to the spouse who owns the policy, but are then taxed in his or her estate. Thus, we are back to the $4 million again. If the non-insured spouse dies first, the cash value of the policy is taxed in that estate and, if marital deduction wills are used, the ownership of the policy might go back to the insured.

Give the $2 million policy to your children. This may be a very good and simple answer. But, it depends on the maturity and stability of your children, and on their outliving you and your spouse. Moreover, in most cases the business owner will want some assurance that the $2 million insurance proceeds will actually be used for estate taxes and not for other needs of the children and their spouses.

Adding to this concern is the fact that, in a typical marital deduction will situation, the estate taxes will not be due until the death of the surviving spouse who may not be the spouse insured in the policy. Suppose the insured spouse dies at age 50: will the children actually hold and invest the insurance proceeds until the death of the second spouse, which might be many years later?

Have the company buy "key person" insurance on your life. Then it will be available to pay estate taxes. But, if you own the company, the insurance proceeds will add to its value for estate tax purposes, causing the policy to pay a tax on itself.

Have the insurance owned by a family partnership that is principally owned by your children. There is a degree of assurance that the insurance will eventually be used for taxes because the partnership agreement will so provide. However, many things can happen and you may not feel comfortable with a partnership. One problem with having the insurance owned by the children, or a partnership of the children, is that a child may die before the surviving parent leaving the insurance to be divided as part of the child's estate.

Use a trust to hold the $2 million policy to make sure the taxes get paid. Of course we deliberately led up to this because a trust can be a very efficient way to get the policy out of both spouses' estates *and* control the destiny of the proceeds—ensure that the $2 million will really be used to pay the estate tax on the basis. In contrast, a gift of insurance to children, or to a legal entity controlled by them, will eliminate it from the parents' estates, but does not give assurance that the proceeds will be used to pay the parents' estate taxes.

A trust works here because it is a distinct legal entity governed by rules you build into the trust instrument. The trustee (who manages the trust) is legally bound to follow your directions, and a trust can be designed to last for a long time. A trust set up to hold the $2 million policy can be designed to escape your estate, your spouse's estate, and even your children's estates if you want it that way. In summary, tax-free insurance should be held in most cases by a trust.

Gifts to a Crummy Trust

In 1962, a Mr. D. Clifford Crummy set up a very significant trust for his family. In so doing he solved a very serious problem for persons who wish to set up trusts with annual gifts equal to the $10,000 annual exclusion. (In 1962, the annual exclusion was $3,000.)

The problem arose from the fact that for a gift to qualify for the $10,000 annual exclusion it must be a gift of a "present interest" in legal terms: as a practical matter it must be an outright gift to an individual donee. For openers, a gift of $10,000 to a trust is not an outright gift to an individual donee. Why? It's in trust and the donee can't lay his hands on it. Mr. Crummy and his advisors solved this problem by providing that the beneficiary of the trust can withdraw the amount of any transfer to the trust within a given period. If the Beneficiary does not elect to withdraw, the gift stays in the trust. After some legal battling, the United States Court of Appeals finally held, in 1968, that Mr. Crummy's gifts to the trust did qualify for the (then $3,000) annual exclusion because the beneficiary could have taken the gift outright had he or she wished to do so. In legal effect, it was a "present interest," an outright gift to the child.

The court held that by not withdrawing the gift during the stated time period it was the beneficiary, the child, who made the gift to the trust and not the parent. Thus, the parent can set up the terms that govern the use of the gift for a generation or two, and still eliminate it from the parent's estate, and even the child's estate if desired.

Let us consider the ramifications.

In Chapter 3 we discussed the great tax benefit of making annual $10,000 gifts of stock to the children, $20,000 if both spouses join. There is a concern about what the children, or their spouses, heirs, or creditors might do with the stock if some disaster occurred. In part, we can solve the problem by use of a stock restrictive agreement (see Exhibit 3.1) or a corporate bylaw (see Exhibit 3.2). But these are limited in effect to some form of first refusal option or buy-out, which require cash to implement. A good practical restriction on transfer, but not a total solution.

Suppose you are giving $20,000 worth of your business to a 16-year-old child; your tax advisor has told you that this will eliminate $20,000 and all future value growth of the stock from your estate, a long-term policy of such gifts may save your company from foundering under a great burden of estate taxes. Is a stock restrictive agreement signed by a minor enforceable? Is such a gift wise from the child's standpoint? You have to make this decision, but you can also use Mr. Crummy's trust concept to meet some of your personal concerns. Here is the procedure:

1. Adopt a corporate bylaw (see Exhibit 3.2) to assure yourself a first refusal right on any transfer, no matter what happens.

2. Transfer the $20,000 of stock to a trust of which a trusted person is the trustee. Notify the child and your spouse of the child's right to withdraw the gift in 30 days. As a practical matter, this withdrawal will not happen, and the stock will stay in the trust. If the child does elect to withdraw, give the child no more gifts.

3. The trustee agrees to hold the stock until the child is 25 years old or some other age selected by you. At that point the stock is transferred to the child, who remains subject to the restrictive bylaw.

4. Set up the trust so that if the child dies before the designated age, the child may direct by will the disposition of the stock among his or her spouse or children, if any. If there are no children or spouse, the stock goes to your other childrens trust.

5. File gift tax returns with your spouse to make a split gift election. Under the split gift election, each spouse is entitled to the $10,000 annual exclusions to the extent of the gifts to the trust. This gives you the $20,000 total gift referred to in 2.

There are, of course, many variations on this theme which the lawyer who prepares the trust can review with you.

How to Shelter Insurance in a Crummy Trust

Now let us get back to insurance to fund taxes. Earlier in this chapter, we reviewed potential difficulties in the use of life insurance to fund taxes. For example, if you own the insurance, it is taxed in your estate, thereby doubling the amount needed to pay the taxes on the business. Or, if you give the insurance to a spouse or child, there is no assurance that the insurance proceeds will actually be used to fund estate taxes on the business. Then why not give cash to a trust like Mr. Crummy's, and let the trust own the insurance? In fact, such an arrangement is very useful—and very popular. It permits purchase and wise control of life insurance to fund estate taxes and other estate needs. The trust provides that the policy proceeds are available for use by the trustee to help the estate pay your taxes.

How to Leverage Your Dollars

The key factor here is leverage—leverage of the $10,000 annual exclusion. If the aim is to prefund estate taxes so the business won't be crippled, the insurance trust is a very efficient device. To many owners of a successful business, the $10,000 or $20,000 per year in exclusions may seem to have a minor impact on the big picture estate tax problems, like pumping a trickle of water to bail out a flooded cellar. Figure 5.1 demonstrates the estate tax funding leverage of various ways of using the $10,000 exclusion each year for 10 years. To keep things simple, we assume the business owner and spouse both die in ten years.

Figure 5.1 illustrates the funding leverage produced by life insurance as compared to other ways of making $10,000 annual gifts. Remember the point of the current discussion is funding of tax payments, not reducing or delaying taxes. Table 5.1 contains the facts pictured in Figure 5.1 and explains the dramatic leverage gained by use of an insurance trust.

In Case #1 assume that annual gifts of liquid securities to a child have removed $145,000 from your estate and thus saved $73,000 of taxes and that the donee retains the $145,000 to help pay estate taxes. The sum of the two—money available and tax saved—is the "tax funding" benefit.

Case #2 is similar but, instead of liquid assets you give closely-held stock. In our example the tax savings is greater because the closely-held stock grows faster than the securities. But the overall "tax funding" effect is less because the closely-held stock can't be used to pay estate taxes.

Case #3 shows that insurance excluded from the estate provides the greatest leverage because it makes a large amount of cash available *and* reduces the estate by the value of the liquid assets used to purchase insurance.

Figure 5.1. Leverage Effect on Tax Funding of
Alternate Uses of $10,000 per Year Gifts

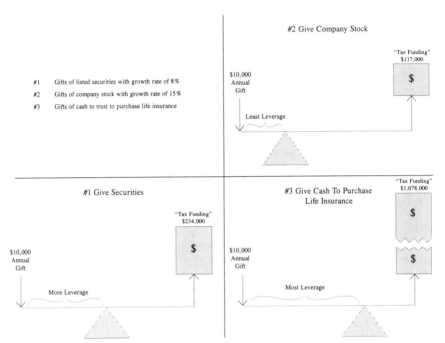

Copyright G. Shattuck 1992

The exact amount of leverage, of course, depends on the age of the insured party, years to death, and the kind of insurance purchased. In case #3, the "growth rate" is based on the proceeds of insurance in 10 years.

In each case, the leverage attained by 10 years of $10,000 gifts, total $100,000, is the tax saved by the gifts plus the fund of liquid assets on hand to help pay estate taxes. In summary:

Case	"Tax Funding"	"Leverage"
Case #1–Give cash or securities	$ 234,000	2.34:1
Case #2–Give Stock of Company	$ 117,000	1.17:1
Case #3–Give to Life Insurance Trust	$1,078,000	10.78:1

Note that, here, the leverage is tax funding leverage which we define to include tax reduction and cash then available to pay taxes. Obviously, different assumptions on growth rates, insurance cost, and time of death will vary the results of our example.

Table 5.1. Tax Funding from Life Insurance Trust

Case #	(1) Annual Gift	(2) Growth Rate	(3) Accum. Val. 10 Years	(4) Tax Saved* Assuming Death	(5) Cash Avail. in 10 Years	(6) Tax Funding = (4) + (5)
#1 Gifts of Securities	$10,000	8%	$ 156,000	$ 78,000	$ 156,000	$ 234,000
#2 Gifts of Closely-Held Stock	$10,000	15%	$ 233,000	$117,000	None	$ 117,000
#3 Gifts of Cash to Buy Life Insurance	$10,000	N/A	$1,000,000**	$ 78,000	$1,000,000	$1,078,000

* Tax saved is 50% of the presumed reduction in estate after 10 years of growth of gifts.
** Face value of insurance, assuming the insured dies in 10 years.

49

Insure the Real Risk to Provide Cash
When the Estate Tax Is Due

If you own a $300,000 house, and a $25,000 barn in the back lot, which would you insure if you had to make a choice? Don't even answer.

Now, suppose you are funding for estate taxes and have three choices on where to place life insurance:

Choice	Estate Tax Needs
#1–Male spouse dies first	None
#2–Female spouse dies first	None
#3–Surviving spouse dies, whichever dies first	Big tax

Which event would you insure if your purpose is to have money to pay estate taxes on the ultimate transfer of your business to your children? Remember, if you have correct marital deduction wills:

• there is no tax if the husband dies first,

• there is no tax if the wife dies first, but

• there is a big tax when the surviving spouse dies.

That is the event you want to insure, the second spouse's death *if* your purpose is to provide cash when the taxes are due.

Insurance companies have a policy designed to meet this need, sometimes called a joint life policy, sometimes a survivor policy. From a tax-funding standpoint, there are two major advantages:

• the cash is provided when needed, whether a year from now or 30 years from now;

• the cost of protection is very low due to the fact that the insurance company is measuring the risk of two lives.

Following is a relative table of cost based on comparable $1,000,000 policies.

	Annual Cost per $Million of	
Age of Insured	**Single Life**	**Joint Life**
40	$14,300	$ 7,300
50	$24,700	$12,600
60	$41,400	$22,100

These estimates are based on the policy in each case being paid up in 15 years, and, of course, depend on the insurance company's actual earnings or dividend experience over the years. Although the above premium costs are estimates, the relative difference between two single life policies and one joint life policy is dramatic.

If you now couple a joint life policy with a trust for the children holding the policy, you get a very efficient way of funding for taxes. A warning: this is a very complex area of tax law. Preparation of such a trust requires the help of legal counsel and of an insurance person who is expert in this field.

Other Insurance Uses

The previous Section presumes that the purpose of obtaining life insurance is to have cash on hand to pay estate taxes. If that is so, and if you are married, then joint life insurance provides a very good answer. But, it is not always the best answer. Consider the following situations:

- There is a need for cash to pay estate taxes but you want to provide ample financial security for your spouse. The joint life policy does not meet that need because it pays only after your spouse's death too. Then consider a policy on one spouse's life which is owned by a trust. At the insured spouse's death, the policy pays into the trust which provides income, and principal if needed, for the life of the surviving spouse. Then the principal, including any investment appreciation, is available to pay estate taxes at the spouse's death. Such a trust can be designed to escape tax in both spouse's estates. The drawback here is that such a single life policy is more costly for a given amount of insurance coverage than a joint life policy.

- Each spouse wants an insurance policy on his or her life payable for the benefit of the other. Here, each spouse sets up a trust as discussed in the previous scenario. But your lawyer should carefully check out "the reciprocal trust" rules in designing this for you. The IRS does not look kindly on contemporaneous transfers between spouses that avoid taxes.

- Your plan is to have the business go to Child A after you both die. The other assets go to Child B. (See Chapter 4.) If you don't have enough assets, apart from the business, to give Child B an equal value when you both die, consider a joint life policy in trust for Child B. When you both die, A gets the business and B gets the other assets plus tax-free cash or a trust fund of approximately equal value to the business going to A. This concept was introduced in Chapter 4. Can you achieve absolute dollar equality in such a case? You probably cannot because of not knowing now how much the business will be worth at your death. But remember cash is cash and the value of a family business is a highly judgmental matter. All one can do is set up the plan now in a fair way and then try to keep it in adjustment. Your insurance advisor will be able to suggest ways of adjusting the insurance amount as you go along. Your lawyer may design an "equalizer" clause in the insurance trust to adjust if the business is then worth much less than the insurance amount.

One thing to be careful of is the tax apportionment clause in your wills. Be sure that the source of payment of the eventual estate tax is planned for and provided in your wills. Do not leave this important consideration up to a form clause in your will, as many do. It would be unfair to leave to Child A a business worth $2 million subject to tax and to Child B a tax-free trust of $2 million. If there was a $1 million tax on the business, to be borne by Child A, your plan of fair division would go awry. See Chapter 19 for a more complete discussion of the tax apportionment issue.

Summary

Both single life insurance and joint life insurance are useful, each in its own place. As the owner of a family business, your task is to make sure that *you* have insured the right risk. Your advisers can suggest and guide, but they don't know what you and your spouse want. So focus on the risk and then select the insurance—with guidance from expert advisors.

This chapter is about funding, providing for estate taxes. It is not about purchasing insurance as a protection mechanism, "If I die what will happen to my spouse and children?" That is a crucially important issue, but not one that is directly answered here.

Our premise is that estate taxes on a business value should be viewed as a current cost of doing business. If the cost is deferred till the estate tax is due, the business may not be able to pay the cost of transferring its value to your heirs. One excellent way to fund the estate tax cost now is by using life insurance which is free of estate taxes. For the married couple, joint life insurance is an excellent, cost-effective way to provide funds for eventual taxes. Business owners should always seek to have the insurance owned by a party or entity other than the insured or spouse. The insurance trust is an effective way to achieve this, but it should not be used without:

- benefit of legal counsel who is an expert in tax law as well as the trust rules of the state where you reside, and
- the assistance of an insurance expert who can lead you through the many options and variables, and guide you around the pitfalls.

6 ——————————————

How to Defer Tax
Payments to the IRS

It is difficult for the owner of a family business currently to predict and then
to provide for the costs of eventual success. The early years are devoted to
struggle to stay solvent, and the growth to eventual success is slow. When
the time comes to look at estate planning, the current value or the projected
growth in value may make total insurance funding of estate taxes impractical.
Or, we may be dealing with second-generation or third-generation owners.
They may already own huge values which were successfully passed down to
them by a prior generation. At some point, unfortunately, if a business
continues and prospers, the estate taxes will come due.

How does such an estate pay its taxes? That is the focus of this chapter
and chapter 7.

Recognizing the Impact of Taxes

The estate taxes discussed in this book are a combination of federal and
state taxes, the federal tax making up the largest part. In some states, the
combined federal and state taxes total can exceed 60 percent for large
estates. We use 50 percent here for illustrative purposes because it makes
tables and graphs more intelligible. The federal tax used to be due 18
months after death, then 15 months, and now it is due nine months after
death. That is a short period in which the return should be filed, all elections
made, and the tax paid. An extension of up to six months to file the return
may be obtained from the IRS, but the tax money is due in the nine months.

Assume you own a business worth $1,000,000 and have no marital
deduction for estate tax purposes because your spouse has predeceased you
or you are single. What kind of tax burden does your growing business add to

**Figure 6.1. How Your Tax Obligation Can Grow
Over the Life Span of the Business Owner
and Spouse**

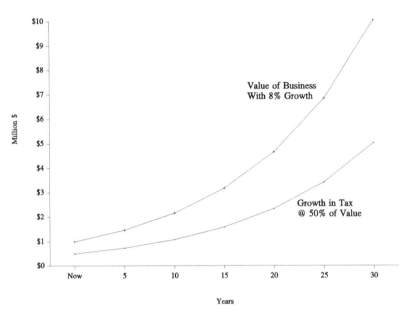

your estate when you die? Assume you have enough liquid assets to pay the tax due on nonbusiness property.

Suppose the business grows at 8 percent per year. Keeping all else constant, the 50 percent toll is illustrated in Figure 6.1. Thus, at least half of all future value growth will eventually go to the government in taxes. Furthermore the tax amount is due at a time now unknown; tomorrow? next year? ten years from now?

Pretty steep growth! At 8 percent growth, the dollar doubles every nine years. Based on past history, about 5 percent of the growth shown on Figure 6.1 is just inflation in the dollar, leaving 3 pecent for the "real" growth of your business.

Over a 30-year life expectancy for both spouses, it is not far fetched that a well-run family business would grow from $1 million to $10 million in dollar value and from $0.5 million to $5 million in tax exposure. Table 6.1, below, shows the effect of growth at varying rates; the tax is 50 percent of those figures. Unless otherwise provided for, the eventual estate tax will be at least 50 percent of these values.

Table 6.1. Business Values at Varying Growth Rates
Starting at $1 Million

Growth Rate	Business Value in Millions of Dollars			
	5 years	10 years	15 years	20 years
5 %	$1.3	$1.6	$2.1	$ 2.7
7.5%	$1.4	$2.1	$3.0	$ 4.2
10 %	$1.6	$2.6	$4.2	$ 6.7
12.5%	$1.8	$3.2	$5.9	$10.5
15 %	$2.0	$4.0	$8.1	$16.4

Payment Options for the Estate Tax

Suppose the value of the business interest in your estate is $4 million. The estate tax attributable to the business, due nine months after death, is $2,000,000. How do your heirs meet this obligation? What are their options?

- *Use other estate assets to pay the tax on the business value*? Let us assume for purposes of Chapters 6 and 7 that the other assets are not adequate to do this and accomplish your wishes and other obligations. Remember there is a tax due on the other assets too.

- *Sell the business interest to outsiders*? Yes, this is possible, but the premise of this book is that you as the owner want to keep the business for the family.

- *Borrow $2 million from a bank to pay the tax*? Where does the estate get the funds to pay the principal and interest on the loan? Will a bank lend to an estate for this purpose?

- *Sell $2 million of stock back to the business*? Does the business have $2 million to spare? What does selling part of your stock back to the business do to proportionate ownership among the family? With respect to nonrelated shareholders?

- *Ask the IRS to defer tax collectionz*? Yes, this is possible, and we discuss such deferral in the next section.

- *Elect to defer tax payment for up to 14 years*? Yes, in certain situations a closely held business can elect to defer estate tax payment for up to 14 years after due date—with interest. This is also discussed in this chapter.

- *Distribute cash from the business to owners, including the estate as majority owner*? Yes, this is feasible for an S Corporation, partnership, or proprietorship. See Chapter 7 discussion of this option.

- *Choose other payment options?* Yes, certainly there are other options, but the main ones in concept are listed above.

These options have time dimensions: First, you can file them away in your head somewhere and hope that your heirs and the estate's executor will think of them and use one or more as may seem available. Second, you can put them on the front burner now and plan your affairs so your estate can qualify and make use of those that are most relevant to your situation. A great deal is at stake here, if it is your desire that the business remain in the family. The following sections of this chapter discuss the options in detail and enable you, the owner, to plan for this future cost.

Deferring Tax with IRS Permission

Yes, this is an option. There is a specific provision in the Internal Revenue Code for extension of tax payments for up to nine years with interest where the estate can show reasonable cause for the delay. Reasonable cause has been interpreted by the IRS as a situation where the estate does not have enough cash to pay the tax when due after considering the needs of the spouse, beneficiaries, and other creditors of the estate. This seems to fit the case of our $4 million business interest: The sum of $2 million is just not available nine months after the owner dies. So what are the financial implications to the estate of obtaining the IRS permission to defer?

The first is that the tax is usually paid in 10 equal installments, the first 10 percent on the due date of the return. Hence the deferral of the 90 percent balance is for nine years after the due date. The second financial implication is that interest must be paid on the deferred balance with each annual tax payment, just like a bank term loan. The applicable rate is a published federal rate, which is adjusted quarterly, plus three percentage points. The average of this published rate for the twelve months prior to June 30, 1992, was 6.25 percent, to which should be added the three points making a total rate of 9.25 percent. For advance planning purposes we like to use a 10 percent rate which is more reflective of a longer past history. Assuming a 10 percent rate, the payment schedule on $2 million tax is shown in Table 6.2. This nine-year deferral puts the payment of estate taxes on a more realistic basis.

How to Deduct the Interest on Deferred Tax

Is that interest deductible in some way? Having the interest deductible would of course reduce the payment burden still further. Is the interest deductible for the estate's income tax purposes? The answer here is yes. Such interest is deductible against the estate's income; but it is not likely that the estate would have that much income. However, the estate tax rates

Table 6.2. Deferred Tax Payment Schedule
(Interest not Deducted)

Payment Date	Principal Paid	Principal Balance	Interest Paid	Total Payment
Return Date	$ 200,000	$1,800,000	$ 0	$ 200,000
1 year	200,000	1,600,000	180,000	380,000
2 years	200,000	1,400,000	160,000	360,000
3 years	200,000	1,200,000	140,000	340,000
4 years	200,000	1,000,000	120,000	320,000
5 years	200,000	800,000	100,000	300,000
6 years	200,000	600,000	80,000	280,000
7 years	200,000	400,000	60,000	260,000
8 years	200,000	200,000	40,000	240,000
9 years	200,000	0	20,000	220,000
Total Payments	$2,000,000		$900,000	$2,900,000

are higher than income tax rates (55 percent versus 31 percent) so it would be more advantageous to deduct the interest as an estate administration expense in calculating the estate tax, rather than the income tax.

Can the interest on the deferred tax payments somehow be deducted for estate tax purposes? Yes, such interest is deductible as an estate administration expense to arrive at estate tax. However, you cannot deduct the same interest in calculating both taxes. You have to elect which deduction you want. One more important point: under IRS rules, you cannot deduct the whole nine years' interest, $900,000 in the foregoing table, up front when the return is filed. You can only deduct the interest as it's actually paid, installment by installment. For instance, the first interest payment of $180,000, shown in Table 6.2 as payable at the end of one year, would be deducted from the $4 million value of the business to reduce the $2 million estate tax by $90,000. But you have already paid $180,000, which is too much because the estate has been reduced thus:

Taxable estate before interest payment	$4,000,000
Interest payment	180,000
Revised estate	$3,820,000
Revised tax 50% (instead of	$1,910,000
the original $2 million)	

As you can see, the estate paid too much interest in the payment at the end of year one because the initial tax has been reduced by deducting the interest. This happens each year as each interest payment is made. Thus a "circular" calculation is needed where the interest depends on the tax due, which in turn depends on the interest paid and deducted. Under IRS procedures, you make this adjustment at the first payment to arrive at the next payment, due at the end of the next year, and so on. To permit these adjustments and accompanying reductions in tax, the normal three year period of limitations is extended so the estate can get credit for the tax reduction due to the interest paid after the normal three years limitation period.

As we explained, if, after the first payment of interest, the overall tax has been reduced—the estate paid too much interest. This excess cash payment is credited against the original tax. You get into a chicken and egg situation where the interest is dependent on the reduced tax and vice versa. This gets really complex where we have state taxes and tax credits, plus varying federal and state interest rates. It literally takes a computer to calculate a payment schedule and this must be done each year of payment because the interest rates are subject to change.

Table 6.3 shows a highly simplified payment schedule with approximate figures. Such approximations could not be used for actual tax payment purposes, but may be useful for estate planning or for cash needs projections by an estate. The reduction in total payments each year in Table 6.3, as compared to Table 6.2 above, is due to the deduction each year from the initial taxable estate of an amount equal to the cumulative interest paid.

Table 6.3. Permissive Deferral of $2 Million Estate Tax (Interest Deducted as Administration Expense)

Pmnt. Date	Prin. Paid	Int. Paid	Total Pmnt.
Return Due	$ 200,000	$ 0	$ 200,000
Plus 1 year	200,000	180,000	380,000
Plus 2 years	188,000	151,000	339,000
Plus 3 years	177,000	124,000	301,000
Plus 4 years	166,000	100,000	266,000
Plus 5 years	156,000	78,000	234,000
Plus 6 years	145,000	58,000	203,000
Plus 7 years	135,000	41,000	176,000
Plus 8 years	125,000	25,000	150,000
Plus 9 years	112,000	11,000	123,000
Totals	$1,604,000	$767,000	$2,371,000
Present Value at 10%			$1,705,000

Note: We emphasize that the foregoing Table 6.3 is a rough approximation used to illustrate a principle. Table 6.3 should not be used for actual tax payments.

Thus, the deferral of tax due, with interest deductible against the original tax, can be very valuable to the estate of a business owner. However, there are other factors to consider:

- the executor remains liable for the tax until it is paid, thus any estate distributions are at his or her personal risk until the tax is paid in full,
- in some cases the IRS requires a bond to secure payment of the deferred tax,
- the statute of limitation on additional assessments is extended,
- by virtue of the above, the administration of the estate is extended and made more complex, and expensive.

It is best to provide for the taxes in the first place, but if this is not possible, tax deferral can save the business from being sold or liquidated to pay taxes. Please remember that the nine-year deferral discussed here is with permission of the IRS which is granted only on a showing of reasonable cause for deferral.

Deferring Tax at Estate's Election

The foregoing section deals with deferring the tax, with IRS permission, on a showing of reasonable cause. That is obviously a valuable option where you can justify the need for deferral.

The tax law also provides an additional option to defer the tax on a closely held business for up to 14 years—interest only for the first four years, principal and interest for the next 10 years. This can be elected if the estate qualifies. IRS permission and bonds are not required (but executor's personal liability for any unpaid tax remains). A payment schedule for this elective option is shown on Table 6.4. As in the case of Table 6.3, it assumes that the interest is deductible for estate tax purposes.

Instead of paying $2,000,000 cash at the end of nine months, the estate can elect to pay no tax with the return and then make the payments shown in the last column of Table 6.4. Please note that the deferral here refers to the tax proportionate to the business; the tax attributable to other assets must be paid at the due date of the return. As in the case of the nine year deferral, the interest shown on Table 6.4 is deductible to permit re-calculating and reducing the tax following each interest payment. Part of each interest payment shown in Table 6.4 is transformed into principal on payment, when the calculation is made to deduct the interest. Note: Table 6.4 is also a rough approximation of the payment schedule and is only used for illustrative purposes.

**Table 6.4. Elective Deferral of $2 Million Estate Tax
on Closely-Held Business (Interest Deducted
as Administration Expense)**

Payment Date	Principal Paid	Interest Paid	Total Payment
Return Due	$ 0	$ 0	$ 0
Plus 1 Year	0	200,000	200,000
Plus 2 Years	0	190,000	190,000
Plus 3 Years	0	180,000	180,000
Plus 4 Years	0	170,000	170,000
Plus 5 Years	161,000	161,000	322,000
Plus 6 Years	152,000	137,000	289,000
Plus 7 Years	143,000	114,000	257,000
Plus 8 Years	134,000	94,000	228,000
Plus 9 Years	126,000	76,000	202,000
Plus 10 Years	118,000	59,000	177,000
Plus 11 Years	110,000	44,000	154,000
Plus 12 Years	103,000	31,000	134,000
Plus 13 Years	95,000	19,000	114,000
Plus 14 Years	85,000	8,000	93,000
Totals	$1,227,000	$1,483,000	$2,710,000
Present Value @ 10%			$1,650,000

How to Qualify for Elective Tax Deferral

What does an estate need to qualify for the 14-year tax deferral? Yes, there are some tests, but they are usually not too onerous in the case of the family business. They are:

- The business interest must exceed 35 percent of the total estate, less administrative deductions;

- The business must be closely held; that is, the business may be a proprietorship, partnership, or corporation, but unless the estate owns at least 20 percent of the voting control it may not have more than 15 owners. Members of a family are counted as one owner.

- The business must be an active business. Congress's intent was to help the owners of active businesses, not investment companies, so the tax extension does not apply to tax attributable to passive assets or investment assets.

- Brother-sister companies may be lumped together. Suppose the estate owns two closely held active businesses, each of which comprises only

20 percent of the estate less deductions. In computing the 35 percent requirement described above, if the estate owns at least 20 percent of each business, it can total their values in the estate to see if the 35 percent requirement is met.

- There is no limit on the size of the business. A $1 billion business would qualify if it met the other requirements.

- The deferred tax amount is the proportion of active business value to total estate value.

"Why all this detail?" one might ask. Actually, there's even more detail than in this summary, but the 14-year deferral option is so valuable a tool for the family business that it's worth planning to qualify for it, if other funding and tax reduction devices are not available.

Another Tax Deferral Method

In the previous two sections, we show how an estate can defer paying part of the estate tax on the basis of reasonable cause if that can be shown, or by electing to pay over 14 years if the requirements for election are met. In effect, the estate is borrowing from the IRS at tax subsidized interest rates. One more option should be mentioned: If an asset of the estate is a business which has credit, be it a corporation or partnership, the business itself can borrow the tax amount from a lending institution and either lend the cash to the estate, or redeem stock or a partnership interest from the estate.

Assume that the tax is $2 million and that the business can borrow that sum, payable annually with 10 percent interest over 14 years. The corporation borrows the $2 million and redeems $2 million of stock from the estate. Chapter 7 details how such a redemption may be done. The tax is paid on the due date and the IRS is out of the picture. Instead the corporation owes the money to the lender. The corporation's payment schedule is shown in Table 6.5. Here, a 14-year payment schedule is used to get a comparison with the 14-year tax deferral in Table 6.4; in practice the business would repay its loan on a 10-year basis, or whatever term it could negotiate with the lender.

In Table 6.5 as compared to Tables 6.3 and 6.4, the corporation is deducting interest against its 40 percent income tax rate not the 50 percent tax rate assumed in 6.3 and 6.4. Hence the corporation receives less benefit from deducting the interest. But it is probably still better than paying the tax at due date.

Summary

Most estates, in one way or another, can be planned to meet the cash demands for estate taxes when the tax is due. But sometimes planning options are not available or have not kept pace with growth in values. This is

**Table 6.5. How Corporate Borrowing of $2 Million
Enables Estate to Pay Estate Tax on Due Date
(Interest Deducted From Corporate Income)**

Payment Date	Principal Paid	Interest Paid	Total After-Tax Cost
Return Due	$ 0	$ 0	$ 0
Plus 1 Year	143,000	200,000	263,000
Plus 2 Years	143,000	186,000	254,000
Plus 3 Years	143,000	171,000	246,000
Plus 4 Years	143,000	157,000	237,000
Plus 5 Years	143,000	143,000	229,000
Plus 6 Years	143,000	129,000	220,000
Plus 7 Years	143,000	114,000	211,000
Plus 8 Years	143,000	100,000	203,000
Plus 9 Years	143,000	86,000	194,000
Plus 10 Years	143,000	71,000	186,000
Plus 11 Years	143,000	57,000	177,000
Plus 12 Years	143,000	43,000	169,000
Plus 13 Years	143,000	29,000	160,000
Plus 14 Years	143,000	14,000	151,000
Totals	$2,000,000	$1,500,000	$2,900,000
Present Value @ 10%			$1,621,000

especially true where a closely held business forms the bulk of an estate.
Many successful businesses are sold or merged, or go public, because the
estate taxes cannot be paid. Indeed, a sale or merger ultimately may be
forced upon the estate. Short of that, do not overlook, in conjunction with
other planning devices, the means of tax payment deferral which we have
described.

Tables 6.3, 6.4, and 6.5 show a figure for the present value of each
series of payments. This gives a relative value to each means of payment and
also points out the benefits of being able to deduct the interest against the 50
percent estate tax. At 10 percent interest, the after tax rate comes out to 5
percent.

Figure 6.2 is a graph showing the annual after tax cash requirements of
the three alternatives discussed above. The present value, at 10 percent
interest, of each of the alternatives is shown below in Table 6.6.

Graphically, the elective 14-year deferral seems to favor the other
payment schedules; the initial four years' payment are of interest only,
giving the estate and business more time to raise the needed cash. This
reflects itself in the lower present value shown in Table 6.6. Note that in all
three alternatives the present value of the future payments is substantially

**Figure 6.2. After-Tax Cash Payments on Estate
Taxes ($2 Million Initial Tax)**

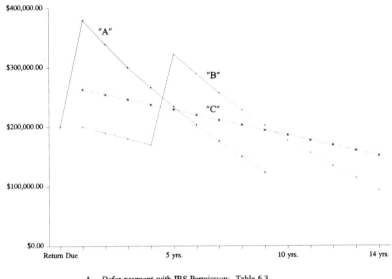

A.   Defer payment with IRS Permission: Table 6.3

KEY: B.   Defer payment by election if business > 35% of estate: Table 6.4

C.   Business borrows cash and redeems stock or lends to estate: Table 6.5

Copyright G. Shattuck 1992

Table 6.6. Present Value of Alternatives

Payment Alternative	See Table #	Present Value at 10%
A. Permissive 9 year payout	6.3	$1,550,000
B. Elective 14 year payment	6.4	1,450,000
C. Corporation borrows funds	6.5	1,621,000
Pay estate tax when due	N/A	$2,000,000

less than the $2.0 million present value of paying the tax when done. This is
because our 10 percent discount rate is higher than the tax subsidized
deferral interest rate.

From a planning standpoint a business owner is well advised to structure things in advance so as to qualify for the 14-year deferral. In all three
payment options, a shorter payment period may be used and the principal
balance can be paid any time.

7

Using the Business as a Source of Tax Funds

So far we have discussed how to:

- defer estate taxes with a marital deduction will,
- reduce taxes with gifts,
- prefund estate taxes with a tax free insurance trust, and
- pay estate taxes over a period of time with deductible interest.

These are all basic elements of estate planning for the family business or closely held business. In all of these, the same rules apply whether the business is a corporation, a partnership, or a sole proprietorship.

Where the issue is, "How to obtain funds from the business," we have different rules for each kind of business entity. In fact, the rules have to be further broken down to account for differences where the ownership is centered in one person or in several. A description of the rules—and opportunities—is the focus of this chapter.

Envision that one of your children is the executor of your estate, which includes stock of your business worth $4 million. The estate tax is $2 million and the executor is looking around for cash to pay the tax. Other assets have been used for debts, expenses, and legacies.

The business has some funds and can borrow more. It is the only logical source of cash to pay the tax, due nine months after death. Even if tax payment is deferred, the cash has to come from somewhere and the estate does not have it. Can the executor just tell the corporate treasurer or financial partner to write a check so the taxes can be paid?

Our discussion of this issue breaks the tax situation down into four types of business entity:

- C Corporation—pays its own corporate tax,

- S Corporation—pays no tax and business income is taxed directly to shareholders,
- S Corporation—formerly a C Corporation,
- Partnership, including a limited liability company.

Each of these has special income tax rules on withdrawal of funds by the owners. Careful attention and expert counsel are required to make sure the estate does not find itself in a serious tax trap.

Tax Rules for C Corporations

Here lies danger. A C Corporation is your typical garden variety corporation which pays a tax on its earnings, and whose shareholders pay a further tax when a dividend is paid to them. A distribution of cash or property from a C Corporation is taxable as a dividend to the estate if the corporation has an earned surplus on its books. This is true even if the estate sells back its stock to the corporation, which we would normally think of as a capital gain. If the transaction is taxed as a dividend, and not as a capital gain sale, the full redemption price is taxable; the estate's cost basis for the stock is irrelevant. If the redemption is taxed as a capital gain, there is normally no income tax at all on the redemption because the estate acquires a new stepped-up basis at the owner's death. Thus an estate which withdraws funds from a corporation to pay estate taxes could incur an income tax on the full amount of cash. There are two exceptions to this:

1. If the estate and family completely terminates their interest in the business, there is no dividend treatment when their stock is redeemed by the corporation.
2. If the business interest comprises more than 35 percent of the estate, stock can be redeemed tax free up to an amount equal to estate taxes and administration expenses. This allows the estate to secure funds from the corporation tax free.

Table 7.1 illustrates the disastrous result of treating a redemption of stock as a taxable dividend. Compare with the capital gain treatment, where there is no tax on the redemption. The basic principles are these:

- in a capital gain transaction the estate's cost basis for the stock is date-of-death value—hence there is no taxable gain when the stock is redeemed by the corporation;
- in a dividend transaction, i.e., redemption treated as a dividend, the entire proceeds are taxable income to the extent of the corporate surplus—here cost basis is irrelevant.

Table 7.1. Example of Taxable vs. Tax Free
Stock Redemption

	Redemption Taxed as a Dividend	Redemption Taxed as Capital Gain
Value of Business in Estate	$4,000,000	$4,000,000
Estate Tax on Business Value	2,000,000	2,000,000
Proceeds of Stock Redemption	2,000,000	2,000,000
Estate's Cost Basis (= Date of Death Value) of the stock redeemed for taxes	NA	2,000,000
Estate's Gain or Income on Redemption	2,000,000	0
Estate's Income Tax @ 31%	620,000	0
Balance Left to Pay on Estate Taxes	$1,380,000	$2,000,000

In order to qualify for the special capital gain treatment, the value of the business must comprise more than 35 percent of the estate, and the redemption must take place within three years and nine months of death of the business owner; but this period can be extended if an election to defer payment of taxes is made as described in the prior chapter.

Is it wise to accumulate cash in a C Corporation to have a fund to pay eventual estate taxes on the owner's estate? No. This is dangerous because the IRS may assert a penalty tax for unreasonable accumulation of income in the corporation. An accumulation to pay estate taxes is not a "reasonable" one so far as the IRS is concerned even though the objective is to have money on hand to pay federal estate taxes.

Tax Rules for S Corporations

An S Corporation is one which has elected to be taxed as though it were a partnership; no "double tax" on its dividends. As in other respects, the tax structure of an S Corporation is vastly superior to that of a C Corporation where estate taxes are concerned. An estate can withdraw cash dividends from an S Corporation tax free up to the amount of its cost basis, i.e., date of death value, with no fear of dividend treatment. But, if there are several shareholders, you can't just distribute cash to one shareholder and not the others; disproportionate dividends may cause loss of subchapter S status.

You may, however, redeem and cancel the estate's stock with no risk of dividend treatment because an S Corporation, that has always been an S Corporation has no earned surplus to be taxed as a dividend.

S Corporation, Formerly C Corporation

If an S Corporation has no earned surplus (from previous C Corporation status), the amount distributed in redemption of stock is tax free as described in the prior section.

However, if an S Corporation does have earned surplus left over from its C Corporation status, distributions are considered made out of the following sources, in the order listed:

1. The Accumulated Adjustment Account ("aaa")—i.e., Subchapter S profits left in the Corporation. To the extent a distribution is considered made out of the AAA, the distribution is taxed in the same manner as if the S Corporation had no earned surplus.

2. Distributions considered in excess of the AAA account are considered made out of earned surplus are taxed as dividends unless the redemption qualifies as tax free as explained in the foregoing discussion on redemption of stock of a C Corporation.

An S Corporation, with the consent of all shareholders to whom distributions are made, can elect to treat distributions as made out of earned surplus before being made out of the AAA. This might be advisable if the redemption to pay taxes qualified as tax free under the C Corporation rules.

Tax Rules for Partnerships

Generally, there are two alternatives for the estate or successors of a deceased partner to withdraw funds to pay estate taxes. Each alternative may have different income tax consequences to both the decedent's estate and the remaining partners. First, the partnership may liquidate the deceased partner's individual interest and the remaining partners continue the operations of the partnership. Second, the estate, or heirs, continue as partners.

If the Remaining Partners Continue Operations

If the partner's individual interest is liquidated and the estate receives one or more payments from the partnership in liquidation of the decedent's interest, the nature of the payments received will determine the taxability. Liquidating payments may be classified as

• payments for the partner's interest in the partnership assets,

- payment for a distributive share of partnership income, or
- a guaranteed payment.

These characterizations of payments from a partnership are significant because they will determine whether the successor will recognize capital gain or loss or ordinary income and whether the remaining partners and the partnership will be entitled to a deduction with respect to such payments. For the most part the nature of such payments can be controlled by the provisions of the partnership agreement.

If the partnership agreement specifies that the deceased partner's interest be bought out, liquidated, then the proceeds are taxed to the estate as a capital gain. This means that the estate realizes no income from the payments because it acquires a new cost basis for the partnership interest. By the same token, the partnership cannot deduct the liquidation payments. This is similar to the rules on capital gains redemptions of stock, discussed above.

If the partnership provides that the payments are distributions of income, or all "guaranteed payments," then such payments are income to the estate and reduce the income of the other partners, in effect are deductible. Thus the agreement can control the tax impact on the estate of a deceased partner and the remaining partners. It can control the mix of capital gains and ordinary income of deductible payments as nondeductible. This assumes an agreement entered into before death.

If the Estate or Heirs Continue in the Partnership

In the event of a partner's death, the estate or other successor may continue as a partner. There are generally no income tax consequences to the estate for withdrawing funds after death, except of course to the extent they represent current untaxed earnings.

Legal Matters

If there are multiple owners of the business, an estate can't just declare dividends, redeem stock, distribute partnership cash at will. The other owners have proportionate rights to the assets and their consent is needed to withdraw funds. Estate tax needs should be addressed in agreement by the shareholders or partners while everyone is around to negotiate.

Summary

The foregoing is a gloss of the complex rules that govern cash withdrawals from business entities. The complexity should not obscure the very real value of being able to look to the business itself as a source of estate tax funds. Where co-owners are involved, a predeath agreement is very important to make sure the funds will be available to an estate when needed.

Withdrawing funds from a corporation can have serious tax consequences. In general this book takes a positive note: how to do it, rather than focus on dire warnings and mazes of technical rules. This chapter, however, must conclude by warning readers that the withdrawal of funds from any business entity, especially a corporation, can have serious income tax consequences. It can be done, but it must be done right. The overall policy of the tax law is to impose a tax on withdrawal of funds from a corporate entity and the need of the owner is not relevant. If an estate is an owner of a business entity, it too must pay attention to the rules—or risk paying a large income tax. The law also sets up exceptions to permit estates with a family business to pay estate taxes, but these exceptions are complex and technical. With expert counsel it is possible to do it right, moreover the penalty for mistakes is severe.

This chapter shows the basic ground rules. It also demonstrates, again, the great value of advance planning by the business owner while he or she is alive.

Part Three

HOW TO FREEZE
YOUR ESTATE

CHAPTER 8.   Determining the Value of Your
              Business for Estate Tax Purposes
CHAPTER 9.   How to Give Away Future
              Company Growth, but Keep Control
              and Security
CHAPTER 10.   Using the Preferred Stock Freeze
              to Save Taxes
CHAPTER 11.   Sale of Stock to Children
CHAPTER 12.   Using the Partnership Freeze
              to Save Taxes
CHAPTER 13.   Will a Freeze Save Your Family
              Business, or Impair It?

In Part One you learned the classic ways to defer taxes and directly reduce your taxable estate. Part Two discussed how to fund and defer payment on the taxes when they inevitably are due.

Part Three takes a different tactic. Here, the theme is "Don't Own It In The First Place." In terms of business succession, the concept is that the current owners' interest be frozen in value so that future appreciation belongs to the next generation of business owners, not in the current owners' estate at all.

Can this be done legally? Yes, but there are rules that you must follow before the IRS will approve. Remember, though, that this book deals with concepts, rather than detailed rules which should be the province of your professional advisers. This is especially true in the area of the so-called estate freeze, which IRS rules have made very complex. No kind of "freeze" transaction should be undertaken without expert tax counsel nor without written independent opinions on value of assets.

Part Three is not a complete explanation, rather it is intended to familiarize you with the correct and practical approaches to freezing the value of your business in your estate.

8

Determining the Value of Your Business for Estate Tax Purposes

The concept of "value" underlies this whole book because the estate and gift tax are computed as a percentage of the "value" of the taxable gift or the taxable estate. Yet value is often very difficult to arrive at, particularly in the case of a closely held business interest. If you own 3,000 shares of General Electric stock, you can look in a newspaper for the value on any particular date. If you own a family construction business with three projects underway, ample resources, and a good earning history, where do you look for value? Your company is unique, personal to the family or families that own it. Who determines the business value?

Someone must because if an interest in the company is in your estate, a value must be put on the estate tax return. That value must withstand the scrutiny of an IRS auditor, who will probably think the business is worth more than you and your family think it is, at least for tax purposes.

Many of the transactions described in this book depend on a current value. If the value you use is too low, the IRS can assess interest and penalties, as well as the extra tax on the increased value. We recommend that appraisals be used in most, if not all, tax-oriented transactions. Depending on the circumstances, the appraisal may be formal and costly, or informal and less costly, but it should always be done by a qualified, unrelated party. Appraisals will be discussed in more detail later in this chapter, but at this point let us state that the term "value" as used here always means value established or confirmed by appraisal.

What Is Value in an Appraisal?

You will not find any citations, laws, or quotes from rules in this book. The one legal quote you should know is the definition of fair market value for gift and estate tax purposes.

> Fair market value is "the price at which the property would change hands between a willing buyer and a willing seller, neither being under any compulsion to buy or sell, and both having reasonable knowledge of relevant facts." Treas. Reg. § 20.2031(b).

Most appraisals you see will state this definition, or paraphrase it, as the basis of what they are doing. Really it's a very nice definition, but how do we apply it to the 532 shares that you now own in the family business (the remaining 468 shares being owned by your spouse and children)? Let's walk quickly through the definition, focusing on several key phrases.

"Price." The price envisioned here is a cash price. It may be that as a practical matter the property could never be sold on a completely cash basis, that an earn-out would be required. Nevertheless, a dollar cash value must be arrived at for gift and estate tax purposes.

"The Property." This is very important. The value of your 532 shares is not 53.2 percent of the value of the whole business, it is the value of just those shares, standing by themselves. In this case, the whole may be worth more than the sum of the parts. This is sometimes reflected in discounts for partial interests, which will be discussed later.

"The Property Would Change Hands." Value is based on a hypothetical sale. We can't say there is no value because there is no chance the property would ever be sold or could ever be sold. The fact that your property, the 532 shares, might be difficult to sell does not eliminate the requirement that a value be established and put on the tax return.

"Willing Buyer," "Willing Seller." The essence of property valuation is imagining the bargaining process between two hypothetical parties, the willing buyer and willing seller. Expert appraisers do this very well. They have banks of data, files of cases and precedents, and the expertise of an established profession. The personal biases of the situation must be eliminated. We all know that your family would never sell the 532 shares in the family company; they might sell the whole thing but never a part. We also know that the willing buyer would be very reluctant to acquire a fractional interest, even a 53.2% controlling interest, in a family company. The appraiser's job is to figure what the hypothetical parties would in fact accept, leaving out the personal feelings.

No "Compulsion." A forced sale by the estate is not envisioned here, nor is a buyer who must buy at all costs.

"Knowledge of Relevant Facts." Facts are the key here. The buyer and the seller are presumed to know all about the company, its finances, markets, competition, management. The appraiser will know the market factors involved and will have some experience in what companies like yours have been appraised for and might sell for. We have to imagine an arms-length bargaining process between knowledgeable people.

Determining the Value of a Business: 3 Case Studies

What is the value, then, of your family or closely held business? Value for tax purposes is the result of a reasoning process, applying actual known sales of similar property by analogy to your situation, to the 532 shares. An appraiser will consider several factors and formulas, discussed later in this chapter, and these usually result in a reasonable range of what the property would be sold for between the willing buyer and seller. The appraiser must then make a good faith judgment in coming up with a concrete number. You cannot say on a tax return that the 532 shares are worth "in a range of $2,000 to $2,500 per share." There has to be a specific number: e.g., $2,350 per share.

Before going into all the details let us illustrate the process with a digest of three actual valuation cases. The first one is the case of a car dealership; the second involves a manufacturing company; and the third describes a real estate company. All happen to be corporations, but the same principles would apply to proprietorships and partnerships.

Case Study #1: Valuation of a Car Dealership

A family-owned car dealership established an employee stock ownership plan (ESOP). Good valuations are vital when an ESOP is created. Initially, the owner of the company usually wants a high value because of the income tax deductions available for the contribution of their stock to the ESOP. Later, when it comes time to buy back the employees' stock he may want a low value. This puts a burden on the appraiser who at all times must seek to arrive at a fair value.

In this car dealership case, the IRS argued that owner had overvalued the stock for deduction purposes. The valuation date was 1973, and the IRS contended that the Arab oil embargo depressed auto sales and thereby reduced the value of an auto dealership. The IRS also based its valuation on the book value of the corporation's assets, and applied a minority discount. The court found that the company's earnings and dividend paying capacity were much more important than book value in determining the company's value. Because the company had an excellent earnings history, the court agreed with the owner's higher valuation. Note that, unlike the estate tax situation, the taxpayer was seeking a high value here to justify an income tax deduction.

Case Study #2: Valuation of a Manufacturing Company

A company manufactured coil springs for the automobile industry. The decedent owned 20 percent of the company at her death and the issue was the value of her 20 percent for purposes of her estate tax. Only one of the company's competitors was a publicly traded firm, and that competitor was engaged in other lines of business, was much larger. In a court case, the estate and the IRS each used an expert appraiser to establish the value of the estate's 20 percent interest.

The IRS appraiser used information from the publicly traded competitor, as well as information from five other manufacturers of parts for the automobile industry in reaching his value. Specifically, he compared the estate's company to the comparable companies using

- ratios of price to current earnings,

- price to 5-year average cash flow, and

- price to book value.

Applying these ratios to the company's own data, he arrived at a rational conclusion as to its value.

The court accepted the IRS expert's opinion, which included a discount for lack of marketability. The IRS expert's appraisal was typical in this setting. It identified comparable publicly traded companies, and then compared several different ratios to the information from the subject company to reach a value. The court rejected the taxpayer's expert testimony because it failed to identify the comparable companies used, and lacked specificity on the comparable ratios used. This was a case of one appraiser doing a job acceptable to the court and the other not doing so. Clearly established valuation guidelines have to be followed.

Case Study #3: Valuation of a Real Estate Company

The decedent owned 27% of a real estate holding company at his death. The company owned several types of parcels, including apartment buildings, office buildings, vacant land, and a motel property. The decedent's estate and the IRS agreed that the net value of the assets owned by the company as of the date of death was $4 million. In other words, there was no dispute that the way to value the overall worth of a real estate holding company, if the decedent owned 100 percent of it, is to appraise the fair market value of each parcel, and subtract from that the outstanding debt. The litigated issues turned on the practice to apply a "discount" to the overall value of the company in arriving at the value of a given block of shares or ownership interest. If a business is worth $1 million, a 27 percent interest does not necessarily have a market value of $270,000. Usually, the value of the actual interest owned by the decedent comes out lower due to various factors, including the fact that an investor would be unwilling to purchase a minority interest when he or she could go out and purchase good property directly.

The key issue in this case was how to value the 27 percent interest owned by the decedent. The taxpayer's family argued that two discounts should apply. First, a discount for "lack of marketability" because it would not be easy to sell a partial interest in a closely held business. Second, the purchaser of the taxpayer's 27 percent interest would acquire only a minority interest in the company, and would not be able to control the management of the company. Thus, the family argued that a "minority discount" should apply. In aggregate, the taxpayer's family took a 60 percent discount from the overall company value in arriving at a value of the stock in question.

The IRS, not surprisingly, thought the family had taken too large a discount. It contended that a 30 percent overall discount was more appropriate. The parties essentially had a battle of appraisers. Unfortunately for the taxpayer, the court gave more weight to the IRS appraisals. Consequently, the court agreed with the IRS, and found the minority interest discount to be 20 percent, and the lack of marketability discount to be 10 percent.

Appraisal Techniques and Valuation Factors

Professional appraisers use a number of techniques. Most of them are based on an IRS rule stating that the value of a closely held business should be ascertained in part by analogy to the stock value of publicly traded companies in the same line of business. The appraiser seeks out so-called "comparable companies" that have a public market and measures them against the company to be appraised. Some of the measures used are described in the following sections.

Price:Earnings Ratio

National Widget Corp., listed on the N.Y. Stock exchange, has 12,000,000 outstanding shares, sales of $800 million, and a book value of $250 million. National Widget has an average profit of $48 million per year. Its stock sells for $48 per share on a given day, and earnings are $4.00 per share. Its price/earnings (price ÷ earnings) ratio is 12:1 for that day.

Your company makes an average of $100,000 per year after taxes. Applying the same 12:1 price/earnings ratio, your company would be worth $1.2 million. Is that fair? Probably not because in other respects—size, financial strength, traded stock, management depth—your company is not really comparable; adjustments must be made.

Book Value Ratio

National Widget has a price-to-book value ratio of 2.3:1 ($576 million ÷ $250 million). Your company has a book value of $800,000, so on this basis it would be worth $1.8 million. Is that fair? Again, probably not, due to the same conditions discussed above. A publicly traded company's stock may have a value on a given day which has little to do with the normal valuation ratios and techniques.

A company's book value is a factor in and of itself. If nothing else, this is a form of reality check in looking at a closely held company. Would a company whose book value (assets less liabilities) is $800,000 really sell on the market for $1.8 million just because National Widget does? Maybe, but the typical buyer of a closely held company is apt to be more asset oriented than someone buying listed stock, who is more earnings oriented.

Cash Flow

Appraisers also look at the cash flow generated by a company and compare it to the price/cash flow ratios of comparable listed companies. Historic cash flow is not easy to establish, but appraisers can do it because of their excellent access to data. Another way to use cash flow is to project it for a number of years into the future and then discount the annual cash flows back to the present at an appropriate (one hopes) discount rate. This looks nice, but it requires some crystal-ball gazing to project future operations and determine an assumed discount rate; in such calculations a point or two either way on the discount rate can make a big difference.

In most mercantile and manufacturing businesses, historic data, such as the price/earnings ratio, seems more reliable. If you are valuing a business with a heavy asset base, such as leased real estate, cash flow projectories have a sounder base.

Income Before Interest and Taxes (IBIT)

Start with net income and add back all income taxes and all interest expenses. The resulting figure is a measure of income actually generated by business operation. This concept takes debt capitalization and income taxes out of the comparison and focuses on operations. First, the appraiser determines a price/IBIT ratio for National Widget and applies this ratio to your company's IBIT to establish its value.

Suppose the price/IBIT ratio for National Widget is 8:1 and your company's income statement looks like this:

Net income after tax	$100,000
Income tax	50,000
Interest expense	40,000
IBIT	$190,000

Then, on the same basis as National Widget, eight times that yields a value of $1,520,000 overall. Then appropriate discounts are applied to arrive at a value for the stock in question.

Comparing Apples and Oranges: Evaluating Comparable Companies to Assess Your Business Value

Use of the factors described above is a way to get a handle on what your company is worth as compared to publicly held companies in the same line of business. Once the appraiser has done this, hopefully using ratios of several comparable public companies, a picture emerges as to what your company is worth on that basis. Admittedly, this is all very inexact, the appraiser having made key judgments all through the process. The appraiser combines facts, assumptions and conclusions to arrive at a final judgment on value.

This is not intended to be a criticism of appraisers, most of whom do a professional job. It is, rather, a commentary on the inherent difficulty of their task. It is a comment on the inherent unfairness of basing a large tax on a number, "value," which is so nebulous when applied to a family business. In planning for succession of a family business the value taxed by the IRS may be absolutely crucial despite the difficulty of establishing a true value.

For example, the use of comparable public companies as benchmarks has some logic, in addition to being mandated by law. However, there are real difficulties with the practical business application of this logic.

Assume a small manufacturing company is being valued. It makes precision parts that are sold to other manufacturers and has sales of $2 million per year, of which $1.8 million comes from just four customers. The company is profitable, well run and after generous compensation to the owner's family makes about $100,000 per year after taxes.

We are now asked to compare this company with others in the same line that do have a public market. There are three major problems inherent in such comparisons.

Problem #1: Business Size Differs Dramatically

The other listed companies, like National Widget, do make a similar product but it accounts for only a fraction of their hundreds of millions in sales. So we look for smaller companies that are not listed on a big exchange but rather have a local over-the-counter market. We find one, the Potsdam Widget Works, Inc., which has 300 shareholders in Potsdam County, North Dakota. It has been struggling for years against competition from National Widget; earnings are low but local pride tends to keep the quoted price high and to equate book value with market value. Actual turnover of shares is very low. The historic Price/Earnings ratio is 25:1, and the Price/Book Value ratio is 1:1. Stock price is established more by bid—asked quotes rather than actual sales.

Which benchmark do we use?

Price:Earnings Ratio	Ratio	Value of Our Company
National Widget	12:1	$1.2 million
Potsdam Widget Works	25:1	$2.5 million
Price:Book Value Ratio		
National Widget	2.3:1	$1.8 million
Potsdam Widget Works	1:1	$0.8 million

Can we just average the findings? The IRS frowns on that, and rightly so. No, it is the job of the appraiser to select a company or companies that is as nearly comparable as possible and then go from there. It is probably the case that people in Potsdam County, North Dakota, disregard earnings and offer to buy and sell based on book value. Neither that fact nor Potsdam's unusually high price/earnings ratio should govern our value.

As to National Widget, how can we really compare a family company with huge multiline companies having tens of thousands of shareholders and stock that is actively traded?

Problem #2: The Property Being Valued Is Not Comparable

Even if we can draw valid comparisons between these companies as companies, we still have the huge conceptual gap in what is the "property" in question. On the stock exchange National Widget listed stock, the "property," consists of units of actively traded shares, which one can sell on a day's notice, in single shares or large blocks. But the "property" we are valuing in the example consists of 532 shares of a small company. In all the company's existence, a share of stock has never been sold. Someone might be interested in purchasing the whole company, but we are not valuing the whole company. We are valuing only those 532 shares. The fact that it is so much more difficult to sell shares of a closely held company is taken into account by a "lack of marketability discount" which is discussed in the next section. If the shares did not represent a controlling interest there would also be a "minority discount."

Problem #3: The Family Business May Not, in Fact, Be Saleable

The market in listed shares is for the most part an economic one made up by judgments, good or bad, made by thousands of owners. As a practical matter, the 532 shares of the family business will never be sold. Can the IRS add a premium because the owners would never sell? No, because we have to assume a "willing seller." Can the estate allege no value at all on the ground that no one would ever buy? No. You have to envision a sale, however difficult that vision is to attain.

Taking Discounts from the Overall Value of Your Company

A fair comparison with public companies is difficult because we are comparing the two different kinds of owners—property owners and different kinds of owners. Over the years, the courts have evolved adjustments for these factors, which usually take the form of "discounts" from the values arrived at by direct comparison with listed companies. These adjustments are discussed in this section.

Lack of Market for Stock

The stock in your family-owned company is not traded on the New York Stock Exchange. Someone buying your stock will pay less for it than they would for the stock of an identical publicly traded company because in your case the buyer will have a much more difficult time turning around and selling the stock. In valuing your stock for tax purposes, you are allowed a discount to reflect the inherent difficulty of marketing your closely held stock. The big question is: How big is the discount?

Appraisers have developed various methods to arrive at the discount. The most reliable method is to examine the discount afforded sales of unregistered common stock of companies that also have registered actively traded common stock. The unregistered shares trade at a substantial discount because they are not marketable in the same fashion, a buyer has to be found and a price negotiated. That discount reflects the general market's perception of the effect of non-marketability on the price of the stock. This discount tends to range between 20 percent and 40 percent.

Minority Discount

Let's say that you own 48 percent of the voting stock of your company. Your son owns the other 52 percent, and you leave all your stock to him. On your estate tax return, your estate will claim a minority discount because a hypothetical buyer of your 48 percent would not be able to control the management of the company, including executive compensation and dividend rates. The courts have recognized a separate discount when a minority interest in a company is involved. Again, quantifying the size of that discount is the key issue, and a range of 10 to 25 percent seems typical.

The availability of the minority discount creates planning opportunities. For instance, you may have given your son 33 percent of your business 25 years ago, and another 19 percent 10 years ago, a total of 52 percent now. Each of those gifts would have been eligible for a minority discount. In addition, at death your remaining 48 percent interest would be subject to a minority discount. The IRS has tried for years to attribute ownership among family members. Thus, it sometimes claims that in valuing the stock passing to your son, you must add together all the stock that will be owned by your son after the transaction is complete. The courts have resisted that approach, holding that with each gift you must assume a hypothetical buyer and a hypothetical seller of that specific "property," leaving out the actual personalities involved. In a recent case, however, the donor on her deathbed gave away a tiny fraction of her stock so that at her death she would own only 49.9 percent of the company. The court refused to allow a minority discount in that particular situation, but the general rule remains that you look only at the property, the shares, transferred.

Another thing to remember about the minority discount is that any price for a stock obtained on a national exchange already reflects some degree of minority discount. That is, the price per share on the New York Stock Exchange for General Motors already incorporates the fact that a purchaser of that share will not obtain control of General Motors. Thus, when an appraiser has determined the value of your company on the basis of comparable publicly traded stock, a large minority discount is more difficult to justify.

Control Premium, the Other Side of the Coin

A corollary to the minority discount is the control premium. Lack of control in the block of stock being valued justifies a discount; but if the block represents control it is worth more than the other stock on a share for share basis. If you own 52 percent of the stock in your company at your death, then the IRS will claim that the hypothetical buyer of those shares would pay more for them because they represent the ability to control the management of the company. This premium applies especially when the aggregate value of the company has been based on comparisons with publicly traded stock, which is assumed to already reflect some minority discount. How much should the premium be? Again, it varies widely. While majority ownership gives you control of the company, general corporate law prohibits you from dealing with the company at the expense of minority shareholders. Thus, it can be argued that the size of the control premium should not be large. Control premiums tend to be less as a percentage than the minority discounts.

Key Person Discount

You started your company several years ago, and it was your expertise and ability that allowed it to grow to its present size. You have developed special relationships with your customers, and you have a unique knowledge of your business. When you die, these things are lost and the hypothetical buyer of your shares will pay less because your death has resulted in the loss of a key employee. Courts have allowed substantial discounts for the loss of a key employee, but the discount could be offset if the company received substantial life insurance proceeds as a result of the death.

Unrealized Gains Discount

Many corporations have assets which are currently worth more than the assets' tax basis. When the assets are sold, or the corporation is liquidated, a tax will be payable on the gain. In other cases, corporations have "recapture" items such as a LIFO inventory reserve, which trigger taxable income or sale or dissolution. Purchasers of corporate business interests are aware of these potential tax charges and seek to negotiate away their impact. In effect, the value of your corporation is reduced by the inherent income tax cost that must be paid upon liquidation of the company, and it should be appropriate to allow a discount to reflect that fact. In the past, the IRS has been reluctant to recognize this discount unless the corporation is actually being liquidated. However, the diminishment of value is a fact that should be considered.

Environmental Liability Discount

A relatively recent phenomenon is the impact of potential environmental liabilities on a corporation's value. Many manufacturing companies probably have a potential environmental liability. The liability usually stems from the staggering costs of cleaning up a site that has been found to be contaminated, or the future cost of investing substantial capital to comply with increasingly stiff and complex environmental regulations.

Buyers take a quick step backwards when they sniff the possibility of an environmental problem. If your company has had environmental problems, or is in the type of business that portends possible future problems, then a valuation discount would seem to be appropriate. The discount could be the present value of future capital expenditures necessary to comply with environmental regulations, or the estimated cost of a clean-up if a known situation exists. We are not aware of any tax case to date in which the court has specifically allowed an environmental liability discount. However, if the liability and clean-up costs are known facts, the appraiser may consider the cost as a liability for valuation purposes. A general discount for unknown but potential liabilities would probably be objected to by the IRS.

Special Cases of Business Valuation

Many industries and business types are governed by valuation principles based on customary benchmarks for active sales and purchases. In these cases the appraiser gives weight to these factors in addition to the comparable companies approach described above. Some of these industries are:

- Insurance Agencies—multiple of annual commission income.

- Engineering, Accounting, and Other Professional and Service Firms—multiple of annual billings.

- Real Estate and Investment Companies—based on value of underlying assets. (The next section of this chapter discusses valuation of these companies in detail.)

- Auto Dealerships—often based on book value of assets, because the dealer franchise is cancellable. (See the case study #1 presented earlier in this chapter.)

In all these cases, appropriate discounts may be used, especially where the owner does not own 100 percent of the stock.

Valuing Investment Companies and Real Estate Companies

Suppose you have a corporation which is not itself in active business, but rather owns a portfolio of listed securities or real property investments. If you just follow the IRS rules, you will value the company based on the underlying value of assets. If the investments are worth $2 million, based on market prices for securities or individual appraisals for real property, is the corporation worth $2 million? Is 50 percent of the stock worth $1 million?

Again, we refer to the comparable companies. In point of fact, the analogy is to mutual funds, of which there are basically two kinds:

1. *Open-End.* This is the typical mutual fund. Its investments are valued for each business day and you can buy or sell shares at will. Here the market value of the fund shares equals the underlying value of the investments it owns.

2. *Closed-End.* This is not typical but there are a number of such funds which do not issue or redeem shares any time you want. The fund has a fixed number of shares which are themselves traded on the market. Some examples are listed in Table 8.1.

Here is a case where even the public, listed companies may trade at a discount from asset value; sometimes at a premium, too. Why a discount? The main reason seems to be that investors, willing buyers, do not regard shares of the portfolio as highly as the individual property underneath because they are only obtaining a minority interest in the enterprise. Why a premium? It may be that the fund's investments are producing rates of return (dividends, mortgage payments, or rents) at rates higher than current income rates. In that case, the earnings capacity of the fund is more important than net asset value. Here apparently, investors are paying a premium for good management or special assets.

Court decisions have allowed substantial discounts for stock of family investment companies, ranging up to 60 percent of the total value of the assets owned by the company. A discount here can be supported by expert appraisers' testimony as well as by numerous court decisions.

Table 8.1. Discounts and Premiums for Public Investment Companies*

Stock Investment Companies

Company	Per Share Value of Assets	Stock Price	Discount or Premium
Adams Express	$19.39	$18.88	− 2.66%
Blue Chip Value	$ 7.91	$ 7.88	− 0.38%
Gemini II Capital	$16.63	$13.25	−20.32%
Gemini II Income	$ 9.91	$13.50	+36.23%
Solomon Fund	$15.00	$13.75	− 8.33%

Real Estate Investment Companies

Company	Value of Assets	Stock Price	Discount or Premium
Southwest Realty Ltd.*	$ 4.69	$ 1.25	−73.35%
USP Real Estate Investment Trust**	$ 7.49	$ 2.88	−61.55%

* As of April 3, 1992.
** As of January 1, 1991.

Valuing Your Business for Estate Tax Planning

In tax planning or estate planning, how does the planner evaluate the business? Do you have to pay for an appraisal?

In most cases, for general planning, you do not need an expert appraisal. Your typical estate or tax planning professional will have a good idea of what the business is worth for tax purposes. It won't be a number you can put on a tax return, but it will be sufficient enough for planning. One way to work with such inexact numbers is to use a high-low method. Work the estate planning numbers using three different values, High, Low, and some middle figure as a best estimate.

For instance, you could use the book value of our little widget company ($.8 million) as the low figure and 10x earnings ($1.2 million) as the high figure. If the planning tests out in that value range, it is probably valid. Remember, values change anyway so one extreme or the other will be nearer correct five years from now than any intermediate, precise, number we pick today.

Penalties and Interest for Inaccurate Business Valuation

It is one thing for the business owner or professional to assume a number for planning purposes or use the "high-low" method, it is quite another to use such a value in an actual transaction or report it on a tax return.

In order to discourage taxpayers from being too aggressive with their valuations, Congress has enacted a special provision that imposes drastic penalties when a taxpayer knowingly undervalues property. Also, in the case where it is to the taxpayer's advantage to overvalue property (as with a charitable gift), the tax law also contains penalties for overvaluation.

The penalty for a gift or estate tax understatement of value only applies if the value claimed on the return is 50 percent or less of the value determined to be correct by the IRS. Thus, if you value your business at $1 million, and the IRS successfully establishes the value at $2 million, then you have made a valuation understatement which is subject to penalty. The penalty is 20 percent of the tax that should have been paid when the return was filed. Thus, if you owe another $500,000 in tax as a result of the IRS valuation (50 percent of the additional $1 million), then you will also owe a penalty of 20 percent of that $500,000, or $100,000. In effect, the IRS redetermination of value results in a much stiffer tax. You will also owe interest on the tax deficiency, which starts to accrue when the tax is due, and compounds daily at a relatively high rate thereafter.

Summary

Much of the tax law, especially the estate and gift tax, is concerned with or is based on value, "fair market value" as defined at the beginning of this chapter. In the case of a transaction or return dependent on value, the use of an independent appraiser is strongly recommended.

For small transactions, an expensive and extensive professional appraisal is not needed. An independent CPA, or banker, or broker should be able to qualify. Be sure the appraisal is in writing. Neither the taxpayer, nor the taxpayer's professional adviser should do the appraisal for return purposes. It is better to pay an independent person, one who is familiar with finances and values, to do it. Penalties await those who do transactions and sign returns without proper value backup.

Value as used in this book is very important. It is also very elusive, subject to a wide range of reasonable results. From a tax planning standpoint, it is advisable to do multiple calculations at a high or low and a midpoint value. If the calculations stand up under all three conditions, it is probably sound for planning purposes.

The freeze transactions described in the balance of Part Three are highly dependent on correct value. If the anticipated benefit to you does not justify the cost of an expert professional appraisal, then you are better not to undertake the transaction.

9

How to Give Away
Future Company Growth, but
Keep Control and Security

The concept of the freeze can best be expressed by an example. Assume a business now worth $2 million is growing at 8 percent per year. The owners are concerned about the impact of estate taxes when the survivor of them dies and leaves the business to the children. Also assume that their other assets are sufficient to pay the tax on such other assets, but not the tax on the increasing business value. Thus, the business itself must eventually pay a tax on 50 percent of its value.

In Figure 9.1 the business, starting at a value of $2 million, grows at 8 percent to a value of over $6 million in 15 years. Allowing for two $600,000 exemptions, the estate tax on it starts at about $400,000 and grows at the same rate to over $2 million. As growth continues, the owners are less and less able to control estate taxes by gifts, insurance funding and other devices. They realize that the business is doomed if it eventually has to pay out such a major part of its then value in taxes.

Suppose the owners can somehow fix, or freeze, the value of the business at the current $2 million and let the children and grandchildren own all the future growth. Would this be worthwhile? For some people the answer is yes. If the estate is frozen at $2 million, the estate taxes always stay at $400,000 (50 percent of value after deducting the two $600,000 exemptions) no matter what the future growth may be. The children or other beneficiaries own all the future growth tax free. Let us describe the concept:

The freeze is a transaction or series of transactions in which the owners receive the current value in a preferred interest and their beneficiaries own all or a major part of the future growth in value.

89

**Figure 9.1. Your Profit Sharing Arrangement with
Uncle Sam—Why a "Freeze Is Desirable**

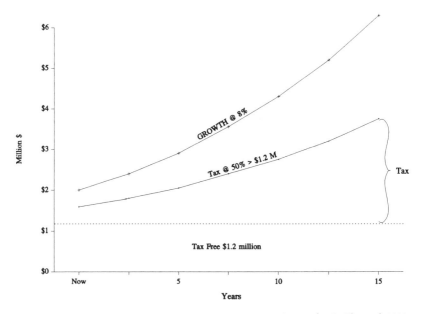

This requires some form of transfer to the children of the growth element of the business, the parents retained interest is designed to have little or no share in growth. Its value is fixed; hence the term "freeze." The American economic system is so flexible that there are myriad ways in which a freeze of value may be accomplished. The balance of this chapter describes gifts as a form of freeze and the next three chapters tell how to freeze using

- preferred stock in a C Corporation,
- sale of common stock in an S Corporation, or
- a preferred interest in a partnership or LLC.

Use Gifts as a Freeze

Yes, gifts to descendants may be a form of freeze and fit the definition above. The future growth in the gifted property belongs to the donee. The donor may retain security and control by keeping at least 51 percent of the voting stock of a corporation or a management interest of a partnership. For the smaller enterprise with a low growth potential, a policy of gifts over a long term, including use of the two $600,000 exemptions, is all the freeze the owner will ever need. See Figures 9.2, 9.3, and 9.4 which show the effect of gifts in varying amounts of stock of the same $2 million dollar business.

- In Figure 9.2 the owner of a $2 million business adopts a program of giving $20,000 per year to each of his or her three children. The gifted shares grow as the business value grows. Here the estate tax saving would be 50 percent of the shaded area.

- Figure 9.3 shows an alternate kind of gift program: have both spouses use their $600,000 exemptions to make a large initial gift of, say, non-voting stock. Here they use up their combined $1.2 million of exemptions and the shaded area shows the growth of that value. Again the tax saved is 50 percent of the shaded area.

- Figure 9.4 has a dramatic look to it: a combined initial gift of $1.2 million and then annual gifts of the $60,000 illustrated in Figure 9.2 will soon eliminate most of the value of the company from the owner's estates. Normally a person whose main asset is a $2 million business is not about to give away 90 percent of it, even if the owner's 10 percent is voting stock and retains control. But what if the owners have another business worth $8 million and the smaller business is separate? Would it make sense from a tax standpoint to give away the smaller business?

Figure 9.2. Freeze by Giving $60,000 of Stock per Year to Three Children

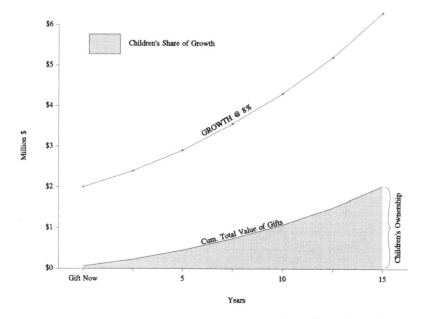

Copyright G. Shattuck 1992

Figure 9.3. Freeze by Giving $1.2 Million of Stock to Children

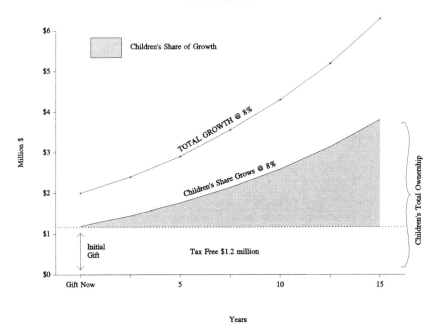

Copyright G. Shattuck 1992

The problem is that with larger businesses, and fast-growing businesses, the increase in value outruns the dollar gift limitations. The moral is to use gifts as far as practical and then, if need be, pass on to a more complex freeze transaction.

Figure 9.5 shows how a larger starting value, $10 million instead of $2 million, reduces the impact of tax free gifts to a relatively small amount. These four illustrations, Figures 9.2–9.5, portray very dramatically the difference in effectiveness of gifts in a small estate versus in a larger estate. You will see that, as the estate becomes larger, as shown in figure 9.5, a more effective, more sophisticated, form of "freeze" becomes desirable.

Revisit the Gift Rules

Gifts are so important in planning for the succession of a small business that it pays to now review the gift rules set forth in Chapter 2. To begin with, gifts of property to persons other than your spouse are subject to gift tax, but with two very important limitations.

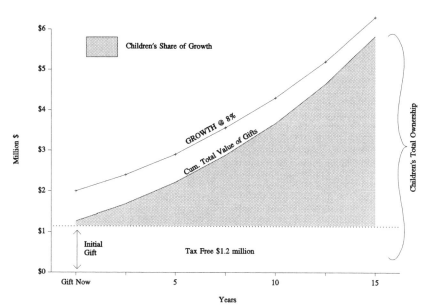

Figure 9.4. Freeze by Giving Stock Worth $1.2 Million Now, Plus $60,000 per Year to Three Children

Copyright G. Shattuck 1992

- you can give $10,000 per year per person each year ($20,000 per person per year if your spouse consents to use of his or her $10,000 exclusion),

- over and above the $10,000 limit referred to above, you have a lifetime $600,000 exemption for federal gift tax purposes ($1,200,000 if spouse consents).

The $10,000 gift and the $600,000 gift have different characteristics. The $10,000 is called an "annual exclusion" and the gifted amounts plus all future increases in value of such property are removed from the donor's estate. If you have an estate of $2 million and make gifts of $20,000 to each of your three children, your estate is now $1,970,000 for tax purposes. Tables 3.3, 3.4, and 3.5 show the dramatic impact of annual gifts if the growth rate of the business is high. These tables are the basis of the graphic illustrations in this chapter.

The $600,000, which we call an "exemption" for purposes of this book, does not work directly to reduce the estate because the same $600,000 is available for estate tax purposes if you do not make a gift of that amount. (See Table 1.1 in Chapter 1.)

**Figure 9.5. Freeze by Giving $1.2 Million of Stock
to Children (Here the Starting Value Is $10 Million,
Instead of $1 Million)**

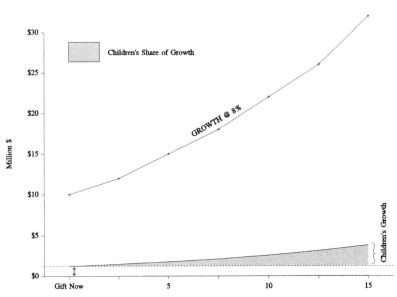

Copyright G. Shattuck 1992

The $600,000 is nonetheless very valuable for lifetime gifts, however, because the value increase of the $600,000 is eliminated from your estate. This is where the freeze concept comes in: a gift of $600,000 share of an expanding business does not eliminate the $600,000 from the estate but it does "freeze" it because the value increase of that property is not accrued by the donor or his estate. The growth is owned by the donee, the recipient of the gift.

Summary Explanation of Figures 9.1-9.5

These figures show in graphic form how gift principles work to freeze future value growth out of your estate. Assume a business interest, corporate or partnership, which is growing in value at the rate of 8 percent per year:

- *Figure 9.1.* This shows the impact of estate taxes as a growing business. The first $1.2 million is tax free assuming the spouses have properly prepared wills. The balance over the $1.2 million is taxable at the second spouse's death. (If the business owner is not married, you start at $600,000 in all these cases instead of $1.2 million).

- *Figure 9.2.* If you and your spouse start now and give $60,000 per year of nonvoting stock to three children, the cumulative effect of the gifts and the growth of the gifts is striking. In 15 years, without fuss or hardship, you can eliminate about a third of the value of the business from your estate. (See also Tables 3.3 and 3.4.)

- *Figure 9.3.* On the same facts, an up-front gift of $1.2 million is even more effective because more growth is given away earlier. Here the $1.2 million is in effect frozen and the value increase is removed from the estate. Remember this effect is over and above the tax savings displayed in Figure 9.2.

- *Figure 9.4.* Here, Figures 9.2 and 9.3 are combined. The business owners make an initial gift of $1.2 million to the children and then $60,000 per year from then on. The shaded portion shows that the taxable part—the narrow wedge at the top of the graph—grows smaller each year as the program continues. Note: the owners can still keep control by giving only nonvoting shares to the children and keeping a few voting shares to maintain voting control as long as they want.

These tables illustrate a very important point to be made before any further discussion of the freeze concept. Where the value of the business interest is in the range of two or three million dollars, a gift program should be thoroughly explored before moving on to other freeze devices which are invariably more complex, more costly, and involve a greater degree of risk.

The corollary of the statement in the preceding paragraph is this. As the value of the business interest grows the effectiveness of gifts decreases and other forms of freeze must be explored. This statement is illustrated by Figure 9.5 which shows the impact of a gift of $1.2 million of stock of a company worth $10 million. The dollar growth of the gifted stock is the same as the gift in Figure 9.3, but the effect on the current owner's estate tax bill is minimal. See also Table 3.5. If the owner of the $10 million business wants to freeze part of the value for estate tax purposes, he or she must do something in addition to gifts.

Economic Weighting

Another form of gift may be called *economic weighting*. This is best illustrated by an example: you own a building used in a business which is now mainly owned by the children. How much rent do you charge? Charge a flat rent with a long term lease. Thus, as time goes on and inflation takes its toll, the economic benefits shift more and more to the children. (See Figure 9.6.) Would we recommend this in all cases? No, probably not. There is a risk of a gift tax if the thing is overdone and such an arrangement may deprive the parents of needed security. However, in describing different aspects of the freeze concept, this economic device deserves some mention.

**Figure 9.6. Shows Eroding Effect of a Long-Term
Lease of Real Property for a Flat Rate, Which Is
Not Adjusted for Inflation. As the Underlying Value
of the Parents (Lessors) Erodes, the Economic
Value to the Children Increases.**

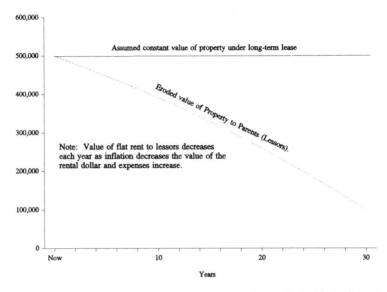

The Concept of the Freeze Is Based on Leverage

This chapter has dealt with simple transfers of business interests as gifts. The concept of leverage, using a $10,000 gift to create a multiple of the $10,000 in benefits is very important. The use of leverage is also explained in Chapter 3, and in Chapter 5. For instance, you may use gifts within the $10,000 annual exclusion to purchase life insurance, or joint life insurance, which pays off at death. Using life insurance, you are leveraging by investing in an asset which has the potential of producing a great multiple of the original gift, all tax free. (See Figure 5.1 and Table 5.1 in Chapter 5.)

Now look at the classic freeze concept: Carve out a secure, income-producing interest, the "frozen" interest, for yourself and give away future growth to children and other descendants. If it is done correctly, the value of the frozen interest remains constant at its current value and future growth is owned by others. In the three chapters that follow, these types of freeze are discussed.

- the preferred stock freeze of a C Corporation,
- sale of stock for an S Corporation, and
- a preferred interest for a partnership.

Figure 9.7 shows generally how these all work. Leverage is created by carving out a preferred and fixed value interest of some kind to the extent of total current value. The growth element is squeezed into a narrow slice which can be given away with little gift tax impact. This squeeze is where the leverage is created. (See Figure 9.7.)

This is the freeze. Chapters 10, 11, and 12 fill out the details with further graphs and illustrations. The owners of a growing business should definitely be familiar with the freeze concept. It is not suitable for all, but very valuable where it does fit.

Figure 9.7. The Freeze, in Concept: Carve Out a Frozen Interest for Yourself and Give the Future Growth Away

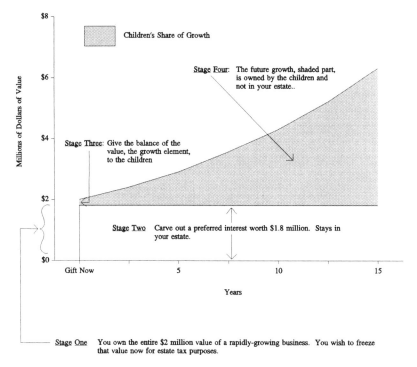

Children's Share of Growth

Stage Four: The future growth, shaded part, is owned by the children and not in your estate..

Stage Three: Give the balance of the value, the growth element, to the children

Stage Two   Carve out a preferred interest worth $1.8 million. Stays in your estate.

Gift Now   5   10   15

Years

Stage One   You own the entire $2 million value of a rapidly-growing business. You wish to freeze that value now for estate tax purposes.

The "Anti-Freeze" Rules

As we might expect, greedy taxpayers and less than scrupulous advisors pushed the freeze concept to the limits, and beyond. The IRS reacted, coming out with adverse rulings in the early 1980s. In late 1987, Congress enacted comprehensive "anti-freeze" legislation, an over-reaction which was punitive and injurious to legitimate business transactions. Finally in 1990, Congress repealed the 1987 legislation and enacted a new set of rules.

These rules are strict, but can be lived with if a legitimate freeze transaction is the objective. *The key to staying out of danger is fair valuation of the frozen (retained) interest and provision for the payment of cumulative annual dividends on the frozen interest.* Such transactions should only be undertaken with expert counsel, qualified appraisers, and an understanding that the rules of the game must carefully be followed.

Summary

Is there a future for the "freeze" concept, particularly the sale of stock to children and the carve out of a preferred interest? Yes, there is. But it must be done correctly and only in situations where other means of business succession are not available. The next four chapters describe freeze transactions in more detail. You will find that these transactions have a cost, but the cost and risk can be far outweighed by benefits if the anticipated growth rate is high enough.

We emphasize that each freeze device should be tested using alternate growth rates. If the growth rate is actually high enough, the result will be a great tax saving, perhaps the key to succession of a growing business. If the growth rate is low you could have a costly disaster on your hands. As you read on, please keep in mind the anticipated growth rate of the business. It is a vital factor.

10

Using the Preferred Stock Freeze to Save Taxes

The preferred stock freeze for a C Corporation is easy to grasp and a good place to start describing the practical applications of the freeze concept. Let us restate the concept of the freeze as described in Chapter 9. The freeze is a transaction or series of transactions in which the owners receive the current value in the form of a preferred interest and their beneficiaries own all or a major part of the future growth in value in the form of common stock or other form of growth interest.

For example, assume your business corporation is worth $2 million and is owned entirely by you and your spouse. It produces an after-tax income of $250,000 per year, and has anticipated growth of 8 percent per year. The estate tax on the $2 million value would be $1 million now, assuming that your $1.2 million of exemptions offset other assets. Depending on how long both spouses live, and assuming growth is a constant 8 percent, the values and taxes could be as follows:

Years From Now	Value	Tax
5	$2.9 million	$1.5 million
10	$4.3 million	$2.2 million
15	$6.3 million	$3.2 million
20	$9.3 million	$4.7 million

This pattern is shown in Part A of Figure 10.1. Part B of 10.1 shows the estate tax effect of using a preferred stock freeze, as discussed below. In Figure 10.1A, the tax on the $2 million business is $1 million and grows at 8 percent per year, right along with business growth—your 50-50 partnership with Uncle Sam. In Part B, you freeze your ownership interest into preferred stock, $1,8 million worth, and give the remaining value in common

Figure 10.1 Effect of a Value "Freeze"

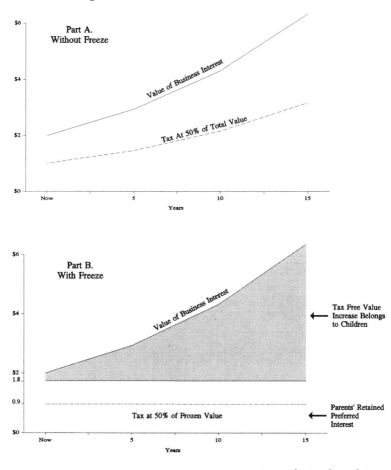

stock to your children. Your taxes are frozen at $900,000 and the rest of the growth belongs to the children or other heirs.

How to Implement a Preferred Stock Freeze

A gift program as discussed in Chapter 9 would help reduce taxes, but you as owners do not wish to give away such a major portion of your capital; you want a secure income plus a capital base if the company is ever sold. One solution would be to recapitalize the corporation into cumulative preferred and common stock. You, the owners, keep the preferred stock and give the common to the children. Table 10.1 illustrates. Although Table 10.1 is over simplified, it shows how the carve out concept works in numbers. Figure

Table 10.1. Preferred Stock Freeze

	Now	Step One, Issue Preferred	Step Two, Give Common	Ten Years Later
Value of Company	$2,000,000	$2,000,000	$2,000,000	$4,300,000
Common Stock				
Owned by Parents	$2,000,000	$ 200,000	0	0
Owned by Children	0	0	$ 200,000	$1,500,000
Preferred Stock				
Owned by Parents	0	$1,800,000	$1,800,000	$1,800,000
Owned by Children	0	0	0	0
Taxed in Parents Estate*	$2,000,000	$2,000,000	$2,000,000	$2,000,000

*The parents will probably have used up part of their two $600,000 exceptions to make the $200,000 gift to the children, so the gift is added back.

10.2 shows it in picture form, giving the estate tax saving after 5, 10, and 15 years growth at 8 percent.

Is that all? No. Assume the preferred stock pays a 12 percent cumulative dividend: $216,000 per year. This must be paid every year, good and bad, so the original owners have to figure that part of the after tax proceeds of the $216,000 may accumulate and be in their estates. Or perhaps the owners would cut their current compensation so they can live on the dividends instead of salary. In any event, the corporate management must figure on paying that $216,000 each and every year, if not the IRS will add it back to the parents' estates anyway, with interest. This is how the IRS rules keep things honest. To be really accepted as having a value of $1.8 million, the preferred must be entitled to a cumulative dividend.

There is another cost. The earnings which provide the $216,000 dividend will be subject to a double tax, one at the corporate level and one at the individual level. Unlike reasonable compensation to employees, dividends are not deductible. Thus the estate tax saving shown on Table 10.1 must be adjusted to account for this factor. Only if the anticipated value growth rate is very high would you use preferred stock for a freeze. With a low growth rate the extra income tax cost exceeds the estate tax saving.

Valuing a Company Before Implementing a Stock Freeze

The preferred stock freeze is a transaction where the owners must definitely have good value data, good appraisals. The IRS (as of the date of

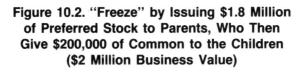

**Figure 10.2. "Freeze" by Issuing $1.8 Million
of Preferred Stock to Parents, Who Then
Give $200,000 of Common to the Children
($2 Million Business Value)**

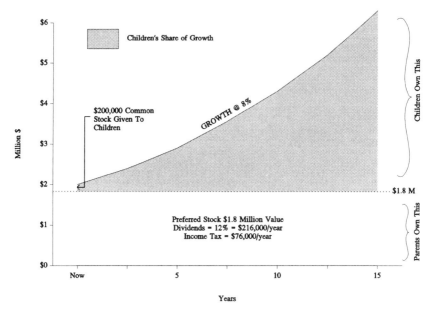

this writing) requires what is called a subtraction approach to valuation. It goes like this:

Step One:	Value of the corporation, overall	$2,000,000
Step Two:	Value of the new preferred stock, subtract	(1,800,000)
Step Three:	The Value of the common by subtraction. This is the value of the gift to the children.	$ 200,000

In arriving at the value of the company as a whole, and of the preferred, we are to use normal valuation methods (see Chapter 8) using such discounts and premiums for each class of stock as may be appropriate. However, in order for the preferred stock to have any value at all, it must provide for a "qualified payment" which in fact must be paid. A "qualified payment" is essentially a fixed cumulative dividend payable on a periodic basis. If the overall company value in Step One is discounted for lack of a market, then the preferred stock in Step Two should also be discounted for lack of a market. In order to keep the gift element to a minimum we need to minimize the overall value in Step One and maximize the value of the preferred in Step Two. In our illustrations we use a 12 percent cumulative rate for the preferred stock. This may be too low or too high a rate in your case, but the dividend rate is a major factor in valuing preferred stock.

Table 10.2 shows how variations in the overall value of the company and variations in value of the preferred stock can drastically affect the amount of the gift value of the common stock. The higher the proportion of preferred used (90 percent of total value in our illustration) the more adverse leverage if either the value of the company or the value of the preferred is challenged by the IRS on audit.

Assume you issue preferred stock and give away the common stock as per the hoped-for result column; the gift amount of $200,000 would be absorbed by the annual exclusions and/or your exemption. But then the IRS audits the value and makes possible value changes as shown in the other five columns. The variance from the hoped-for result is the potential taxable gift which results. If the preferred is not a correctly drafted cumulative preferred, it receives a zero value, with consequences you can deduce from the table.

The variance from the hoped-for result is very important. You may be willing to make a $200,000 gift (first column) but not a $1.3 million gift (last column).

These illustrations focus on the immediate impact which of course must be considered. But do not lose sight of the long range advantage of the value freeze in eliminating estate taxes levied on the business. That may make some risk of up front gift tax acceptable—remember the gift tax itself is removed from your estate after three years.

How Much Leverage?

In the example above, Table 10.1 and Figure 10.2, we used $1.8 million of preferred stock out of a total value of $2 million. This squeezed the common, the growth, interest down to $200,000 which could be given away with no tax. This is a high degree of leverage. In fact, the IRS rules prohibit the growth interest from being less than 10 percent, so the $1.8 million of preferred (90 percent of $2 million value) is the maximum that should be issued.

You can use a lesser degree of leverage, a lesser percent of preferred interest, if you want. The preferred, frozen interest can be at anything up to 10 percent. Table 10.3 and Figure 10.3 show the range of leverage desired. In many cases, you would want to have the preferred *less* than 90 percent of the total value for two reasons:

1. If the preferred dividend has to be set at 10 percent or 12 percent to sustain its value, the corporation may find it difficult to pay an after-tax cumulative 10 percent or 12 percent dividend on 90 percent of its value.

Table 10.2. Valuation Alternatives

	Hoped-For Result	But If Overall Company Value Varies		But If Preferred Value Varies		Both Factors Vary
Value of Company as a Whole	$2,000,000	$2,500,000	$3,000,000	$2,000,000	$2,000,000	$2,500,000
Less Value of Preferred Stock	1,800,000	1,800,000	1,800,000	1,500,000	1,000,000	1,000,000
Balance: Amount of Gift = Value of Common	200,000	700,000	1,200,000	500,000	1,000,000	1,500,000
Variance From Hoped-For Result	—	500,000	1,000,000	300,000	800,000	1,300,000

2. Again, to sustain value, dividend coverage is needed in addition to dividend rate; the coverage is the cushion of income over and above the required cumulative dividend.

Take the corporation in our example. It has a total value of $2 million and after-tax earnings of $250,000 per year. If you issue $1.8 million of preferred stock with a 12 percent dividend, the coverage is:

After tax income	$250,000
Cumulative preferred dividend	(216,000)
Coverage or cushion	$ 34,000

Thus, an investor would say, "Preferred is really not worth $1.8 million because, if earnings decline even a few thousand the company may not be able to pay the dividend. I want more of a cushion." This is a perfectly valid comment and the safety of the preferred, whether we call it "coverage" or "cushion" is a major factor. (See Table 10.3.) This coverage, or cushion test is also very important from your standpoint as owner. If you seek to freeze tax values by limiting yourself to a preferred interest with a fixed income you want to be sure that the income can be relied upon as your future security.

Figure 10.3 pictures the range of options here. Figure 10.3 expands on Table 10.3, showing the entire range of possible preferred capitalization in a freeze. Thus, like a custom tailored suit, the preferred must be designed to fit the owners' particular situation. Remember that if you capitalize with a given percent of value in a preferred interest you need not give away the entire balance, the growth interest, at once. You can retain part of the growth to be given, or realized on, at a future time. The owners could issue $800,000 of preferred to themselves, which would yield a well-covered dividend of $76,000 per year, then give the $1.2 million of common to children and grandchildren. Assuming they had not used up their $1.2 million exemptions, there would be no federal gift tax.

Thus, the design of a preferred stock freeze must balance:

• the estate tax savings resulting from a high amount of low yield preferred,

Table 10.3. Range of Leverage Options and Resulting Earnings Coverage

Preferred Stock as % of Total Value	90%	50%	25%
Preferred Stock amount issued	$1,800,000	$1,000,000	$500,000
Corp. after tax earnings	250,000	250,000	250,000
Preferred Stock dividend at 12%	(216,000)	(120,000)	(60,000)
Coverage amount based on earnings	$ 34,000	$ 130,000	$190,000
Coverage ratio = earnings ÷ dividend	1.2 x	2.1 x	4.2 x

Figure 10.3. Range of Leverage Options in a Freeze Transaction (Value of Business = $2 Million, Earning = $250,000/Year)

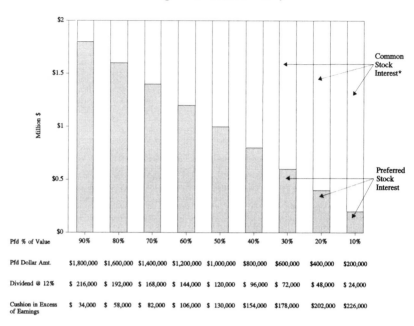

Pfd % of Value	90%	80%	70%	60%	50%	40%	30%	20%	10%
Pfd Dollar Amt.	$1,800,000	$1,600,000	$1,400,000	$1,200,000	$1,000,000	$800,000	$600,000	$400,000	$200,000
Dividend @ 12%	$ 216,000	$ 192,000	$ 168,000	$ 144,000	$ 120,000	$ 96,000	$ 72,000	$ 48,000	$ 24,000
Cushion in Excess of Earnings	$ 34,000	$ 58,000	$ 82,000	$ 106,000	$ 130,000	$154,000	$178,000	$202,000	$226,000

*If the owners issue preferred to themselves, they may retain any part of the common stock interest and give the rest. The growth of the gifted part is removed from the owner's estate.

- the need to sustain the value of the preferred stock, which requires a reasonable dividend rate and earnings coverage,
- the owners' need for personal security by way of a retained preferred stock interest and perhaps some common stock growth, interest.

These considerations are not always compatible, and the key element in resolving them is the corporation's reasonably anticipated rate of growth. The impact of growth rate will be demonstrated in the material that follows.

A Freeze Is Effective at Larger Values

Our illustrations have so far used a $2 million value for the business. This fits with the gift alternative, which is also a viable freeze device at a $2 million value. But suppose the value is $10 million. As we have seen, the straight gift of stock, without the leverage of a freeze, has relatively little impact at that value. (see Figure 9.5). Here is where the freeze leverage really comes in.

Figure 10.4 shows how a freeze works at a $10 million value. Issuance of $9 million of preferred squeezes the value of the growth stock, the common, down to $1 million, which can then be given free of federal tax, using both spouses' $1.2 million of exemptions. The prior section How Much Leverage?, and Figure 10.3, discusses other facets of issuing that much preferred, or a lesser proportion.

Figure 10.5 (a and b) shows, in terms of tax saved on future growth, the effect of the leverage we have discussed where the value is $10 million. The top graph (Figure 9.5) shows the growth removed from your estate by a $1.2 million gift of stock. The lower graph (Figure 10.4) shows a $1.0 million gift of stock after a freeze. The shaded area, in each case, is the future growth owned by the children and not in your estate.

Figure 10.6 shows the same picture as 10.4 but with a 10.5 percent growth rate, instead of the 8 percent used in other examples. Compare the shaded areas to see how the growth rate affects the benefits of a freeze and, as we will learn, the costs of such a freeze are mostly fixed costs.

All of these illustrations show a principle, and are not intended to give a prescription. Using 90 percent of value in preferred stock would not be

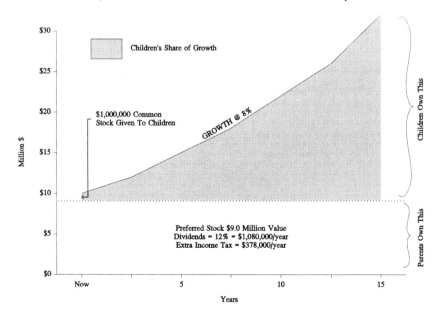

**Figure 10.4. "Freeze" by Issuing $9.0 Million
of Preferred Stock to Payments, Who Then Give
$1,000,000 of Common to Children (C Corporation)
($10 Million Business Value 8% Growth)**

Copyright G. Shattuck 1992

Figure 10.5. Freeze by Giving $1.2 Million of Stock to Children (Here the Starting Value Is $10 Million, Instead of $1 Million)

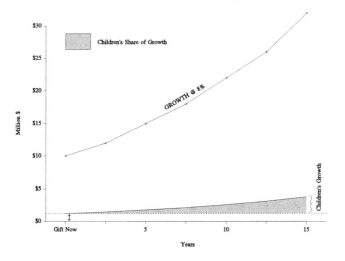

Figure 10.5b. "Freeze" by Issuing $9.0 Million of Preferred Stock to Parents, Who Then Give $1,000,000 of Common to Children (C Corporation) ($10 Million Business Value 8% Growth)

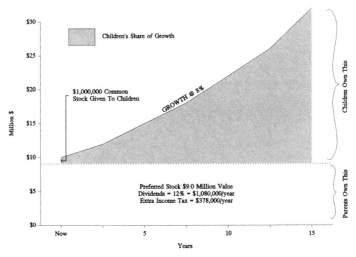

108

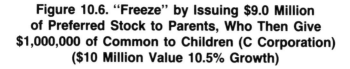

**Figure 10.6. "Freeze" by Issuing $9.0 Million
of Preferred Stock to Parents, Who Then Give
$1,000,000 of Common to Children (C Corporation)
($10 Million Value 10.5% Growth)**

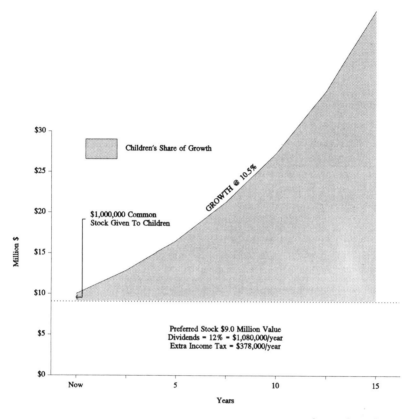

Copyright G. Shattuck 1992

advisable in most cases. The costs and risks outweigh the benefits. The key
to specific calculations appears in Chapter 13.

Issuance of Preferred Stock May Be Tax Free

As discussed above, a preferred stock freeze typically involves the tax
free exchange by a senior shareholder of his or her common stock for voting
preferred stock. The common stock, which represents the future growth in
the corporation's value, is then given to the shareholder's children. For the
exchange of the existing common stock for the preferred stock to qualify for
tax-free income treatment, the recapitalization must qualify as a reorganiza-

tion or a tax free stock dividend for federal tax purposes. To qualify as tax free, the exchange must have the attributes of a recapitalization and a number of statutory tests must be met. Usually, these tests can be met through proper planning, but the counsel of an expert in this area is vital. The preferred stock so issued will have certain negative tax characteristics that must also be evaluated with your expert.

Summary

Valuation is an all important consideration in a preferred stock freeze transaction. Under the new valuation rules, if the retained preferred stock does not provide for a "qualified payment," a reasonable cumulative dividend, it will be considered to have no value. If the preferred does not provide for a qualified payment, virtually the entire value of the corporation would be allocated to the gifted common shares, thereby creating a significant gift tax liability for the senior shareholder.

The preferred stock "freeze" has two real limitations: (i) there is a risk of up front gift tax if the values are wrong, and (ii) the preferred dividends must be paid as long as the preferred is outstanding. Normally, it is best to find some other way to save estate taxes. Nevertheless, there are some limited circumstances where it may make sense:

- The small business, where the potential for a gift tax can be avoided by use of $600,000 exemptions and the owners can waive future salary to make the dividends more palatable;

- The rare situation where there is a high potential for rapid growth but the current low values can reliably be established;

- Where the corporation can never be an S Corporation (alien shareholders, too many shareholders, extra class of stock which can't be eliminated) and the preferred stock "freeze" is the only way to save the business from the ravages of estate taxes.

In no situation should a preferred stock freeze be attempted without expert professional advice and the use of qualified appraisers.

11

Sale of Stock
to Children

This chapter continues the discussion on how to save estate taxes on your business interest by freezing its value in your estate. Chapter 10 shows how preferred stock can be used to allow the parents to retain a secure interest with a fixed income, while allowing descendants to own the future growth in value. Unfortunately, an S Corporation, which is very beneficial taxwise, cannot issue preferred stock. So that type of freeze is not available to owners of an S Corporation.

If you have an S Corporation, you can accomplish the same result another way: sell part or all of the corporate stock to the children in exchange for a long-term secured promissory note. Here the note, with its stream of principal and interest payments, is the secured income-producing interest. The freeze is accomplished because the value of the note is fixed and the children now own the stock which will increase in value.

How to Sell Stock in an S Corporation

Go back to our example in Chapter 10. The business is worth $2 million and produces $250,000 of after tax income per year. Change one thing: it is an S Corporation so, at the corporate level, the $250,000 of after-tax income in the prior example translates in this example to $417,000 of before tax income ($250,000 ÷ 0.6). There is, with limited exceptions, no tax at the corporate level with an S Corporation. Instead, its income flows through to its shareholders and the $417,000 is reported on their personal tax returns.

The owners want to eliminate further value increase from their estate but do not want to freeze value issuing preferred stock as this would cancel the valuable S Corporation status. Here, the owners do something analogous

Table 11.1. Annual Payments on Note of $1.8 Million

Term of Note	Constant %*	Children's Debt Service Payment Per Year
5 years	24.0%	$432,000
10 years	14.8%	$256,000
15 years	12.0%	$216,000
20 years	10.7%	$192,000

*Assumes note amortized in annual payments with interest at 10%. Constant % × note principal = debt service.

to the preferred stock freeze. They *sell* $1.8 million of stock to the children and then *give* them the $200,000 balance. The situation is the same as retaining $1.8 million of preferred stock except that in a sale, the owners retain a secured promissory note from the children instead of stock.

Assume here that the children have no other assets and the money to pay the parents must come from the corporation. With 10 percent interest, the debt service on the $1.8 million note depends on the years duration of the note. Table 11.1 illustrates. For example, look at the 15-year payout in Table 11.1: the children need $215,000 per year to pay the parents the sum due under the note. The S Corporation generates $417,000 pre-tax per year, on which the children owe a tax of $145,000, leaving $272,000 per year available for distribution to the children as stockholders. This assumes a 35 percent individual tax rate. If $216,000 per year is distributed to the children (tax paid because it's an S Corporation), they can use it to pay the $216,000 per year they owe the parents. That "if" is an important word. Such a sale, like use of preferred stock in Chapter 10, must be carefully designed and tested to make sure it is economically feasible and realistic from the IRS viewpoint.

Figures 11.1 and 11.2 show how this kind of freeze works with a company worth $2 million and $10 million respectively.

How does the note payment schedule in Figure 11.1 compare to the $215,000 of dividends on the preferred stock in Chapter 10?

	Preferred Stock C Corp.	Sale of Stock S Corp.
Before tax corporate income	$416,000	$416,000
Corp. tax at 40%	165,000	0
Indiv. tax at 35%	0	145,000
After tax income	250,000	271,000
Preferred dividend or note debt service	216,000	216,000
Safety margin of income	$ 34,000	$ 55,000

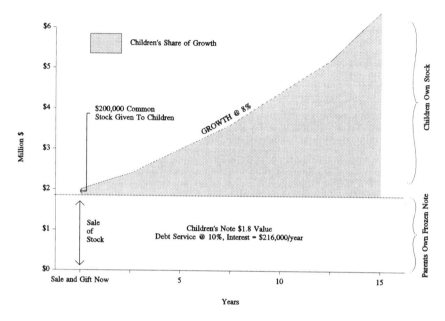

Figure 11.1. Freeze by Selling $1.8 Million of Stock to Children and Giving Them $200,000 of Stock (Pay Over 15 Years @ 10% Interest) (S Corporation)

As noted, Figure 11.1 illustrates the sale transaction based on a $2 million value and a $1.8 million purchase price. Figure 11.2 illustrates a similar transaction with a $10 million value and a $9 million price for the stock. In each case the children pay for the stock over 16 years at 10 percent interest.

What does all this mean? In terms of an actual family situation, the above example means little. It is just how things might work under one given set of facts. On these facts, would you sell to the children? Probably not. Based on the earnings of the company, there is not enough cushion there to feel secure that the annual debt service payments will be made. Can the terms of the sale be altered to result in a more economically viable deal? Yes.

For instance, in either case the owners could reduce the amount of stock converted to a frozen interest (preferred stock or note) and increase the taxable gifts. Or the owners could keep some of the stock and growth—in fact, they might want to as part of a policy of personal security. (See the section on *Leverage* in Chapter 10.)

As stated in Chapter 10, the freeze transaction must be designed like a custom-tailored suit based on the facts and needs at hand. This book pre-

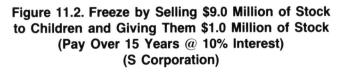

**Figure 11.2. Freeze by Selling $9.0 Million of Stock
to Children and Giving Them $1.0 Million of Stock
(Pay Over 15 Years @ 10% Interest)
(S Corporation)**

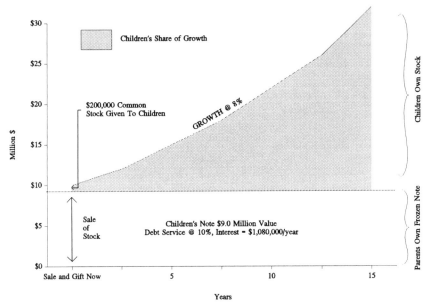

sents the concept of a suit, it shows what a suit looks like, but the book does not attempt to be the tailor. Nor can you buy such a freeze off the rack. You need a custom tailor to create the suit that fits you best.

Valuing an S Corporation Before Selling Stock

As in the case of the preferred stock freeze, using a defensible value is most important. If a parent sells property to his or her child at less than fair value, a gift has in effect been made. Even if the stated price is fair, unfair terms would run danger of being taxed as gifts. For example, the $1.8 million note, if properly secured, may be worth $1.8 million if the going interest rate for such a note is indeed 10 percent. But suppose you use a $1.8 million unsecured note with only 4 percent interest. Clearly that note is not worth $1.8 million at today's rates. The IRS would contend that the parents had made a taxable gift in such case because the note was unsecured and below market interest.

Tax considerations are not the only thing here. The parents are depending on that note for security and income. The figures used in the examples do not have enough earnings coverage of the preferred dividend and debt service, too little room for even a temporary decline in the profits of the company. Structuring a sale transaction would have to take earnings coverage into account just as would the structuring of a preferred stock.

Tax Factors

A sale to children is a taxable event and the parents would have to pay a tax on the interest received as well as a tax on the gain or on the sale of the stock. The installment method could be used to defer the tax on gain (note that any installment sale involving installment obligations in excess of $5 million is subject to special rules requiring the seller to pay interest on the deferred tax liability to the Government).

The key to the sale of S Corporation stock is that the interest on the notes used to acquire the stock is deductible by the children. Under current rulings, such interest is deductible against that corporation's Subchapter S income which flows through to the children. So as long as the company is producing income, the interest paid to the parents is deductible to offset it. However, such interest would probably not be deductible against other earnings or investment income, unless the assets of the S Corporation are used solely in the conduct of a trade or business and the shareholder "materially participates" in the trade or business. These interest rules get changed often by law amendments and by IRS regulations. This is an additional reason why such a transaction should only be taken with professional advice.

Summary

It is possible to "freeze" the value of S Corporation stock by selling all or part to the children. Actually this kind of "freeze" is more effective than one with preferred stock and remains a viable transaction in more instances. Ideally the children should pay for the stock with their own resources, but the sale can be financed in part with future S Corporation distributions.

There is a wide range of possible structures for such a transaction and one combined with a gift program can be very effective. As has been repeatedly stated, the use of professional counsel is imperative.

12

Using the Partnership Freeze to Save Taxes

From a tax standpoint, the partnership is clearly the most flexible and advantageous legal form for a business. In the context of the freeze the partnership lends itself easily to any of the types of freeze described above, the gift of a partnership interest (Chapter 9), the carve out of growth and preferred interests (Chapter 10), and a sale of a partnership interest (Chapter 11).

The Limited Liability Factor

If a partnership is so good taxwise, why do people have corporations? The limitation of personal liability is the main reason asserted for use of a corporation instead of a partnership to own a family business. However, this is not as strong a reason as it may seem to be. The greatest liability risks are insured anyway, be it a corporation or partnership. Corporate protection is eroding in other large risks, e.g., environmental liability, and financing, which requires personal guarantees. The real reason a corporation is so often chosen is convenience, speed, and cost. A corporation can be formed for a few hundred dollars. A partnership agreement, to be done correctly, takes more expertise, thought, time, and cost.

For those concerned with personal liability of owners, a new business ownership vehicle may be available. More than a dozen states have adopted, and others are considering, the limited liability company (LLC). The LLC has the liability protection of the corporate form and can be designed to qualify as a partnership for tax purposes.

Assume that the family business is currently in a partnership form, which in any event is typical of real estate development and ownership, professional businesses, and small service companies. Keep in mind that an

LLC, with limited personal liability, is included here where the word partnership is used.

Carve Out Preferred Partnership Interest

This is a direct analogy to the carve out of a preferred stock interest in a C Corporation. There is one huge advantage: no double tax on business income. A partnership, like an S Corporation, is not subject to tax. Instead, its income flows through to its partners and is reported on their personal returns.

Here the owners have the total partnership valued by an appraiser, then by amendment to the partnership agreement set aside a dollar amount of preferred interest, which is also valued by the appraiser. The preferred interest is entitled to a specified cumulative return in cash each year; it is directly analogous to preferred stock in a corporation. Then the remaining part, the growth part, of the partnership is given to the children; this part is directly analogous to common stock of a corporation.

Appraised value of the partnership as a whole	$2,000,000
Appraised value of the new preferred, fixed value, partnership interest	(1,800,000)
Balance = value of the gift to children of the remaining partnership interest	$ 200,000

What if you do not have a partnership now? The business is owned by you as sole proprietor? Then you form a partnership, carving out the frozen preferred interest for yourself. You give the balance of the partnership to your children, or trusts for them, whose partnership interests will be like common stock, the growth element. Figure 12.1 shows how this will work.

Partnerships are complex and many tax rules apply which these examples do not cover. Such a partnership should be prepared only by an expert. The same is true of an LLC which is taxed like a partnership.

Why Does a Partnership Freeze Work so Well?

The partnership freeze works so well because it combines the ability of a corporation to use a preferred interest with the fact that a partnership (or properly-structured LLC) is not itself subject to a tax on its income. Table 12.1 compares a partnership with a preferred interest to a corporation with preferred stock.

The advantage of the partnership (or LLC) over the corporation here is dramatic. It comes, as Table 12.1 shows, from the fact that the partnership

**Figure 12.1. "Freeze" by Issuing $1.8 Million of
Preferred Partnership Interest to Parents, Who
Then Give the $200,000 Balance of Partnership
to the Children**

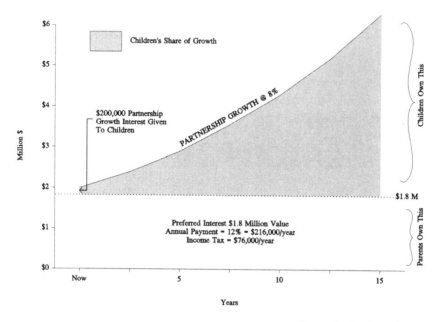

Copyright G. Shattuck 1992

Table 12.1. Partnership versus Corporation

	Partnership with Preferred Interest	Corporation with Preferred Stock
Assume pre-tax income	$416,000	$416,000
Tax on entity (40%)	0	(166,000)
Entity Income after tax	$416,000	$250,000
Preferred distribution/dividend on $1.8 million preferred interest	(216,000)	(216,000)
Balance	$200,000	$ 34,000
Children's tax on their interest @ 35%	(70,000)	*
Balance = cushion or coverage	$130,000	$ 34,000

*It is assumed that the $20,000 would be left in the corporation for business purposes, and not distributed to the children.

does not bear a 40 percent tax as a separate entity nor do the children pay a tax until the parents receive their full preferred distribution.

Note: There is no tax on an S Corporation either, but such a corporation cannot have a preferred interest.

Sell Partnership Interest to Children

Here, as in the case of an S Corporation, the parents could also sell part of their partnership interest to the children, taking back a note which is secured by the childrens' partnership interest. If this course is followed there is no need to have a complex partnership agreement to carve out the preferred interest. In a sale, the childrens' note is the preferred interest. Then the parents give the balance of the partnership to the children, or part of it. The children, as with the S Corporation in Chapter 11, pay partly or wholly out of partnership income. This gives rise to the same constraints on earnings coverage as apply to the preferred stock dividend and to the debt service on the parents' note. The sale of a partnership interest has income tax constraints and valuation constraints similar to those as sale of stock to children.

Limited or General Partnership

A general partnership is an association of two or more persons to act as co-owners of a business for profit. A general partnership, unlike a C Corporation, is not subject to two levels of tax. Instead, its income flows through to its partners and is reported on their personal returns. A major disadvantage of a general partnership is unlimited personal liability for the partners. This disadvantage can be ameliorated somewhat through insurance.

A limited partnership consists of one or more general partners with unlimited liability and one or more limited partners whose liability is limited to the extent of their capital contribution. Limited partnerships are also taxed favorably the same as general partnerships. That is, their income is taxed only once: at the partner level. The limited liability feature of a limited partnership makes it preferable to a general partnership where liability risks cannot be adequately insured. As previously noted, the limited liability company ("LLC"), available in some states, can combine the risk reduction of a corporation with the tax benefits of a partnership.

Family Partnership Rules

Under the family partnership rules, the child recipient of a partnership interest will be treated as a "partner" of the partnership for tax purposes only if he or she has a substantial interest in the capital of the partnership. Under the IRS regulations, a person who receives his interest by way of gift or purchase from another person is not recognized as a partner unless (i) the interest acquired is in a bona fide transaction and not a sham for tax avoidance or evasion, and (ii) the donee or purchaser is the real owner of the interest. Thus, a transfer to a child as partner will not be recognized for tax purposes unless the transfer is complete and vests dominion and control of the partnership interest in the transferee. The family partnership rules cut across both income tax and estate tax plans. These rules are not within the scope of this book, but must be considered by your counsel.

Summary

The general and limited partnership lend themselves very readily to a freeze transaction. In comparison with the C Corporation and the S Corporation, the structured partnership is highly advantageous. An LLC, designed to be taxed as a partnership, can use the same advantages and still provide limited liability to the owners.

13

Will a Freeze Save Your Family Business, or Impair It?

Thus far we have painted the freeze with a broad brush, showing the general concept and how it can help avert estate taxes. We have compared it to a custom suit, which must be carefully tailored in order to fit correctly. Our graphs show the tax savings, but not the potential costs of achieving the savings.

The more we analyze the so-called freeze, the more it resembles the concept time—crystal clear at first glance but blurring when you give it some deep thought. One fact does emerge: the freeze in some form can be very useful, even essential in some cases. A further analogy is considering a new, radical medical procedure. You and a medical specialist examine the whole situation in detail and study all the pros and cons, benefits, risks, and possible side effects before making a decision.

This chapter is not a substitute for that skilled practitioner. Rather, it presents a way to look at the issue, to start to evaluate it. More than all other chapters of this book, this one depends on numbers. You will see why the freeze can be such a valuable tool in succession planning.

Most books and articles you read on the freeze tell you why you can't do it, why "you can't get there from here." By contrast, we focus you on the better issue "When to do it."

A Basic Example of Freeze Alternatives

This example expands on those previously used. Here assume you own a business worth $4 million, which earns $952,000 before tax. Your other property offsets the $1.2 million exemptions of yourself and your spouse, so

123

let us eliminate that factor from future illustrations, and apply the 50% tax rate to the full business value. Your business is growing rapidly and you would like to have it continue in the family after you and your spouse die.

You have had two heart attacks and your spouse does not qualify as a "non-smoker." You can get life insurance to pay estate taxes—but only at a prohibitive cost. You have read this book so far and have learned that, at age 60, a joint life insurance payable on the last to die of yourself and your wife would normally cost about $22,000 per year per million of coverage. You know that you can put this into a tax free trust, having read Chapter 5, so the full insurance proceeds are available to pay estate taxes. With some shock you learn that given your health, such insurance will cost you $29,000 per year per million. That is $58,000 in after tax dollars each year for insurance to fund the 50 percent tax on your current $4 million of business value. This may be a feasible number for you if it would settle the tax funding problem once and for all.

Now your business is growing rapidly. It is not difficult to calculate that with its 10 percent growth rate the business could be worth $13 million at the end of your 12-year life expectancy. If you set out to fund your anticipated 50 percent tax burden, you have to purchase at least $6.5 million of insurance at a current cost of $188,000 per year in after tax dollars.

Are you and your spouse prepared to commit to spending $188,000 per year in after tax dollars to fund the estate tax potentially due when you both die? At some level of cost, insurance may be the best deal you'll ever have, but consider these other alternatives:

- Give your children $1.2 million of nonvoting stock now, plus $20,000 per year per child hereafter. Chapters 12, 3, and 9 show the value of this—but gifts do not solve the tax problem of a $4 million business with 10 percent growth.

- If the business is a C Corporation, issue preferred stock, give away the common stock, and freeze your estate at the preferred's value.

- If the business is an S Corporation, sell nonvoting common stock to your children, give away the common and freeze your estate to the extent of the value of the stock sold.

- If the business is a partnership or limited liability company, amend the agreement or articles to carve out a preferred interest, give away the growth interest and freeze your estate at such interest's value.

These four alternatives have been described in the preceding chapters. The last three will now be analyzed from a financial standpoint. Our analysis is in the form of computer generated spreadsheets which cannot give the full picture in your specific case, but can give you a basis for formulating your own study.

How to Execute a Preferred Stock Freeze

Let us go back to the graphic illustration of a freeze, except here we use a $4 million business value and a 10 percent growth rate.

- Figure 13.1 shows how the freeze would work, assuming 90% of value is issued in preferred stock, the maximum leverage. The shaded area is the future growth eliminated from your estate.

- Figure 13.2 shows the range of leverage alternatives using preferred stock. This helps select a capital structure for the company which makes economic sense.

- Figure 13.3 compares the benefits of the preferred stock freeze with its costs. Here it is the *cost* that is shown in the shaded area.

You have seen pictures of the freeze concept in our graphic illustrations. You have seen the concept condensed in various tables. The rest of this chapter shows numerically how freeze concepts work in practice. The sched-

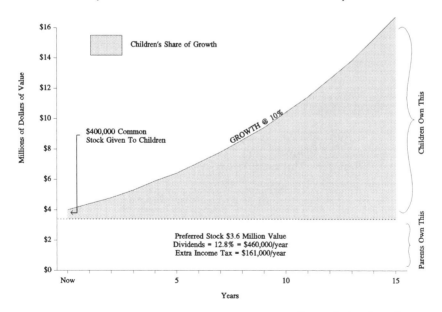

**Figure 13.1. "Freeze" by Issuing $3.6 Million
of Preferred Stock to Parents, Who Then Give
$400,000 of Common to Children (C Corporation)
($4 Million Business Value 10% Growth)**

Copyright G. Shattuck 1992

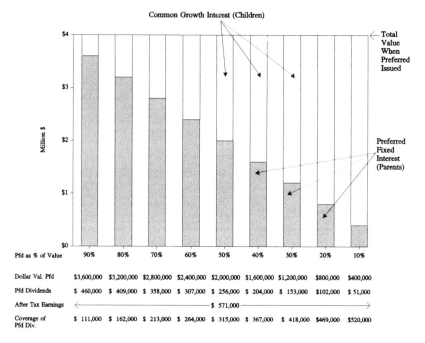

**Figure 13.2. Freeze Leverage Alternatives Using
Preferred Stock (Corp. After Tax Earnings
= $571,000) (Preferred Div. Rate = 12.78%)
(C Corporation)**

Pfd as % of Value	90%	80%	70%	60%	50%	40%	30%	20%	10%
Dollar Val. Pfd	$3,600,000	$3,200,000	$2,800,000	$2,400,000	$2,000,000	$1,600,000	$1,200,000	$800,000	$400,000
Pfd Dividends	$ 460,000	$ 409,000	$ 358,000	$ 307,000	$ 256,000	$ 204,000	$ 153,000	$102,000	$ 51,000
After Tax Earnings					$ 571,000				
Coverage of Pfd Div.	$ 111,000	$ 162,000	$ 213,000	$ 264,000	$ 315,000	$ 367,000	$ 418,000	$469,000	$520,000

The table helps decide how much preferred may safely be issued as the estate tax decreases
from issuing more preferred.

Copyright G. Shattuck 1992

ules show the projected benefits of the freeze and in a hypothetical way show
the detriments. The following sample shows how the preferred stock schedules work. These have the same factual assumptions as Figures 13.1, 13.2,
and 13.3. In fact, the Figures are pictures of the numbers in the schedules.

Table 13.1 shows you how to read Tables 13.2, 13.3, and 13.4 which
illustrate a preferred stock freeze.

Table 13.2 assumes that the parents own a C corporation worth
$4,000,000, which is growing at 5 percent per year. They recapitalize the cor-
poration and issue $3.6 million of preferred stock which has a 12.78 percent
cumulative dividend rate. The parents then give all the common stock to the
children. Thereafter, the company pays a cumulative preferred dividend of
$460,000 a year to the parents. This dividend incurs a personal income tax of
$161,000 per year, which is a "cost" of the transaction. The estate tax saved
on the growth, less this "cost," less any gift tax, gives the net benefit of the

Figure 13.3. Cost: Benefit Comparison Estate Tax Benefit vs. Extra Income Tax Cost

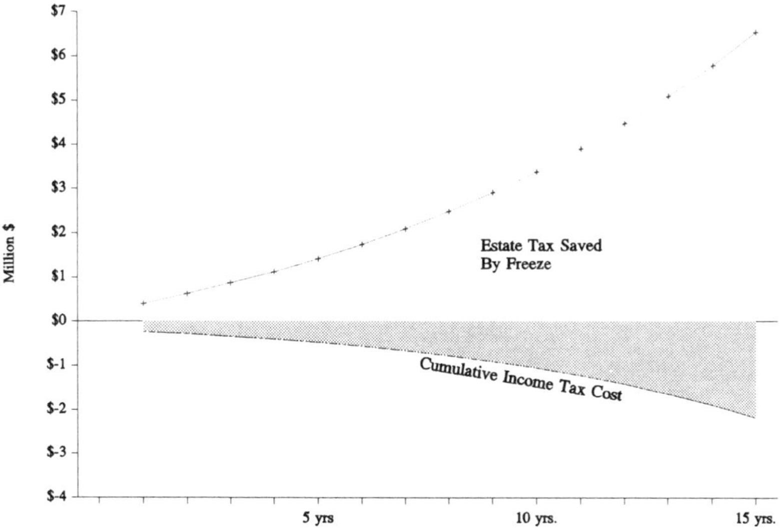

This is based on Figure 13.1 and a 10% annual growth rate in value. The net benefit is shown in Schedule II, below. At a lower growth rate the net benefit declines and can turn into a detriment, See Schedule I.

Copyright G. Shattuck 1992

transaction if death occurs in any given year. For example, if the owner on Table 13.2 died at year #10

the estate tax saved would be	$1,458,000
the cumulative income tax cost to that point would be	(2,333,000)
therefore the net benefit of the transaction would be	$ 875,000

In this illustration, the parents made a gift of $400,000 to the children, because they retained $3.6 million of preferred stock out of a total business value of $4 million. This gift element may be varied by increasing the proportion of preferred stock (up to 90 percent of total value) or by giving away a smaller percentage of future growth. (See Figure 13.2.) This is where judgment comes in, determining the right "mix" of factors for the parents' situation.

The use of a computer to calculate projected results enables the owner to explore "tailoring" the transaction to see if desired results can be achieved by changing the mix of elements. The format in our Tables is one way to look at these transactions in an actual case, your professional advisors might use revised or different schedules.

The figures and tables are by no means intended to "sell" a preferred stock freeze to you as a business owner, but only to fully explain and illustrate such a transaction. Despite seeming positive results at the higher growth rates, a preferred stock freeze would make sense only in very unusual circumstances.

Table 13.1. Sample of Tables 13.2, 13.3, 13.4
(Based on Table 13.2)

ASSUMPTIONS:

A. GROWTH RATE		5.00%
B. COMPANY VALUE AS OF START	$4,000,000	
C. % COMMON OWNERSHIP BEFORE RECAP.	100.00%	
D. ESTATE TAX RATE		50.00%
E. OWNER'S PREFERRED STOCK VALUE	$3,600,000	
F. PREFERRED DIVIDEND		$460,141
G. INCOME TAX RATE		35.00%
H. INTEREST RATE		8.00%
I. DIVIDEND RATE		12.7817%

	YEAR 1	YEAR 2	
I. ESTATE TAX SAVINGS			
Total Company Value at Beginning of Year	$4,000,000	$4,200,000	← Represents 5% growth.
Total Company Value at End of Year	4,200,000	4,410,000	
Company Value Includible in Estate Before Recapitalization	4,200,000	4,410,000	
Company Value Includible in Estate After Recapitalization and Gift	3,600,000	3,600,000	
Estate Tax Before Recapitalization	2,100,000	2,205,000	← 50% of Company Value
Estate Tax After Recapitalization	1,800,000	1,800,000	← 50% of $3,600,000
Estate Tax Savings	$ 300,000	$ 405,000	
II. INCOME TAX COST			
Preferred Dividend	$460,141	$460,141	← Dividend on preferred
Tax Cost of Dividend	161,049	161,049	← tax cost of paying dividend
Cumulative Tax Cost	161,049	322,099	
Cumulative Combined Tax and Interest Cost	$161,049	$334,983	← tax cost of paying dividend and loss of income on that amount
III. NET BENEFIT (DETRIMENT) *	$ 138,951	$ 70,017	← estate tax benefit less income tax cost
IV. PREFERRED DIVIDEND, AFTER TAX CUMULATIVE AMOUNT	$299,092	$598,184	← accumulated preferred dividends, assuming they are not consumed or given away, these are includible in estate

Note: The Net Benefit as shown above is before any gift tax on the common stock. Also, the accumulated preferred dividends, unless consumed or given away, are also subject to estate tax.

          At a 5% growth rate there is a detriment after a few years rather than a net benefit because the extra income tax cost of the dividend outweighs the estate tax saving.

Sale of S Corporation—Illustrated

Preferred stock has the limitation that there is a double tax on the preferred dividends, one at the corporate level and a second at the level of the individual preferred shareholder who receives the dividends. This cash

Table 13.2

PREFERRED STOCK 'FREEZE' ILLUSTRATIONS

ASSUMPTIONS:

A. GROWTH RATE	5.00%
B. COMPANY VALUE AS OF START	$4,000,000
C. % COMMON OWNERSHIP BEFORE RECAP.	100.00%
D. ESTATE TAX RATE	50.00%
E. OWNER'S PREFERRED STOCK VALUE	$3,600,000
F. PREFERRED DIVIDEND	$460.141
G. INCOME TAX RATE	35.00%
H. INVESTMENT EARNINGS RATE	8.00%
I. DIVIDEND RATE	12.7817%

SCHEDULE DESCRIPTION:

This illustration assumes that the owners issue $3,600,000 of 12.7817% cumulative preferred to themselves and give the common stock to the children. The growth is owned by the children and the parents save the estate tax on the growth, (See I). The cost is the double tax on the preferred dividend, (See II). The parents will have the preferred dividends after tax, (See IV), which if not consumed will be in their estates too. The same principle can be applied to partnerships. This analysis does not include any gift tax on transfer of common stock to the children.

	YEAR 1	YEAR 2	YEAR 3	YEAR 4	YEAR 5	YEAR 6	YEAR 7	YEAR 8	YEAR 9	YEAR 10	YEAR 11	YEAR 12	YEAR 13	YEAR 14	YEAR 15	YEAR 16	YEAR 17
I. ESTATE TAX SAVINGS																	
Total Company Value at Beginning of Year	4,000,000	4,200,000	4,410,000	4,630,500	4,862,025	5,105,126	5,360,383	5,628,402	5,909,822	6,205,313	6,515,579	6,841,357	7,183,425	7,542,597	7,919,726	8,315,713	8,731,498
Total Company Value at End of Year	4,200,000	4,410,000	4,630,500	4,862,025	5,105,126	5,360,383	5,628,402	5,909,822	6,205,313	6,515,579	6,841,357	7,183,425	7,542,597	7,919,726	8,315,713	8,731,498	9,168,073
Company Value Includible in Estate Before Recapitalization	4,200,000	4,410,000	4,630,500	4,862,025	5,105,126	5,360,383	5,628,402	5,909,822	6,205,313	6,515,579	6,841,357	7,183,425	7,542,597	7,919,726	8,315,713	8,731,498	9,168,073
Company Value Includible in Estate After Recapitalization	3,600,000	3,600,000	3,600,000	3,600,000	3,600,000	3,600,000	3,600,000	3,600,000	3,600,000	3,600,000	3,600,000	3,600,000	3,600,000	3,600,000	3,600,000	3,600,000	3,600,000
Estate Tax Before Recapitalization	2,100,000	2,205,000	2,315,250	2,431,013	2,552,563	2,680,191	2,814,201	2,954,911	3,102,656	3,257,789	3,420,679	3,591,713	3,771,298	3,959,863	4,157,856	4,365,749	4,584,037
Estate Tax After Recapitalization	1,800,000	1,800,000	1,800,000	1,800,000	1,800,000	1,800,000	1,800,000	1,800,000	1,800,000	1,800,000	1,800,000	1,800,000	1,800,000	1,800,000	1,800,000	1,800,000	1,800,000
Estate Tax Savings	300,000	405,000	515,250	631,013	752,563	880,191	1,014,201	1,154,911	1,302,656	1,457,789	1,620,679	1,791,713	1,971,298	2,159,863	2,357,856	2,565,749	2,784,037
II. INCOME TAX COST																	
Preferred Dividend	460,141	460,141	460,141	460,141	460,141	460,141	460,141	460,141	460,141	460,141	460,141	460,141	460,141	460,141	460,141	460,141	460,141
Tax Cost of Dividend	161,049	161,049	161,049	161,049	161,049	161,049	161,049	161,049	161,049	161,049	161,049	161,049	161,049	161,049	161,049	161,049	161,049
Cumulative Tax Cost	161,049	322,099	483,148	644,198	805,247	966,297	1,127,346	1,288,395	1,449,445	1,610,494	1,771,544	1,932,593	2,093,642	2,254,692	2,415,741	2,576,791	2,737,840
Cumulative Combined Tax and Interest Cost	161,049	334,983	522,831	725,707	944,813	1,181,447	1,437,012	1,713,023	2,011,114	2,333,052	2,680,746	3,056,255	3,461,805	3,899,799	4,372,832	4,883,708	5,435,454
III. NET BENEFIT (DETRIMENT) *	138,951	70,017	(7,581)	(94,694)	(192,250)	(301,256)	(422,811)	(558,112)	(708,458)	(875,263)	(1,060,067)	(1,264,543)	(1,490,507)	(1,739,936)	(2,014,976)	(2,317,959)	(2,651,418)
IV. PREFERRED DIVIDEND, AFTER TAX																	
CUMULATIVE AMOUNT	299,092	598,184	897,275	1,196,367	1,495,459	1,794,551	2,093,642	2,392,734	2,691,826	2,990,918	3,290,010	3,589,101	3,888,193	4,187,285	4,486,377	4,785,468	5,084,560

* Note that the benefit increases as the projected growth rate increases. Initial gift tax not included.

129

Table 13.3

PREFERRED STOCK "FREEZE" ILLUSTRATIONS

ASSUMPTIONS:

A. GROWTH RATE	10.00%
B. COMPANY VALUE AS OF START	$4,000,000
C. % COMMON OWNERSHIP BEFORE RECA	100.00%
D. ESTATE TAX RATE	50.00%
E. OWNER'S PREFERRED STOCK VALUE	$3,600,000
F. PREFERRED DIVIDEND	$460,141
G. INCOME TAX RATE	35.00%
H. INVESTMENT EARNINGS RATE	8.00%
I. DIVIDEND RATE	12.7817%

SCHEDULE DESCRIPTION:

This illustration assumes that the owners issue $3,600,000 of 12.7817% cumulative preferred to themselves and give the common stock to the children. The growth is owned by the children and the parents save the estate tax on the growth, (See I). The cost is the double tax on the preferred dividend, (See II). The parents will have the preferred dividends after tax, (See IV), which if not consumed will be in their estates too. The same principle can be applied to partnerships.

This analysis does not include any gift tax on transfer of common stock to the children.

	YEAR 1	YEAR 2	YEAR 3	YEAR 4	YEAR 5	YEAR 6	YEAR 7	YEAR 8	YEAR 9	YEAR 10	YEAR 11	YEAR 12	YEAR 13	YEAR 14	YEAR 15	YEAR 16	YEAR 17
I. ESTATE TAX SAVINGS																	
Total Company Value at Beginning of Year	4,000,000	4,400,000	4,840,000	5,324,000	5,856,400	6,442,040	7,086,244	7,794,868	8,574,355	9,431,791	10,374,970	11,412,467	12,553,714	13,809,085	15,189,993	16,708,993	18,379,892
Total Company Value at End of Year	4,400,000	4,840,000	5,324,000	5,856,400	6,442,040	7,086,244	7,794,868	8,574,355	9,431,791	10,374,970	11,412,467	12,553,714	13,809,085	15,189,993	16,708,993	18,379,892	20,217,881
Company Value Includible in Estate Before Recapitalization	4,400,000	4,840,000	5,324,000	5,856,400	6,442,040	7,086,244	7,794,868	8,574,355	9,431,791	10,374,970	11,412,467	12,553,714	13,809,085	15,189,993	16,708,993	18,379,892	20,217,881
Company Value Includible in Estate After Recapitalization and Gift	3,600,000	3,600,000	3,600,000	3,600,000	3,600,000	3,600,000	3,600,000	3,600,000	3,600,000	3,600,000	3,600,000	3,600,000	3,600,000	3,600,000	3,600,000	3,600,000	3,600,000
Estate Tax Before Recapitalization	2,200,000	2,420,000	2,662,000	2,928,200	3,221,020	3,543,122	3,897,434	4,287,178	4,715,895	5,187,485	5,706,233	6,276,857	6,904,542	7,594,997	8,354,496	9,189,946	10,108,941
Estate Tax After Recapitalization	1,800,000	1,800,000	1,800,000	1,800,000	1,800,000	1,800,000	1,800,000	1,800,000	1,800,000	1,800,000	1,800,000	1,800,000	1,800,000	1,800,000	1,800,000	1,800,000	1,800,000
Estate Tax Savings	400,000	620,000	862,000	1,128,200	1,421,020	1,743,122	2,097,434	2,487,178	2,915,895	3,387,485	3,906,233	4,476,857	5,104,542	5,794,997	6,554,496	7,389,946	8,308,941
II. INCOME TAX COST																	
Preferred Dividend	460,141	460,141	460,141	460,141	460,141	460,141	460,141	460,141	460,141	460,141	460,141	460,141	460,141	460,141	460,141	460,141	460,141
Tax Cost of Dividend	161,049	161,049	161,049	161,049	161,049	161,049	161,049	161,049	161,049	161,049	161,049	161,049	161,049	161,049	161,049	161,049	161,049
Cumulative Tax Cost	161,049	322,099	483,148	644,198	805,247	966,297	1,127,346	1,288,395	1,449,445	1,610,494	1,771,544	1,932,593	2,093,642	2,254,692	2,415,741	2,576,791	2,737,840
Cumulative Combined Tax and Interest Cost	161,049	334,983	522,831	725,707	944,813	1,181,447	1,437,012	1,713,023	2,011,114	2,333,052	2,680,746	3,056,255	3,461,805	3,899,799	4,372,832	4,883,708	5,435,454
III. NET BENEFIT (DETRIMENT) *	238,951	285,017	339,169	402,493	476,207	561,675	660,422	774,155	904,781	1,054,432	1,225,487	1,420,602	1,642,737	1,895,198	2,181,664	2,506,238	2,873,486
IV. PREFERRED DIVIDEND, AFTER TAX																	
CUMULATIVE AMOUNT	299,092	598,184	897,275	1,196,367	1,495,459	1,794,551	2,093,642	2,392,734	2,691,826	2,990,918	3,290,010	3,589,101	3,888,193	4,187,285	4,486,377	4,785,468	5,084,560

* Note that the benefit increases as the projected growth rate increases. Initial gift tax not included.

Table 13.4

PREFERRED STOCK "FREEZE" ILLUSTRATIONS

ASSUMPTIONS:

A. GROWTH RATE	15.00%
B. COMPANY VALUE AS OF START	$4,000,000
C. % COMMON OWNERSHIP BEFORE RECA	100.00%
D. ESTATE TAX RATE	50.00%
E. OWNER'S PREFERRED STOCK VALUE	$3,600,000
F. PREFERRED DIVIDEND	$460,141
G. INCOME TAX RATE	35.00%
H. INVESTMENT EARNINGS RATE	8.00%
I. DIVIDEND RATE	12.7817%

SCHEDULE DESCRIPTION:

This illustration assumes that the owners issue $3,600,000 of 12.7817% cumulative preferred to themselves and give the common stock to the children. The growth is owned by the children and the parents save the estate tax on the growth, (See I). The cost is the double tax on the preferred dividend, (See II). The parents will have the preferred dividends after tax, (See IV), which if not consumed will be in their estates too. The same principle can be applied to partnerships. This analysis does not include any gift tax on transfer of common stock to the children.

	YEAR 1	YEAR 2	YEAR 3	YEAR 4	YEAR 5	YEAR 6	YEAR 7	YEAR 8	YEAR 9	YEAR 10	YEAR 11	YEAR 12	YEAR 13	YEAR 14	YEAR 15	YEAR 16	YEAR 17
I. ESTATE TAX SAVINGS																	
Total Company Value at Beginning of Year	4,000,000	4,600,000	5,290,000	6,083,500	6,996,025	8,045,429	9,252,243	10,640,080	12,236,091	14,071,505	16,182,231	18,609,566	21,401,000	24,611,150	28,302,823	32,548,247	37,430,483
Total Company Value at End of Year	4,600,000	5,290,000	6,083,500	6,996,025	8,045,429	9,252,243	10,640,080	12,236,091	14,071,505	16,182,231	18,609,566	21,401,000	24,611,150	28,302,823	32,548,247	37,430,483	43,045,056
Company Value Includible in Estate Before Recapitalization	4,600,000	5,290,000	6,083,500	6,996,025	8,045,429	9,252,243	10,640,080	12,236,091	14,071,505	16,182,231	18,609,566	21,401,000	24,611,150	28,302,823	32,548,247	37,430,483	43,045,056
Company Value Includible in Estate After Recapitalization and Gift	3,600,000	3,600,000	3,600,000	3,600,000	3,600,000	3,600,000	3,600,000	3,600,000	3,600,000	3,600,000	3,600,000	3,600,000	3,600,000	3,600,000	3,600,000	3,600,000	3,600,000
Estate Tax Before Recapitalization	2,300,000	2,645,000	3,041,750	3,498,013	4,022,714	4,626,122	5,320,040	6,118,046	7,035,753	8,091,115	9,304,783	10,700,500	12,305,575	14,151,412	16,274,123	18,715,242	21,522,528
Estate Tax After Recapitalization	1,800,000	1,800,000	1,800,000	1,800,000	1,800,000	1,800,000	1,800,000	1,800,000	1,800,000	1,800,000	1,800,000	1,800,000	1,800,000	1,800,000	1,800,000	1,800,000	1,800,000
Estate Tax Savings	500,000	845,000	1,241,750	1,698,013	2,222,714	2,826,122	3,520,040	4,318,046	5,235,753	6,291,115	7,504,783	8,900,500	10,505,575	12,351,412	14,474,123	16,915,242	19,722,528
II. INCOME TAX COST																	
Preferred Dividend	460,141	460,141	460,141	460,141	460,141	460,141	460,141	460,141	460,141	460,141	460,141	460,141	460,141	460,141	460,141	460,141	460,141
Tax Cost of Dividend	161,049	161,049	161,049	161,049	161,049	161,049	161,049	161,049	161,049	161,049	161,049	161,049	161,049	161,049	161,049	161,049	161,049
Cumulative Tax Cost	161,049	322,099	483,148	644,198	805,247	966,297	1,127,346	1,288,395	1,449,445	1,610,494	1,771,544	1,932,593	2,093,642	2,254,692	2,415,741	2,576,791	2,737,840
Cumulative Combined Tax and Interest Cost	161,049	334,983	522,831	725,707	944,813	1,181,447	1,437,012	1,713,023	2,011,114	2,333,052	2,680,746	3,056,255	3,461,805	3,899,799	4,372,832	4,883,708	5,435,454
III. NET BENEFIT (DETRIMENT) *	338,951	510,017	718,919	972,306	1,277,902	1,644,674	2,083,027	2,605,023	3,224,639	3,958,063	4,824,037	5,844,245	7,043,770	8,451,613	10,101,291	12,031,534	14,287,074
IV. PREFERRED DIVIDEND, AFTER TAX																	
CUMULATIVE AMOUNT	299,092	598,184	897,275	1,196,367	1,495,459	1,794,551	2,093,642	2,392,734	2,691,826	2,990,918	3,290,010	3,589,101	3,888,193	4,187,285	4,486,377	4,785,468	5,084,560

* Note that the benefit increases as the projected growth rate increases. Initial gift tax not included.

cost of the freeze transaction using preferred stock makes such a freeze prohibitively expensive.

An S corporation gets around the double tax problem, but involves another problem: an S corporation cannot have two classes of stock with different economic characteristics. Thus, you cannot carve out a preferred stock interest in an S corporation.

Here the concept is to *sell* subchapter S stock to the children and have them pay for it, at least in part, with dividends on that stock. This involves a long-term note arrangement of some kind. It only makes sense if you have an appraised value low enough in relation to earnings to enable the children to use their dividends to make the note payments.

Tables 13.6, 13.7 and 13.8 assume the same company value as in the preferred stock illustration and that the owners sell $3.6 million worth of stock to the children in exchange for a long term secured note. Instead of "frozen" preferred stock, the owners receive "frozen" notes from the children. The sale transaction illustrated in Tables 13.6-13.8 is not exactly parallel to the preferred stock freeze because these schedules assume that the parents keep the remaining $400,000 worth of stock. Table 13.6, assuming a 5 percent growth rate, is illustrated on the next sheet. The actual Tables 13.6–13.8 follow that.

Although the preferred stock schedules and the sale schedules are not directly comparable to each other (since they illustrate two different kinds of transactions), they do have these elements in common:

- $4 million overall value of the business,
  $3.6 million of "frozen" interest (preferred stock or notes) retained by the parents, and

- cash payments by the corporation of $460,000 per year to effect the transaction.

The $460,000 was selected as the common element because it happens to be the annual debt service constant (12.781 percent) on a note for $3.9 million payable at 10 percent interest in annual installments over 16 years. To get a comparable cash outlay for the preferred stock freeze, we used a 12.781 percent preferred stock dividend rate.

Before you examine Tables 13.6, 13.7 and 13.8 in detail, turn to page 2 of Table 13.7 (sale of stock which has a 10 percent growth rate). Look at the last three lines of numbers for year #10. Now look at the comparable numbers in Table 13.4:

	Table 13.3 Preferred Stock Freeze	Table 13.7 Sale of Stock
Estate Tax Saving	$3,387,000	$2,869,000
Income Tax Cost	(2,333,000)	(381,000)
Net Benefit (Detriment)	$1,054,000	$2,488,000

Table 13.5

ASSUMPTIONS:		
GROWTH RATE	5.00%	
COMPANY VALUE	4,000,000	
PORTION OF COMPANY SOLD	3,600,000	
SUBCHAPTER S EARNINS	952,000	
% OF STOCK SOLD	90.00%	
# OF YEARS PAYABLE	16	
INTEREST RATE	10.00%	
ESTATE TAX RATE	50.00%	
INCOME TAX RATE	35.00%	
AMORTIZATION CONSTANT	12.7817%	

I. BASIC DATA AND ESTATE TAX SAVINGS	YEAR 1	YEAR 2
SUBCHAPTER S EARNINGS, 5% GROWTH	952,000	1,000,000
TOTAL INCOME TAX WITHOUT SALE @ 35%	333,000	350,200
TOTAL COMPANY VALUE AT BEGINNING OF YEAR	4,000,000	4,200,000
TOTAL COMPANY VALUE AT END OF YEAR	4,200,000	4,410,500
100% OF GROWTH	200,000	210,500
10.00% OF GROWTH AFTER SALE, TO PARENTS	20,000	21,000
GROWTH TO CHILDREN	180,000	189,000
ESTATE TAX SAVED	$ 90,000	$ 95,000

II. CHILDRENS' TAX PICTURE		
SUBCHAPTER S EARNINGS, 90.00% OF TOTAL	857,000	900,000
INTEREST DEDUCTION	360,000	350,000
TAXABLE INCOME	497,000	550,000
TAX @ 35%	174,000	193,000
DEBT SERVICE	460,000	460,000
TOTAL DIVIDEND NEEDED BY CHILDREN	$634,000	$653,000
TOTAL DIVIDEND AS A % OF CHILDREN'S SUBCHAPTER S EARNINGS	73.98%	72.52%

III. PARENTS' TAX PICTURE *	YEAR 1	YEAR 2
SUBCHAPTER S EARNINGS, 10.00% OF TOTAL	95,000	100,000
INTEREST INCOME	360,000	350,000
50% OF PRINCIPAL RECEIVED	50,000	55,000
TOTAL TAXABLE INCOME	505,000	505,000
TAX @ 35%	177,000	177,000
DEBT SERVICE INCOME RECEIVED,	460,000	460,000
SAME % OF SUBCHAPTER S INCOME AS CHILDREN	70,000	73,000
TOTAL CASH RECEIVED	531,000	533,000
NET AFTER TAX CASH FLOW	$354,000	$355,000

IV. NET BENEFIT **		
ESTATE TAX SAVED ON YEAR'S GROWTH	90,000	95,000
CUMULATIVE ESTATE TAX SAVINGS	90,000	185,000
PARENTS INCOME TAX	- 177,000	177,000
CHILDREN'S INCOME TAX	174,000	193,000
TOTAL INCOME TAX AFTER SALE	351,000	369,000
TOTAL INCOME TAX WITHOUT SALE	333,000	350,000
ADDITIONAL INCOME TAX DUE TO SALE	18,000	19,000
ADDITIONAL INCOME TAX COST ACCUMULATED AT 8%	18,000	38,000
CUMULATIVE ESTATE TAX SAVINGS ADDITIONAL INCOME TAX COST ACCUMULATED AT 8%	90,000	185,000
	18,000	38,000
NET BENEFIT (DETRIMENT)	$ 72,000	$146,000

Sample of Tables 13.6, 13.7 & 13.8
(Based on Table 13.6)

← total growth in value

← parents' remaining share of growth
← childrens' growth in purchased stock

← 50% of childrens' growth

← needed by children to pay their income tax and their debt service to parents
← this % will decline if earnings increase

← this assumes that parents' basis is 50% of value of stock

← constant debt service from children
← parents' share of company income

← this will be accumulated and added to parents' estates unless it is consumed

← this is basically a tax on ½ the principal received in the note payments

← this excludes consideration of the parents accumulated cash flow, which is a part of their estates

On this basis the sale of stock in an S Corporation is more than twice as efficient as the use of preferred stock in a C Corporation; the common element being the $460,000 that the business must pay out each year to make the transaction work.

The difference in effect is remarkable and it is due to the income tax advantages of an S Corporation. In our sale example, here, we assumed the parents *kept $400,000 worth of common* in addition to the note. If they gave the common to the children, as with the preferred freeze, the net benefit of the sale could be even larger. Now go to the explanation of the stock sale on the next sheet, Table 13.5, and then the following schedules.

Table 13.6

SALE OF SUBCHAPTER S STOCK "FREEZE" ILLUSTRATIONS

ASSUMPTIONS:

GROWTH RATE	5.00%
COMPANY VALUE	4,000,000
PORTION OF COMPANY SOLD	3,600,000
SUBCHAPTER S EARNINGS	952,382
% OF STOCK SOLD	90.00%
# OF YEARS PAYABLE	16
INTEREST RATE, NOTE	10.00%
ESTATE TAX RATE	50.00%
INCOME TAX RATE	35.00%
AMORTIZATION CONSTANT	12.7817%

SCHEDULE DESCRIPTION:

Here the parents sell 90% of the Company to the children for $3,600,000 payable over 16 years with interest at 10%. The parents keep the remaining 10%. This eliminates 90% of the future stock growth from the parents' estate, (See I). The children pay for the stock with Subchapter S dividends, (See II). The parents have a large after tax cash flow which if not consumed will be in their estates too, (See III). (An installment note over $5 million is subject to special tax rules which are not included in this illustration.)

I. BASIC DATA AND ESTATE TAX SAVINGS

	YEAR 1	YEAR 2	YEAR 3	YEAR 4	YEAR 5	YEAR 6	YEAR 7	YEAR 8	YEAR 9	YEAR 10	YEAR 11	YEAR 12	YEAR 13	YEAR 14	YEAR 15	YEAR 16	YEAR 17
SUBCHAPTER S EARNINGS, 5% GROWTH	952,382	1,000,001	1,050,001	1,102,501	1,157,626	1,215,508	1,276,283	1,340,097	1,407,102	1,477,457	1,551,330	1,628,896	1,710,341	1,795,858	1,885,651	1,979,934	2,078,930
TOTAL INCOME TAX WITHOUT SALE @ 35%	333,334	350,000	367,500	385,875	405,169	425,428	446,699	469,034	492,486	517,110	542,965	570,114	598,619	628,550	659,978	692,977	727,626
TOTAL COMPANY VALUE AT BEGINNING OF YEAR	4,000,000	4,200,000	4,410,000	4,630,500	4,862,025	5,105,126	5,360,383	5,628,402	5,909,822	6,205,313	6,515,579	6,841,357	7,183,425	7,542,597	7,919,726	8,315,713	8,731,498
TOTAL COMPANY VALUE AT END OF YEAR	4,200,000	4,410,000	4,630,500	4,862,025	5,105,126	5,360,383	5,628,402	5,909,822	6,205,313	6,515,579	6,841,357	7,183,425	7,542,597	7,919,726	8,315,713	8,731,498	9,168,073
10% OF GROWTH	200,000	210,000	220,500	231,525	243,101	255,256	268,019	281,420	295,491	310,266	325,779	342,068	359,171	377,130	395,986	415,786	436,575
10% OF GROWTH AFTER SALE, TO PARENTS	20,000	21,000	22,050	23,153	24,310	25,526	26,802	28,142	29,549	31,027	32,578	34,207	35,917	37,713	39,599	41,579	43,657
GROWTH TO CHILDREN	180,000	189,000	198,450	208,373	218,791	229,731	241,217	253,278	265,942	279,239	293,201	307,861	323,254	339,417	356,388	374,207	392,917
ESTATE TAX SAVED	90,000	94,500	99,225	104,186	109,396	114,865	120,609	126,639	132,971	139,620	146,601	153,931	161,627	169,708	178,194	187,104	196,459

II. CHILDRENS TAX PICTURE

	YEAR 1	YEAR 2	YEAR 3	YEAR 4	YEAR 5	YEAR 6	YEAR 7	YEAR 8	YEAR 9	YEAR 10	YEAR 11	YEAR 12	YEAR 13	YEAR 14	YEAR 15	YEAR 16	YEAR 17
SUBCHAPTER S EARNINGS, 90% OF TOTAL	857,144	900,001	945,001	992,251	1,041,864	1,093,957	1,148,655	1,206,087	1,266,392	1,329,711	1,396,197	1,466,007	1,539,307	1,616,272	1,697,086	1,781,940	1,871,037
INTEREST DEDUCTION	360,000	349,986	338,971	326,854	313,525	298,864	282,736	264,996	245,481	224,015	200,403	174,429	145,858	114,430	79,859	41,831	418,309
TAXABLE INCOME	497,144	550,015	606,030	665,397	728,339	795,093	865,919	941,092	1,020,911	1,105,696	1,195,794	1,291,578	1,393,449	1,501,843	1,617,227	1,740,110	1,452,728
TAX @ 35%	174,000	192,505	212,111	232,889	254,918	278,283	303,072	329,382	357,319	386,994	418,528	452,052	487,707	525,645	566,029	609,038	508,455
DEBT SERVICE	460,140	460,140	460,140	460,140	460,140	460,140	460,140	460,140	460,140	460,140	460,140	460,140	460,140	460,140	460,140	460,140	0
TOTAL DIVIDEND NEEDED BY CHILDREN	634,140	652,645	672,250	693,029	715,058	738,422	763,211	789,522	817,459	847,133	878,668	912,192	947,847	985,785	1,026,169	1,069,178	508,455
TOTAL DIVIDEND AS A % OF CHILDRENS SUBCHAPTER S EARNINGS	73.98%	72.52%	71.14%	69.84%	68.63%	67.50%	66.44%	65.46%	64.55%	63.71%	62.93%	62.22%	61.58%	60.99%	60.47%	60.00%	27.18%

Table 13.6 (Cont'd.)

SALE OF SUBCHAPTER S STOCK "FREEZE" ILLUSTRATION – (CONTINUED)

	YEAR 1	YEAR 2	YEAR 3	YEAR 4	YEAR 5	YEAR 6	YEAR 7	YEAR 8	YEAR 9	YEAR 10	YEAR 11	YEAR 12	YEAR 13	YEAR 14	YEAR 15	YEAR 16	YEAR 17
III. PARENTS TAX PICTURE *																	
SUBCHAPTER S EARNINGS, 10% OF TOTAL	95,238	100,000	105,000	110,250	115,763	121,551	127,628	134,010	140,710	147,746	155,133	162,890	171,034	179,586	188,565	197,993	207,893
INTEREST INCOME	360,000	349,986	338,971	326,854	313,525	298,864	282,736	264,996	245,481	224,015	200,403	174,429	145,858	114,430	79,859	41,831	0
50% OF PRINCIPAL RECEIVED	50,070	55,077	60,585	66,643	73,307	80,638	88,702	97,572	107,329	118,062	129,868	142,855	157,141	172,855	190,140	209,154	0
TOTAL TAXABLE INCOME	505,308	505,063	504,555	503,747	502,595	501,052	499,066	496,577	493,521	489,823	485,404	480,174	474,033	466,871	458,565	448,979	207,893
TAX @ 35%	176,858	176,772	176,594	176,311	175,908	175,368	174,673	173,802	172,732	171,438	169,892	168,061	165,912	163,405	160,498	157,143	72,763
DEBT SERVICE INCOME RECEIVED	460,140	460,140	460,140	460,140	460,140	460,140	460,140	460,140	460,140	460,140	460,140	460,140	460,140	460,140	460,140	460,140	0
SAME % OF SUBCHAPTER S INCOME AS CHILDREN	70,457	72,520	74,697	76,999	79,448	82,047	84,796	87,723	90,828	94,129	97,625	101,350	105,323	109,529	114,025	118,796	56,505
TOTAL CASH RECEIVED	530,597	532,660	534,837	537,139	539,588	542,187	544,936	547,863	550,968	554,269	557,765	561,490	565,463	569,669	574,165	578,936	56,505
NET AFTER TAX CASH FLOW	353,739	355,888	358,243	360,827	363,679	366,818	370,263	374,060	378,236	382,830	387,874	393,429	399,551	406,264	413,668	421,793	(16,257)
IV. NET BENEFIT **																	
ESTATE TAX SAVED ON YEAR'S GROWTH	90,000	94,500	99,225	104,186	109,396	114,865	120,609	126,639	132,971	139,620	146,601	153,931	161,627	169,708	178,194	187,104	196,459
CUMULATIVE ESTATE TAX SAVINGS	90,000	184,500	283,725	387,911	497,307	612,172	732,781	859,420	992,391	1,132,010	1,278,611	1,432,541	1,594,168	1,763,877	1,942,071	2,129,174	2,325,633
PARENTS INCOME TAX	176,858	176,772	176,594	176,311	175,908	175,368	174,673	173,802	172,732	171,438	169,892	168,061	165,912	163,405	160,498	157,143	72,763
CHILDRENS INCOME TAX	174,000	192,505	212,111	232,889	254,918	278,283	303,072	329,382	357,319	386,994	418,528	452,052	487,707	525,645	566,029	609,038	508,455
TOTAL INCOME TAX AFTER SALE	350,858	369,277	388,705	409,200	430,827	453,651	477,745	503,184	530,051	558,432	588,419	620,113	653,619	689,050	726,527	766,181	581,218
TOTAL INCOME TAX WITHOUT SALE	333,334	350,000	367,500	385,875	405,169	425,428	446,699	469,034	492,486	517,110	542,965	570,114	598,619	628,550	659,978	692,977	727,626
ADDITIONAL INCOME TAX DUE TO SALE	17,524	19,277	21,205	23,325	25,658	28,223	31,046	34,150	37,565	41,322	45,454	49,999	54,999	60,499	66,549	73,204	(146,408)
ADDITIONAL INCOME TAX COST ACCUMULATED AT 8%	17,524	38,203	62,464	90,786	123,707	161,827	205,819	256,434	314,514	380,997	456,931	543,485	641,963	753,819	880,674	1,024,332	959,870
CUMULATIVE ESTATE TAX SAVINGS	90,000	184,500	283,725	387,911	497,307	612,172	732,781	859,420	992,391	1,132,010	1,278,611	1,432,541	1,594,168	1,763,877	1,942,071	2,129,174	2,325,633
ADDITIONAL INCOME TAX COST ACCUMULATED AT 8%	17,524	38,203	62,464	90,786	123,707	161,827	205,819	256,434	314,514	380,997	456,931	543,485	641,963	753,819	880,674	1,024,332	959,870
NET BENEFIT (DETRIMENT)	72,476	146,297	221,261	297,125	373,600	450,345	526,962	602,985	677,876	751,013	821,680	889,056	952,205	1,010,058	1,061,397	1,104,842	1,365,763

* After the childrens' notes are paid in Year 16, the parents' cash flow is whatever dividends are paid on all the stock. The note proceeds, after tax, are part of their estate unless consumed.

** Note that the benefit increases as the projected growth rate increases, and of course increases greatly in Year 17, after the notes are paid off.

135

Table 13.7

SALE OF SUBCHAPTER S STOCK "FREEZE" ILLUSTRATIONS

ASSUMPTIONS:

GROWTH RATE	10.00%
COMPANY VALUE	4,000,000
PORTION OF COMPANY SOLD	3,600,000
SUBCHAPTER S EARNINGS	952,382
% OF STOCK SOLD	90.00%
# OF YEARS PAYABLE	16
INTEREST RATE, NOTE	10.00%
ESTATE TAX RATE	50.00%
INCOME TAX RATE	35.00%
AMORTIZATION CONSTANT	12.7817%

SCHEDULE DESCRIPTION:

Here the parents sell 90% of the Company to the children for $3,600,000 payable over 16 years with interest at 10%. The parents keep the remaining 10%. This eliminates 90% of the future stock growth from the parents' estate, (See I). The children pay for the stock with Sub-chapter S dividends, (See II). The parents have a large after tax cash flow which if not consumed will be in their estates too, (See III). (An installment note over $5 million is subject to special tax rules which are not included in this illustration.)

	YEAR 1	YEAR 2	YEAR 3	YEAR 4	YEAR 5	YEAR 6	YEAR 7	YEAR 8	YEAR 9	YEAR 10	YEAR 11	YEAR 12	YEAR 13	YEAR 14	YEAR 15	YEAR 16	YEAR 17
I. BASIC DATA AND ESTATE TAX SAVINGS																	
SUBCHAPTER S EARNINGS, 10% GROWTH	952,382	1,047,620	1,152,382	1,267,620	1,394,382	1,533,821	1,687,203	1,855,923	2,041,515	2,245,667	2,470,234	2,717,257	2,988,983	3,287,881	3,616,669	3,978,336	4,376,170
TOTAL INCOME TAX WITHOUT SALE @ 35%	333,334	366,667	403,334	443,667	488,034	536,837	590,521	649,573	714,530	785,983	864,582	951,040	1,046,144	1,150,758	1,265,834	1,392,418	1,531,659
TOTAL COMPANY VALUE AT BEGINNING OF YEAR	4,000,000	4,400,000	4,840,000	5,324,000	5,856,400	6,442,040	7,086,244	7,794,868	8,574,355	9,431,791	10,374,970	11,412,467	12,553,714	13,809,085	15,189,993	16,708,993	18,379,892
TOTAL COMPANY VALUE AT END OF YEAR	4,400,000	4,840,000	5,324,000	5,856,400	6,442,040	7,086,244	7,794,868	8,574,355	9,431,791	10,374,970	11,412,467	12,553,714	13,809,085	15,189,993	16,708,993	18,379,892	20,217,881
10% OF GROWTH	400,000	440,000	484,000	532,400	585,640	644,204	708,624	779,487	857,436	943,179	1,037,497	1,141,247	1,255,371	1,380,908	1,518,999	1,670,899	1,837,989
10% OF GROWTH AFTER SALE, TO PARENTS	40,000	44,000	48,400	53,240	58,564	64,420	70,862	77,949	85,744	94,318	103,750	114,125	125,537	138,091	151,900	167,090	183,799
GROWTH TO CHILDREN	360,000	396,000	435,600	479,160	527,076	579,784	637,762	701,538	771,692	848,861	933,747	1,027,122	1,129,834	1,242,818	1,367,099	1,503,809	1,654,190
ESTATE TAX SAVED	180,000	198,000	217,800	239,580	263,538	289,892	318,881	350,769	385,846	424,431	466,874	513,561	564,917	621,409	683,550	751,905	827,095
II. CHILDRENS TAX PICTURE																	
SUBCHAPTER S EARNINGS, 90% OF TOTAL	857,144	942,858	1,037,144	1,140,858	1,254,944	1,380,439	1,518,483	1,670,331	1,837,364	2,021,100	2,223,210	2,445,531	2,690,084	2,959,093	3,255,002	3,580,502	3,938,553
INTEREST DEDUCTION	360,000	349,986	338,971	326,854	313,525	298,864	282,736	264,996	245,481	224,015	200,403	174,429	145,858	114,430	79,859	41,831	418,309
TAXABLE INCOME	497,144	592,872	698,173	814,005	941,419	1,081,575	1,235,747	1,405,335	1,591,883	1,797,085	2,022,807	2,271,102	2,544,226	2,844,663	3,175,143	3,538,671	3,520,244
TAX @ 35%	174,000	207,505	244,361	284,902	329,497	378,551	432,511	491,867	557,159	628,980	707,983	794,886	890,479	995,632	1,111,300	1,238,535	1,232,085
DEBT SERVICE	460,140	460,140	460,140	460,140	460,140	460,140	460,140	460,140	460,140	460,140	460,140	460,140	460,140	460,140	460,140	460,140	0
TOTAL DIVIDEND NEEDED BY CHILDREN	634,140	667,645	704,501	745,041	789,637	838,691	892,651	952,007	1,017,299	1,089,120	1,168,122	1,255,026	1,350,619	1,455,772	1,571,440	1,698,675	1,232,085
TOTAL DIVIDEND AS A % OF CHILDRENS SUBCHAPTER S EARNINGS	73.98%	70.81%	67.93%	65.31%	62.92%	60.76%	58.79%	57.00%	55.37%	53.89%	52.54%	51.32%	50.21%	49.20%	48.28%	47.44%	31.28%

Table 13.7 (Cont'd.)

SALE OF SUBCHAPTER S STOCK "FREEZE" ILLUSTRATION – (CONTINUED)

	YEAR 1	YEAR 2	YEAR 3	YEAR 4	YEAR 5	YEAR 6	YEAR 7	YEAR 8	YEAR 9	YEAR 10	YEAR 11	YEAR 12	YEAR 13	YEAR 14	YEAR 15	YEAR 16	YEAR 17
III. PARENTS TAX PICTURE *																	
SUBCHAPTER S EARNINGS, 10% OF TOTAL	95,238	104,762	115,238	126,762	139,438	153,382	168,720	185,592	204,152	224,567	247,023	271,726	298,898	328,788	361,667	397,834	437,617
INTEREST INCOME	360,000	349,986	338,971	326,854	313,525	298,864	282,736	264,996	245,481	224,015	200,403	174,429	145,858	114,430	79,859	41,831	0
50% OF PRINCIPAL RECEIVED	50,070	55,077	60,585	66,643	73,307	80,638	88,702	97,572	107,329	118,062	129,868	142,855	157,141	172,855	190,140	209,154	0
TOTAL TAXABLE INCOME	505,308	509,825	514,793	520,259	526,271	532,884	540,158	548,160	556,962	566,644	577,295	589,010	601,897	616,073	631,666	648,819	437,617
TAX @ 35%	176,858	178,439	180,178	182,091	184,195	186,509	189,055	191,856	194,937	198,325	202,053	206,154	210,664	215,626	221,083	227,087	153,166
DEBT SERVICE INCOME RECEIVED	460,140	460,140	460,140	460,140	460,140	460,140	460,140	460,140	460,140	460,140	460,140	460,140	460,140	460,140	460,140	460,140	0
SAME % OF SUBCHAPTER S INCOME AS CHILDREN	70,457	74,182	78,281	82,788	87,735	93,195	99,191	105,788	113,039	121,019	129,786	139,450	150,077	161,764	174,613	188,732	136,887
TOTAL CASH RECEIVED	530,597	534,322	538,421	542,928	547,874	553,335	559,330	565,927	573,179	581,159	589,926	599,589	610,217	621,904	634,753	648,872	136,887
NET AFTER TAX CASH FLOW	353,739	355,883	358,243	360,838	363,680	366,825	370,275	374,071	378,242	382,833	387,873	393,436	399,553	406,278	413,669	421,785	(16,279)
IV. NET BENEFIT **																	
ESTATE TAX SAVED ON YEAR'S GROWTH	180,000	198,000	217,800	239,580	263,538	289,892	318,881	350,769	385,846	424,431	466,874	513,561	564,917	621,409	683,550	751,905	827,095
CUMULATIVE ESTATE TAX SAVINGS	180,000	378,000	595,800	835,380	1,098,918	1,388,810	1,707,691	2,058,460	2,444,306	2,868,736	3,335,610	3,849,171	4,414,088	5,035,497	5,719,047	6,470,951	7,298,047
PARENTS INCOME TAX	176,858	178,439	180,178	182,091	184,195	186,509	189,055	191,856	194,937	198,325	202,053	206,154	210,664	215,626	221,083	227,087	153,166
CHILDRENS INCOME TAX	174,000	207,505	244,361	284,902	329,497	378,551	432,511	491,867	557,159	628,980	707,983	794,886	890,479	995,632	1,111,300	1,238,535	1,232,085
TOTAL INCOME TAX AFTER SALE	350,858	385,944	424,538	466,992	513,691	565,061	621,567	683,723	752,096	827,305	910,036	1,001,039	1,101,143	1,211,258	1,332,383	1,465,622	1,385,251
TOTAL INCOME TAX WITHOUT SALE	333,334	366,667	403,334	443,667	488,034	536,837	590,521	649,573	714,530	785,983	864,582	951,040	1,046,144	1,150,758	1,265,834	1,392,418	1,531,659
ADDITIONAL INCOME TAX DUE TO SALE	17,524	19,277	21,205	23,325	25,658	28,223	31,046	34,150	37,565	41,322	45,454	49,999	54,999	60,499	66,549	73,204	(146,408)
ADDITIONAL INCOME TAX COST ACCUMULATED AT 8%	17,524	38,203	62,464	90,786	123,707	161,827	205,819	256,434	314,514	380,997	456,931	543,485	641,963	753,819	880,674	1,024,332	959,870
CUMULATIVE ESTATE TAX SAVINGS	180,000	378,000	595,800	835,380	1,098,918	1,388,810	1,707,691	2,058,460	2,444,306	2,868,736	3,335,610	3,849,171	4,414,088	5,035,497	5,719,047	6,470,951	7,298,047
ADDITIONAL INCOME TAX COST ACCUMULATED AT 8%	17,524	38,203	62,464	90,786	123,707	161,827	205,819	256,434	314,514	380,997	456,931	543,485	641,963	753,819	880,674	1,024,332	959,870
NET BENEFIT (DETRIMENT)	162,476	339,797	533,336	744,594	975,211	1,226,983	1,501,872	1,802,026	2,129,791	2,487,739	2,878,679	3,305,686	3,772,125	4,281,678	4,838,373	5,446,619	6,338,176

* After the childrens' notes are paid in Year 16, the parents' cash flow is whatever dividends are paid on all the stock. The note proceeds, after tax, are part of their estate unless consumed.

** Note that the benefit increases as the projected growth rate increases, and of course increases greatly in Year 17, after the notes are paid off.

Table 13.8

SALE OF SUBCHAPTER S STOCK "FREEZE" ILLUSTRATIONS

ASSUMPTIONS:

GROWTH RATE	15.00%
COMPANY VALUE	4,000,000
PORTION OF COMPANY SOLD	3,600,000
SUBCHAPTER S EARNINGS	952,382
% OF STOCK SOLD	90.00%
# OF YEARS PAYABLE	16
INTEREST RATE, NOTE	10.00%
ESTATE TAX RATE	50.00%
INCOME TAX RATE	35.00%
AMORTIZATION CONSTANT	12.7817%

SCHEDULE DESCRIPTION:

Here the parents sell 90% of the Company to the children for $3,600,000 payable over 16 years with interest at 10%. The parents keep the remaining 10%. This eliminates 90% of the future stock growth from the parents' estate, (See I). The children pay for the stock with Subchapter S dividends, (See II). The parents have a large after tax cash flow which if not consumed will be in their estates too, (See III).
(An installment note over $5 million is subject to special tax rules which are not included in this illustration.)

	YEAR 1	YEAR 2	YEAR 3	YEAR 4	YEAR 5	YEAR 6	YEAR 7	YEAR 8	YEAR 9	YEAR 10	YEAR 11	YEAR 12	YEAR 13	YEAR 14	YEAR 15	YEAR 16	YEAR 17
I. BASIC DATA AND ESTATE TAX SAVINGS																	
SUBCHAPTER S EARNINGS, 15% GROWTH	952,382	1,095,239	1,259,525	1,448,454	1,665,722	1,915,580	2,202,917	2,533,355	2,913,358	3,350,362	3,852,916	4,430,854	5,095,482	5,859,804	6,738,775	7,749,591	8,912,030
TOTAL INCOME TAX WITHOUT SALE @ 35%	333,334	383,334	440,834	506,959	583,003	670,453	771,021	886,674	1,019,675	1,172,627	1,348,521	1,550,799	1,783,419	2,050,931	2,358,571	2,712,357	3,119,210
TOTAL COMPANY VALUE AT BEGINNING OF YEAR	4,000,000	4,600,000	5,290,000	6,083,500	6,996,025	8,045,429	9,252,243	10,640,080	12,236,091	14,071,505	16,182,231	18,609,566	21,401,000	24,611,150	28,302,823	32,548,247	37,430,483
TOTAL COMPANY VALUE AT END OF YEAR	4,600,000	5,290,000	6,083,500	6,996,025	8,045,429	9,252,243	10,640,080	12,236,091	14,071,505	16,182,231	18,609,566	21,401,000	24,611,150	28,302,823	32,548,247	37,430,483	43,045,056
100% OF GROWTH	600,000	690,000	793,500	912,525	1,049,404	1,206,814	1,387,836	1,596,012	1,835,414	2,110,726	2,427,335	2,791,435	3,210,150	3,691,673	4,245,423	4,882,237	5,614,573
10% OF GROWTH AFTER SALE, TO PARENTS	60,000	69,000	79,350	91,253	104,940	120,681	138,784	159,601	183,541	211,073	242,733	279,143	321,015	369,167	424,542	488,224	561,457
GROWTH TO CHILDREN	540,000	621,000	714,150	821,273	944,463	1,086,133	1,249,053	1,436,411	1,651,872	1,899,653	2,184,601	2,512,291	2,889,135	3,322,505	3,820,881	4,394,013	5,053,115
ESTATE TAX SAVED	270,000	310,500	357,075	410,636	472,232	543,066	624,526	718,205	825,936	949,827	1,092,301	1,256,146	1,444,568	1,661,253	1,910,441	2,197,007	2,526,558
II. CHILDRENS TAX PICTURE																	
SUBCHAPTER S EARNINGS, 90% OF TOTAL	857,144	985,715	1,133,573	1,303,609	1,499,150	1,724,022	1,982,626	2,280,020	2,622,022	3,015,326	3,467,625	3,987,768	4,585,934	5,273,824	6,064,897	6,974,632	8,020,827
INTEREST DEDUCTION	360,000	349,986	338,971	326,854	313,525	298,864	282,736	264,996	245,481	224,015	200,403	174,429	145,858	114,430	79,859	41,831	418,309
TAXABLE INCOME	497,144	635,729	794,602	976,755	1,185,625	1,425,159	1,699,890	2,015,024	2,376,541	2,791,311	3,267,222	3,813,339	4,440,076	5,159,394	5,985,038	6,932,801	7,602,518
TAX @ 35%	174,000	222,505	278,111	341,864	414,969	498,806	594,961	705,258	831,789	976,959	1,143,528	1,334,669	1,554,026	1,805,788	2,094,763	2,426,480	2,660,881
DEBT SERVICE	460,140	460,140	460,140	460,140	460,140	460,140	460,140	460,140	460,140	460,140	460,140	460,140	460,140	460,140	460,140	460,140	0
TOTAL DIVIDEND NEEDED BY CHILDREN	634,140	682,645	738,251	802,004	875,109	958,945	1,055,101	1,165,398	1,291,929	1,437,099	1,603,667	1,794,809	2,014,166	2,265,928	2,554,903	2,886,620	2,660,881
TOTAL DIVIDEND AS A % OF CHILDRENS SUBCHAPTER S EARNINGS	73.98%	69.25%	65.13%	61.52%	58.37%	55.62%	53.22%	51.11%	49.27%	47.66%	46.25%	45.01%	43.92%	42.97%	42.13%	41.39%	33.17%

Table 13.8 (Cont'd.)

SALE OF SUBCHAPTER S STOCK "FREEZE" ILLUSTRATION – (CONTINUED)

	YEAR 1	YEAR 2	YEAR 3	YEAR 4	YEAR 5	YEAR 6	YEAR 7	YEAR 8	YEAR 9	YEAR 10	YEAR 11	YEAR 12	YEAR 13	YEAR 14	YEAR 15	YEAR 16	YEAR 17
III. PARENTS TAX PICTURE *																	
SUBCHAPTER S EARNINGS, 10% OF TOTAL	95,238	109,524	125,953	144,845	166,572	191,558	220,292	253,336	291,336	335,036	385,292	443,085	509,548	585,980	673,877	774,959	891,203
INTEREST INCOME	360,000	349,986	338,971	326,854	313,525	298,864	282,736	264,996	245,481	224,015	200,403	174,429	145,858	114,430	79,859	41,831	0
50% OF PRINCIPAL RECEIVED	50,070	55,077	60,585	66,643	73,307	80,638	88,702	97,572	107,329	118,062	129,868	142,855	157,141	172,855	190,140	209,154	0
TOTAL TAXABLE INCOME	505,308	514,587	525,508	538,342	553,405	571,060	591,730	615,903	644,146	677,114	715,563	760,370	812,547	873,265	943,877	1,025,944	891,203
TAX @ 35%	176,858	180,105	183,928	188,420	193,692	199,871	207,105	215,566	225,451	236,990	250,447	266,129	284,392	305,643	330,357	359,081	311,921
DEBT SERVICE INCOME RECEIVED	460,140	460,140	460,140	460,140	460,140	460,140	460,140	460,140	460,140	460,140	460,140	460,140	460,140	460,140	460,140	460,140	0
SAME % OF SUBCHAPTER S INCOME AS CHILDREN	70,457	75,845	82,033	89,109	97,228	106,545	117,239	129,480	143,541	159,678	178,197	199,433	223,794	251,796	283,905	320,756	295,612
TOTAL CASH RECEIVED	530,597	535,985	542,173	549,249	557,368	566,684	577,379	589,620	603,681	619,818	638,337	659,573	683,933	711,936	744,044	780,895	295,612
NET AFTER TAX CASH FLOW	353,739	355,880	358,245	360,829	363,676	366,813	370,274	374,053	378,230	382,828	387,890	393,443	399,542	406,293	413,688	421,815	(16,309)
IV. NET BENEFIT **																	
ESTATE TAX SAVED ON YEAR'S GROWTH	270,000	310,500	357,075	410,636	472,232	543,066	624,526	718,205	825,936	949,827	1,092,301	1,256,146	1,444,568	1,661,253	1,910,441	2,197,007	2,526,558
CUMULATIVE ESTATE TAX SAVINGS	270,000	580,500	937,575	1,348,211	1,820,443	2,363,509	2,988,036	3,706,241	4,532,177	5,482,004	6,574,305	7,830,450	9,275,018	10,936,270	12,846,711	15,043,718	17,570,275
PARENTS INCOME TAX	176,858	180,105	183,928	188,420	193,692	199,871	207,105	215,566	225,451	236,990	250,447	266,129	284,392	305,643	330,357	359,081	311,921
CHILDRENS INCOME TAX	174,000	222,505	278,111	341,864	414,969	498,806	594,961	705,258	831,789	976,959	1,143,528	1,334,669	1,554,026	1,805,788	2,094,763	2,426,480	2,660,881
TOTAL INCOME TAX AFTER SALE	350,858	402,611	462,038	530,284	608,660	698,676	802,067	920,825	1,057,241	1,213,949	1,393,975	1,600,798	1,838,418	2,111,431	2,425,120	2,785,561	2,972,802
TOTAL INCOME TAX WITHOUT SALE	333,334	383,334	440,834	506,959	583,003	670,453	771,021	886,674	1,019,675	1,172,627	1,348,521	1,550,799	1,783,419	2,050,931	2,358,571	2,712,357	3,119,210
ADDITIONAL INCOME TAX DUE TO SALE	17,524	19,277	21,205	23,325	25,658	28,223	31,046	34,150	37,565	41,322	45,454	49,999	54,999	60,499	66,549	73,204	(146,408)
ADDITIONAL INCOME TAX COST ACCUMULATED AT 8%	17,524	38,203	62,464	90,786	123,707	161,827	205,819	256,434	314,514	380,997	456,931	543,485	641,963	753,819	880,674	1,024,332	959,870
CUMULATIVE ESTATE TAX SAVINGS	270,000	580,500	937,575	1,348,211	1,820,443	2,363,509	2,988,036	3,706,241	4,532,177	5,482,004	6,574,305	7,830,450	9,275,018	10,936,270	12,846,711	15,043,718	17,570,275
ADDITIONAL INCOME TAX COST ACCUMULATED AT 8%	17,524	38,203	62,464	90,786	123,707	161,827	205,819	256,434	314,514	380,997	456,931	543,485	641,963	753,819	880,674	1,024,332	959,870
NET BENEFIT (DETRIMENT)	252,476	542,297	875,111	1,257,425	1,696,736	2,201,683	2,782,217	3,449,807	4,217,663	5,101,007	6,117,373	7,286,965	8,633,055	10,182,451	11,966,037	14,019,386	16,610,405

* After the childrens' notes are paid in Year 16, the parents' cash flow is whatever dividends are paid on all the stock. The note proceeds, after tax, are part of their estate unless consumed.

** Note that the benefit increases as the projected growth rate increases, and of course increases greatly in Year 17, after the notes are paid off.

Tables 13.6, 13.7, and 13.8 are complex but the overall tax impact of such a sale is complex, too. It is important to keep in mind that the common factor is the $460,000 per year paid out by the business.

Another very important difference is that the note payments stop at some point (year #16 in our illustrations) but the preferred dividends go on indefinitely.

The Partnership Freeze

The partnership freeze is very similar to preferred stock with one huge difference. In a C Corporation which issues preferred stock, the corporation must pay a corporate tax of 40 percent *before* it pays the preferred dividend. Thus, in order to pay a preferred dividend of $460,000 it must generate pretax income of $766,902 ($460,141 ÷ 0.60).

In a partnership which pays $460,000 in guaranteed payments need only generate $460,000 to cover the payments, as compared to the $766,902 for a C Corporation.

Compare Tables 13.9, 13.10, and 13.11 (partnership) with Tables 13.2, 13.3, and 13.4 (C Corporation). The difference is dramatic because the corporate double tax has been eliminated.

What do all those numbers tell us? Let us look at the bottom line, what we call the net benefit. The first thing we notice is that the sale of stock of an S Corporation is a far superior freeze than the use of preferred in a regular C Corporation. This is condensed in Table 13.12. (See page 144.)

The next thing, it leaps out, the value of a freeze under the best of circumstances depends upon the growth rate of the business value. At no anticipated growth, or even 5 percent, a freeze is probably not worth the bother. Part C of Table 13.12 (page 144) shows the bottom line on a freeze of a partnership or limited liability company (LLC). The partnership freeze is analyzed in Tables 13.9, 13.10, and 13.11. They assume that the parents form a partnership in which they retain a $3.6 million "frozen" preferred interest. The partnership is obligated to pay them a 12.781 percent return, $460,000 per year, on a cumulative basis, the same $460,000 used as a benchmark in the preceding tables.

The $460,000 can be paid out as a first charge on the partnership's earnings without any "double tax" and without any tax impact on the other partners, the children. Deductibility of interest is not a consideration. Nor do the parents realize any taxable gain. This is why the partnership freeze is so efficient compared to the other forms.

Tables 13.9, 13.10, and 13.11, following, by their sheer brevity as compared to the others demonstrate the efficiency point. The surge in popularity of LLCs, allowing tax benefits plus limited personal liability, make the partnership form ever more attractive for the future.

Table 13.9

PARTNERSHIP "FREEZE" ILLUSTRATIONS

ASSUMPTIONS:

A GROWTH RATE	5.00%
B COMPANY VALUE AS OF START	$4,000,000
C % COMMON OWNERSHIP BEFORE RECAP.	100.00%
D ESTATE TAX RATE	50.00%
E OWNERS' PREFERRED INTEREST VALUE	$3,600,000
F PREFERRED DIVIDEND	$460,141
G PARTNERSHIP INCOME TAX RATE	0.00%
H INVESTMENT EARNINGS RATE	8.00%
I DIVIDEND RATE	12.7817%
J INCOME TAX RATE	35.00%

SCHEDULE DESCRIPTION:

This illustration assumes that the owners amend the partnership agreement and carve out a $3,600,000 preferred interest with a 12.7817% cumulative guaranteed payment for themselves, and give the balance of the partnership to the children. The growth is owned by the children and the parents save the estate tax on the growth, (See I). There is no partnership tax cost on guaranteed payment, (See II). The parents will have the guaranteed payments after tax, (See IV), which if not consumed will be in their estates too. This analysis does not include any gift tax on transfer of the balance of the partnership to the children.

	YEAR 1	YEAR 2	YEAR 3	YEAR 4	YEAR 5	YEAR 6	YEAR 7	YEAR 8	YEAR 9	YEAR 10	YEAR 11	YEAR 12	YEAR 13	YEAR 14	YEAR 15	YEAR 16	YEAR 17
I. ESTATE TAX SAVINGS																	
Total Company Value at Beginning of Year	4,000,000	4,200,000	4,410,000	4,630,500	4,862,025	5,105,126	5,360,383	5,628,402	5,909,822	6,205,313	6,515,579	6,841,357	7,183,425	7,542,597	7,919,726	8,315,713	8,731,498
Total Company Value at End of Year	4,200,000	4,410,000	4,630,500	4,862,025	5,105,126	5,360,383	5,628,402	5,909,822	6,205,313	6,515,579	6,841,357	7,183,425	7,542,597	7,919,726	8,315,713	8,731,498	9,168,073
Company Value Includible in Estate Before Recapitalization	4,200,000	4,410,000	4,630,500	4,862,025	5,105,126	5,360,383	5,628,402	5,909,822	6,205,313	6,515,579	6,841,357	7,183,425	7,542,597	7,919,726	8,315,713	8,731,498	9,168,073
Company Value Includible in Estate After Recapitalization and Gift	3,600,000	3,600,000	3,600,000	3,600,000	3,600,000	3,600,000	3,600,000	3,600,000	3,600,000	3,600,000	3,600,000	3,600,000	3,600,000	3,600,000	3,600,000	3,600,000	3,600,000
Estate Tax Before Recapitalization	2,100,000	2,205,000	2,315,250	2,431,013	2,552,563	2,680,191	2,814,201	2,954,911	3,102,656	3,257,789	3,420,679	3,591,713	3,771,298	3,959,863	4,157,856	4,365,749	4,584,037
Estate Tax After Recapitalization	1,800,000	1,800,000	1,800,000	1,800,000	1,800,000	1,800,000	1,800,000	1,800,000	1,800,000	1,800,000	1,800,000	1,800,000	1,800,000	1,800,000	1,800,000	1,800,000	1,800,000
Estate Tax Savings	300,000	405,000	515,250	631,013	752,563	880,191	1,014,201	1,154,911	1,302,656	1,457,789	1,620,679	1,791,713	1,971,298	2,159,863	2,357,856	2,565,749	2,784,037
II. INCOME TAX COST																	
Guaranteed Payment	460,141	460,141	460,141	460,141	460,141	460,141	460,141	460,141	460,141	460,141	460,141	460,141	460,141	460,141	460,141	460,141	460,141
Partnership's Tax Cost of Guaranteed Payment	0	0	0	0	0	0	0	0	0	0	0	0	0	0	0	0	0
Cumulative Tax Cost	0	0	0	0	0	0	0	0	0	0	0	0	0	0	0	0	0
Cumulative Combined Tax and Interest Cost	0	0	0	0	0	0	0	0	0	0	0	0	0	0	0	0	0
III. NET BENEFIT (DETRIMENT) *	300,000	405,000	515,250	631,013	752,563	880,191	1,014,201	1,154,911	1,302,656	1,457,789	1,620,679	1,791,713	1,971,298	2,159,863	2,357,856	2,565,749	2,784,037
IV. GUARANTEED PAYMENT, AFTER TAX CUMULATIVE AMOUNT	299,092	598,184	897,275	1,196,367	1,495,459	1,794,551	2,093,642	2,392,734	2,691,826	2,990,918	3,290,010	3,589,101	3,888,193	4,187,285	4,486,377	4,785,468	5,084,560

* Note that the benefit increases as the projected growth rate increases. Initial gift tax not included.

Table 13.10

PARTNERSHIP "FREEZE" ILLUSTRATIONS

ASSUMPTIONS:

A. GROWTH RATE	10.00%
B. COMPANY VALUE AS OF START	$4,000,000
C. % COMMON OWNERSHIP BEFORE RECAP.	100.00%
D. ESTATE TAX RATE	50.00%
E. OWNERS' PREFERRED INTEREST VALUE	$3,600,000
F. PREFERRED DIVIDEND	$460,141
G. PARTNERSHIP INCOME TAX RATE	0.00%
H. INVESTMENT EARNINGS RATE	8.00%
I. DIVIDEND RATE	12.7817%
J. INCOME TAX RATE	35.00%

SCHEDULE DESCRIPTION:

This illustration assumes that the owners amend the partnership agreement and carve out a $3,600,000 preferred interest with a 12.7817% cumulative guaranteed payment for themselves, and give the balance of the partnership to the children. The growth is owned by the children and the parents save the estate tax on the growth, (See I). There is no partnership tax cost on guaranteed payment, (See II). The parents will have the guaranteed payments after tax, (See IV), which if not consumed will be in their estates too. This analysis does not include any gift tax on transfer of balance of the partnership to the children.

	YEAR 1	YEAR 2	YEAR 3	YEAR 4	YEAR 5	YEAR 6	YEAR 7	YEAR 8	YEAR 9	YEAR 10	YEAR 11	YEAR 12	YEAR 13	YEAR 14	YEAR 15	YEAR 16	YEAR 17
I. ESTATE TAX SAVINGS																	
Total Company Value at Beginning of Year	4,000,000	4,400,000	4,840,000	5,324,000	5,856,400	6,442,040	7,086,244	7,794,868	8,574,355	9,431,791	10,374,970	11,412,467	12,553,714	13,809,085	15,189,993	16,708,993	18,379,892
Total Company Value at End of Year	4,400,000	4,840,000	5,324,000	5,856,400	6,442,040	7,086,244	7,794,868	8,574,355	9,431,791	10,374,970	11,412,467	12,553,714	13,809,085	15,189,993	16,708,993	18,379,892	20,217,881
Company Value Includible in Estate Before Recapitalization	4,400,000	4,840,000	5,324,000	5,856,400	6,442,040	7,086,244	7,794,868	8,574,355	9,431,791	10,374,970	11,412,467	12,553,714	13,809,085	15,189,993	16,708,993	18,379,892	20,217,881
Company Value Includible in Estate After Recapitalization and Gift	3,600,000	3,600,000	3,600,000	3,600,000	3,600,000	3,600,000	3,600,000	3,600,000	3,600,000	3,600,000	3,600,000	3,600,000	3,600,000	3,600,000	3,600,000	3,600,000	3,600,000
Estate Tax Before Recapitalization	2,200,000	2,420,000	2,662,000	2,928,200	3,221,020	3,543,122	3,897,434	4,287,178	4,715,895	5,187,485	5,706,233	6,276,857	6,904,542	7,594,997	8,354,496	9,189,946	10,108,941
Estate Tax After Recapitalization	1,800,000	1,800,000	1,800,000	1,800,000	1,800,000	1,800,000	1,800,000	1,800,000	1,800,000	1,800,000	1,800,000	1,800,000	1,800,000	1,800,000	1,800,000	1,800,000	1,800,000
Estate Tax Savings	400,000	620,000	862,000	1,128,200	1,421,020	1,743,122	2,097,434	2,487,178	2,915,895	3,387,485	3,906,233	4,476,857	5,104,542	5,794,997	6,554,496	7,389,946	8,308,941
II. INCOME TAX COST																	
Guaranteed Payment	460,141	460,141	460,141	460,141	460,141	460,141	460,141	460,141	460,141	460,141	460,141	460,141	460,141	460,141	460,141	460,141	460,141
Partnership's Tax Cost of Guaranteed Payment	0	0	0	0	0	0	0	0	0	0	0	0	0	0	0	0	0
Cumulative Tax Cost	0	0	0	0	0	0	0	0	0	0	0	0	0	0	0	0	0
Cumulative Combined Tax and Interest Cost	0	0	0	0	0	0	0	0	0	0	0	0	0	0	0	0	0
III. NET BENEFIT (DETRIMENT) *	400,000	620,000	862,000	1,128,200	1,421,020	1,743,122	2,097,434	2,487,178	2,915,895	3,387,485	3,906,233	4,476,857	5,104,542	5,794,997	6,554,496	7,389,946	8,308,941
IV. GUARANTEED PAYMENT, AFTER TAX																	
CUMULATIVE AMOUNT	299,092	598,184	897,275	1,196,367	1,495,459	1,794,551	2,093,642	2,392,734	2,691,826	2,990,918	3,290,010	3,589,101	3,888,193	4,187,285	4,486,377	4,785,468	5,084,560

* Note that the benefit increases as the projected growth rate increases. Initial gift tax not included.

Table 13.11

PARTNERSHIP "FREEZE" ILLUSTRATIONS

ASSUMPTIONS:

A. GROWTH RATE	15.00%
B. COMPANY VALUE AS OF START	$4,000,000
C. % COMMON OWNERSHIP BEFORE RECAP.	100.00%
D. ESTATE TAX RATE	50.00%
E. OWNERS' PREFERRED INTEREST VALUE	$3,600,000
F. PREFERRED DIVIDEND	$460,141
G. PARTNERSHIP INCOME TAX RATE	0.00%
H. INVESTMENT EARNINGS RATE	8.00%
I. DIVIDEND RATE	12.7817%
J. INCOME TAX RATE	35.00%

SCHEDULE DESCRIPTION:

This illustration assumes that the owners amend the partnership agreement and carve out a $3,600,000 preferred interest with a 12.7817% cumulative guaranteed payment for themselves, and give the balance of the partnership to the children. The growth is owned by the children and the parents save the estate tax on the growth, (See I). There is no partnership tax cost on guaranteed payment, (See II). The parents will have the guaranteed payments after tax, (See IV), which if not consumed will be in their estates too. This analysis does not include any gift tax on transfer of the balance of the partnership to the children.

	YEAR 1	YEAR 2	YEAR 3	YEAR 4	YEAR 5	YEAR 6	YEAR 7	YEAR 8	YEAR 9	YEAR 10	YEAR 11	YEAR 12	YEAR 13	YEAR 14	YEAR 15	YEAR 16	YEAR 17
I. ESTATE TAX SAVINGS																	
Total Company Value at Beginning of Year	4,000,000	4,600,000	5,290,000	6,083,500	6,996,025	8,045,429	9,252,243	10,640,080	12,236,091	14,071,505	16,182,231	18,609,566	21,401,000	24,611,150	28,302,823	32,548,247	37,430,483
Total Company Value at End of Year	4,600,000	5,290,000	6,083,500	6,996,025	8,045,429	9,252,243	10,640,080	12,236,091	14,071,505	16,182,231	18,609,566	21,401,000	24,611,150	28,302,823	32,548,247	37,430,483	43,045,056
Company Value Includible in Estate Before Recapitalization	4,600,000	5,290,000	6,083,500	6,996,025	8,045,429	9,252,243	10,640,080	12,236,091	14,071,505	16,182,231	18,609,566	21,401,000	24,611,150	28,302,823	32,548,247	37,430,483	43,045,056
Company Value Includible in Estate After Recapitalization and Gift	3,600,000	3,600,000	3,600,000	3,600,000	3,600,000	3,600,000	3,600,000	3,600,000	3,600,000	3,600,000	3,600,000	3,600,000	3,600,000	3,600,000	3,600,000	3,600,000	3,600,000
Estate Tax Before Recapitalization	2,300,000	2,645,000	3,041,750	3,498,013	4,022,714	4,626,122	5,320,040	6,118,046	7,035,753	8,091,115	9,304,783	10,700,500	12,305,575	14,151,412	16,274,123	18,715,242	21,522,528
Estate Tax After Recapitalization	1,800,000	1,800,000	1,800,000	1,800,000	1,800,000	1,800,000	1,800,000	1,800,000	1,800,000	1,800,000	1,800,000	1,800,000	1,800,000	1,800,000	1,800,000	1,800,000	1,800,000
Estate Tax Savings	500,000	845,000	1,241,750	1,698,013	2,222,714	2,826,122	3,520,040	4,318,046	5,235,753	6,291,115	7,504,783	8,900,500	10,505,575	12,351,412	14,474,123	16,915,242	19,722,528
ii. INCOME TAX COST																	
Guaranteed Payment	460,141	460,141	460,141	460,141	460,141	460,141	460,141	460,141	460,141	460,141	460,141	460,141	460,141	460,141	460,141	460,141	460,141
Partnership's Tax Cost of Guaranteed Payment	0	0	0	0	0	0	0	0	0	0	0	0	0	0	0	0	0
Cumulative Tax Cost	0	0	0	0	0	0	0	0	0	0	0	0	0	0	0	0	0
Cumulative Combined Tax and Interest Cost	0	0	0	0	0	0	0	0	0	0	0	0	0	0	0	0	0
III. NET BENEFIT (DETRIMENT) *	500,000	845,000	1,241,750	1,698,013	2,222,714	2,826,122	3,520,040	4,318,046	5,235,753	6,291,115	7,504,783	8,900,500	10,505,575	12,351,412	14,474,123	16,915,242	19,722,528
IV. GUARANTEED PAYMENT, AFTER TAX																	
CUMULATIVE AMOUNT	299,092	598,184	897,275	1,196,367	1,495,459	1,794,551	2,093,642	2,392,734	2,691,826	2,990,918	3,290,010	3,589,101	3,888,193	4,187,285	4,486,377	4,785,468	5,084,560

* Note that the benefit increases as the projected growth rate increases. Initial gift tax not included.

Table 13.12 Freeze Comparisons

The Net Benefit (Detriment)
on a $3.9 Million Freeze

	Death In:	*5 yrs*	*10 yrs*	*15 yrs*
A. *Preferred Stock*				
Table 13.2 5% Value Growth		$ (192,000)	(875,000)	(2,015,000)
Table 13.3 10% Value Growth		$ 476,000	1,054,000	2,182,000
Table 13.4 15% Value Growth		$1,278,000	3,958,000	10,101,000
B. *Sale of Stock to Children*				
Table 13.6 5% Value Growth		$ 374,000	751,000	1,061,000
Table 13.7 10% Value Growth		$ 975,000	2,488,000	4,838,000
Table 13.8 15% Value Growth		$1,697,000	5,101,000	12,000,000
C. *Partnership or LLC*				
Table 13.9 5% Value Growth		$ 752,000	1,458,000	2,358,000
Table 13.10 10% Value Growth		$1,421,000	3,387,000	6,555,000
Table 13.11 15% Value Growth		$2,223,000	6,291,000	14,474,000

A word of caution: the drafting of such a partnership requires really expert counsel to steer a course around other complex income tax and estate tax rules. The cost of achieving a perfectly drafted partnership agreement is another cost of the partnership freeze—a cost which should not lightly be undertaken.

Summary of the Estate Freeze for Different Business Forms

What accounts for the wide differences in results in the three different business forms?

- The main factor is the extra tax on the C Corporation: accumulating this tax with interest mounts up fast to diminish the result of the estate tax saving. Only at high growth rates does the estate tax saving offset this income tax cost (which is a constant).
- A factor that makes the sale of stock less attractive than the partnership freeze is the capital gain tax that must be borne by the parents selling the stock. The full impact of this capital gain tax shows up in the later years of the schedules.
- The key factor in the sale of stock of an S Corporation is the deduct-

ibility of interest against the S Corporation income, which is assumed in the schedules. If the corporate income declines, the children still have to make the note payments to the parents from other resources and may not be able to deduct the interest against other income. Also, the law on deductibility of interest could change, as it has in the past.

- The high leverage (high percent of frozen interest) used in the examples has an effect on the overall results. Convenient for illustration, such leverage need not be used in all transactions.

- In determining net benefit, none of the tables take into account the estate tax impact of the accumulated distributions to the owners of the frozen interest. We have not included this as a factor (even though it is shown in the schedules) because of the wide variety of things that could be done with such funds.

- Finally, the format of the analysis used in the schedules is a major factor. The format we have developed for use here is one way of looking at the freeze alternatives, but not the only valid way. The reader contemplating a freeze transaction should work closely with his or her professional advisors to develop a format for analysis which is tailored to the specific situation at hand.

Interpretation of Tables

Tables 13.1–13.11 are submitted, not to show an ideal transaction, but rather to propose a model to help design a transaction. These tables deal with income and estate taxes but do not address economic validity, the common sense of the transaction. Specifically, from the parents' viewpoint we need to examine the likelihood that the preferred dividends will be paid or that the note will be paid in full.

Table 13.13 examines the same transaction in a different way. It seeks to determine if the transaction makes economic sense, to answer the question "when can subchapter S dividends on a share of stock enable the children to pay the debt service to purchase the stock?" If we assume level earnings, no growth, the answer may be never. If we assume some growth in value and earnings there is a point at which a share can pay for itself with corporate distribution in a properly structured transaction. Table 13.3 aggregates 16 years of projected results for both the sale of subchapter S stock and the use of preferred stock. The idea here is to test the economic validity of the deal, rather than tax savings. It is another way of looking at the "coverage" and "leverage" issues discussed above.

This format will enable the reader to test out various blends of factors (e.g., varying interest rates or preferred dividend rates) in designing a freeze transaction. The long-term economic safety and reality of what you are doing must override all presumed tax benefits.

Table 13.13. Can the Corporate Income Support
the Transaction (Assume No Income Growth)
(02/05/92)

ASSUMPTIONS

1. BEFORE TAX INCOME	$952,382	5. ESTATE TAX RATE	50%
2. VALUE OF CORPORATION	$4,000,000	6. SALE TERMS	16 YEARS @ 10%
3. CORPORATE TAX RATE	40%	7. CONSTANT PAYMENT	12.78%
4. INDIVIDUAL TAX RATE	35%	8. PREFERRED DIVIDEND RATE	12.78%

DESCRIPTION	SCENARIO 1 SALE OF N% OF STOCK AND GIVE BALANCE – S CORP	DESCRIPTION	SCENARIO 2 ISSUE PREFERRED N% OF VALUE AND GIVE BALANCE – C CORP
TOTAL VALUE	$4,000,000	TOTAL VALUE	$4,000,000
STOCK SOLD	3,600,000	PREFERRED STOCK DIVIDEND	3,600,000
GIFT	400,000	GIFT OF COMMON STOCK	400,000
DEBT SERVICE PER YEAR @ 12.78%	460,000	PREFERRED DIVIDEND @ 12.78%	460,000
DEBT SERVICE IN 16 YEARS	7,361,000	PREFFERED DIVIDEND IN 16 YEARS	7,361,000
INCOME BEFORE TAX 16 YEARS	15,238,112	INCOME BEFORE TAX 16 YEARS	15,238,112
INTEREST DEDUCTION 16 YEARS	3,761,000	INTEREST DEDUCTION 16 YEARS	0
TAXABLE INCOME 16 YEARS	11,477,112	TAXABLE INCOME 16 YEARS	15,238,112
TAX @ 35%	4,016,989	TAX @ 40%	6,095,245
AFTER TAX INCOME, SUB S	11,221,473	AFTER TAX INCOME IN CORPORATION	9,142,867
DEBT SERVICE 16 YEARS	7,361,000	PREFERRED DIVIDEND	7,361,000
AFTER TAX INCOME – DEBT SERVICE	3,860,473	AFTER TAX INCOME – PREFERRED DIVIDEND	1,781,867
PARENTS' TAX = 35% DEBT SERVICE	2,576,350	PARENTS' TAX = 35% OF DIVIDEND	2,576,350
CHILDRENS' TAX, ABOVE	4,016,989	CHILDRENS' TAX, ABOVE	6,095,245
TOTAL TAX AFTER TRANSCATION	6,593,339	TOTAL TAX AFTER TRANSCATION	8,671,595
TAX ON INCOME WITHOUT TRANSACTION	5,333,339	TAX OF CORPORATION WITHOUT PREFERRED	6,095,245
EXTRA TAX DUE TO TRANSACTION*	1,260,000	EXTRA TAX DUE TO TRANSACTION*	2,576,350
TOTAL INCOME AFTER 16 YEARS	15,238,112	TOTAL CORP INCOME AFTER 16 YEARS	9,142,867
CHILDRENS' TAX	4,016,989	– PREFERRED DIVIDEND	7,361,000
SUB S INCOME AFTER, 16 YEARS	11,221,473		
– DEBT SERVICE	7,361,000	PREFERRED DIVIDEND COVERAGE	1.24:1
DEBT SERVICE COVERAGE	1.5:1	*EXTRA INCOME ON PREFERRED CONTINUES	
		FOREVER; EXTRA INCOME TAX ON PRUCHASE STOPS	
		AFTER 16 YEARS.	

Freeze Analysis Summary

If nothing else the foregoing analysis and tables show us the following:

- It is extremely important to test the economic validity of the freeze arrangement. (See Table 13.13.)
- The anticipated rate of growth also determines whether a "freeze" makes sense. Table 13.14 summarizes how rate of growth affects alternate freeze devices at varying growth rates.
- Figures 13.4, 13.5, and 13.6 are graphs of the corresponding schedules'

Table 13.14. Net Benefit of "Freeze" at Year Ten

Net Benefit Tenth Year
Growth Rate of:

	5%	10%	15%
C Corporation, Preferred & Gift			
Table 13.2	($875,000)		
Table 13.3		$1,054,000	
Table 13.4			$3,958,000
S Corporation, Sale			
Table 13.6	751,000		
Table 13.7		2,488,000	
Table 13.8			5,101,000
Partnership, Preferred & Gift			
Table 13.9	1,458,000		
Table 13.10		3,987,000	
Table 13.11			6,291,000

net benefits. They show that the partnership or LLC is clearly the best vehicle to achieve a freeze; the S Corporation is good but less so; the C Corporation is not a good candidate for a freeze except in very unusual circumstances. These figures also bring out the importance of the anticipated growth rate.

The value of the freeze concept can be summarized in four questions and answers which follow:

Q. Can I use gifts to freeze the value of my estate for tax purposes?

A. Yes, gifts are a form of freeze and are very effective for businesses up to a certain size of business.

Q. Beyond gifts, what is available? I have heard that Congress killed the freeze.

A. Certain forms of freeze transactions are still available if you follow carefully the rules laid out by the IRS.

Q. When does a freeze make sense?

A. Only in situations where there is a fairly high value growth rate and where the business owner is willing to play by the rules set forth by Congress and the IRS. Penalties for doing it incorrectly are high.

Q. How can I do it safely?

A. Play strictly by the rules and have independent expert appraisals to guide you and your advisors.

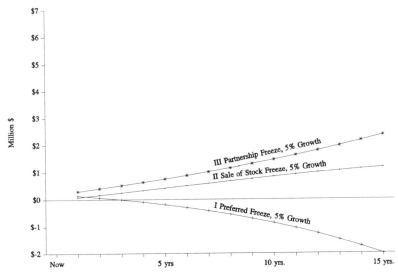

Figure 13.4. Relative Net Benefit of Preferred Freeze, Sale of Stock Freeze, and Partnership Freeze ($4.0 Million Initial Value) (5% Growth Rate)

Copyright G. Shattuck 1992

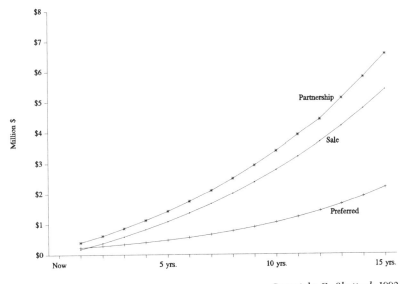

Figure 13.5. Relative Net Benefit of Preferred Freeze, Sale of Stock Freeze, and Partnership Freeze ($4.0 Million Initial Value) (10% Growth Rate)

Copyright G. Shattuck 1992

Figure 13.6. Relative Net Benefit of Preferred Freeze, Sale of Stock Freeze, and Partnership Freeze ($4.0 Million Initial Value) (15% Growth Rate)

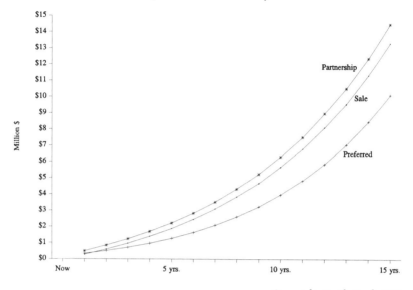

Copyright G. Shattuck 1992

Part Four

HOW TO KEEP
YOUR KEY EMPLOYEES

CHAPTER 14. Offering Stock Options, Restricted Stock, and Phantom Stock as Incentives to Key Employees.

CHAPTER 15. How Key Employees Can Acquire Stocks Painlessly—Use the Bonus-Out.

CHAPTER 16. The ESOP and the Stock Bonus Plan.

CHAPTER 17. Comparing Stock-Based Incentive Plans.

Parts One, Two, and Three focus on the estate tax burden, and on how to lessen it or to alleviate the immediate post-death tax impact. These are essential parts of planning for the succession of a family business, but not the whole of it.

Part Four derives from the presumption that any business large enough to pose an estate tax problem upon the death of the owner is a business that depends greatly on key employees other than the owner. In terms of succession planning, key employees become even more key and more essential after the owner dies. In Chapter 1, we emphasized the importance of the marital deduction which provides for the surviving spouse's needs, and defers the impact of estate tax until the spouse's death. But who runs the show in the interim between the

151

original owner's death and the surviving spouse's death? The spouse? Are the children old enough? Are they qualified to manage the business? Is management ability hereditary?

The main points of Part Four are that

- the successful business has a number of key employees who really make it tick, and

- in addition to fair pay and treatment, an ownership interest is a valuable incentive to key employees.

One note before we begin. Part 4 deals with key employees, *who may or may not be the owner's children.* In fact, the methods of getting ownership to key employees which are described below can be a very effective additional way to get stock ownership out of the owner's estate and into the childrens' hands. We have learned that gifts, while effective, are subject to certain dollar limitations. If the children are bona fide employees, transfers to them as employees can go beyond the gift limitation. Part Four shows how to use this additional way to transfer stock ownership to children.

14

Offering Stock Options, Restricted Stock, and Phantom Stock as Incentives to Key Employees

In the case study that appears as Part Six of this book, you will read the story of Jim and Kate Wolczk who have built up a very valuable electronics business. Their executive vice president is Bob Lewis who, as "Mr. Inside," really runs the three manufacturing plants while Jim and Kate do work such as R&D management, financing, and marketing. Without Bob Lewis they could be in deep trouble. If Bob left now, Jim could keep things going while the search process for a replacement was carried out. But what if Jim died or was disabled during the replacement process? What if Bob died when they need him most?

The Wolczk's daughter, Molly Wolczk, BS, MBA, as head of the international division, is also a key employee and is thought of as an eventual successor to Bob Lewis. Management ability may not be hereditary, but Molly has proven herself in her years with the company. Jim and Kate look to her as the future CEO.

Stock ownership by key employees has been described as a golden handcuff. That may well be so, but a competitor or other company which covets a key person can always try to outbid your handcuff. If dollars were the only issue, stock ownership for key people would have little value in retaining them. However, the Bob Lewises of the world are not just hacks, for sale to the highest bidder. Ownership, a piece of the company they identify with, can mean more to them than its dollar equivalent.

Who, how, and how much? These are questions that each owner must answer based on the personnel and other facts, but some guidance on the "how" factor is available. Four possibilities come to mind where the objective is to get incentive stock into the hands of key employees:

- Outright ownership with restrictions on transfer to outsiders;
- Ownership subject to some performance or other contingency, known as "restricted stock";
- Stock options, rights to acquire stock, which also may be subject to contingencies when issued (i.e., restricted stock); and
- Phantom stock, or shadow stock, which is really deferred cash compensation using stock performance as an index of amount.

The purpose of each of these devices is to provide incentive to key employees—to give them "a piece of the action", as it were. The Bob Lewis in our example is more likely to stay around if he owns a share of the company than if he does not.

Molly Wolczk, the daughter, is a different case. True, stock-based compensation may help keep her on board, but it also presents an opportunity for her parents to reduce their estate by getting stock into her hands, provided that they meet the IRS criteria of reasonable compensation.

These four basic ways of getting stock into employees hands are described in detail in this chapter.

Offer Key Employees Outright Stock Ownership

This is very similar to taking certain key employees in as partners in a partnership. In some cases they could be corporate directors too, subject always to the owner's need to keep control. As in the case of gifts of stock to children to reduce estate taxes, the stock in the hands of such employees should be subject to a restrictive agreement or bylaws (see Chapter 3, Exhibits 3.1 and 3.2), which are designed to prevent transfer to outsiders.

It also is advisable to arrange for what will happen when such an employee retires, or dies. Consider these alternatives:

- The company can retain an option to repurchase the stock when the employee dies or retires;
- The employee and the employee's estate can be given an option to "put" (i.e., sell) the stock back to the company at retirement or death;
- Each party can be given an option as described above, the company to buy and the employee to sell, and, if it turns out that neither party exercises its options, the employee could bequeath the stock to his or her heirs who would continue with the same restrictions as to disposition of stock by them;

- The parties could agree that such stock shall automatically be purchased at retirement or death, no option either way.

In all these cases, the company and the employee have to consider how to fix a value (a purchase price) for the stock, and how to fund that purchase price. "Value" is discussed in Chapter 8.

Typically, an agreement to repurchase stock will provide for redemption of the key employee's stock at termination of employment, retirement, total disability, or death. The buyout at death often is funded, at least in part, by company-owned insurance on the life of the employee; the insurance proceeds can cover the entire purchase price, or can be a source of the down payment with a corporate note issued for the balance. At termination, retirement, or disability, where no insurance proceeds are available, the stock usually will be redeemed in exchange for an installment note payable with interest over a period of years. The stock sold is pledged as security for payment.

The key in any repurchase is that the purchase price be based on a formula that fairly reflects the value of the stock at the time of the acquisition by the employee and the buyout by the employer. This is what gives the employee the incentive he or she has a piece of the action. Developing a fair formula is easier said than done, however, because, in addition to being fair, the formula price must be easy to ascertain. Book value has the advantage of being fairly easy to ascertain, when based on the most recent year-end or month-end statement. However, at a given point, book value (assets less liabilities) may not reflect the future earning power or the intangible values, of the company. A formula based on capitalization of earnings meets this need, but can be volatile in this economic climate where earnings can take wide swings from year to year and the price/earnings ratios of comparable companies varies with an edgy stock market. Consider a formula that contains two factors (i) book value which has been adjusted to reflect appraised value of certain assets such as real property, and (ii) a capitalization of average earnings. The weighting of these factors would be adjusted based on the nature of each individual company and the judgment of the person designing the formula.

In any event, assuming the formula was negotiated fairly, if a key employee acquires stock at a value determined by a formula (be it too high or too low) and then sells by the same formula (be it too high or too low), then the actual formula may not be crucial. For example, if a formula provides a relatively "low" value, the company benefits from a lower repurchase price, but the employee was originally able to buy at a lower price.

Developing a fair formula can get so complex that the parties may need the services of an independent appraiser or expert to help arrive at the formula. If stock is issued to a family member, such as Molly Wolczk in our example, it is important to be extremely careful to have a fair price arrangement. Otherwise, the IRS will see gift and estate tax problems.

Offer Key Employees Restricted Stock

The preceding section describes instances where an employee acquires stock based on a fair and reasonable value and he or she is the true owner of the stock for all purposes (subject to an agreement restricting transfer or providing for a buyout).

With restricted stock, the employee usually acquires stock at some discount from true value. This is a benefit, an incentive compensation device. If the Wolczks' company is worth $4 per share, they can (after observing corporate formalities required by state law) issue such stock to Bob Lewis at only $1 per share. Suppose, for example, they issue to him 50,000 shares for which he pays only $50,000. Bob receives $200,000 worth of stock for $50,000.

There is a catch, however. By agreement with Bob, the Wolczks tell him his stock is "restricted" so that he has to stay with the company at least 10 years before he gets the full benefit of ownership. The agreement provides that Bob's ownership interest "vests" (i.e., becomes nonforfeitable) as follows:

Bob's Subsequent Service	% Vested
0–2 years	0%
2 years	20%
4 years	40%
6 years	60%
8 years	80%
10 years	100%

Suppose Bob quits, or is terminated for cause, three years after he first acquires the stock. In that case, 20 percent of his stock is vested and his to keep. The remaining 80 percent is forfeited to the company and Bob is repaid what he paid for those shares (i.e., $1 per share). At the time Bob leaves the company, the stock has increased in value from $4 per share to $6 per share. Table 14.1 shows how Bob prospers.

Bob's 50,000 shares could be covered by an agreement such as the one described later in Section 14.3. For instance, if Bob retired from the company 15 years after acquiring the stock, at Bob's subsequent death, or on attaining age 65 (in either of which cases the stock would be 100 percent vested), the company would be required to repurchase his stock at the then value determined by a formula. The price then could vary greatly depending on the company's performance. Bob is really a shareholder. He has taken the risks of a shareholder, and receives the rewards if all goes well. How is this handled from a tax standpoint? The rules bear attention.

Table 14.1. Stock Vesting Example

	Shares	Value
Issued stock now valued @ $6	50,000	$300,000
Stock forfeited because Bob left after 2 years	(40,000)	(240,000)
Bob's "vested" stock	10,000	$ 60,000
Bob's original cost for the 10,000 shares		(10,000)
Bob's gain, paid over a period of three years		$ 50,000

Note: Bob also would receive back the $40,000 he had paid for the 40,000 forfeited shares.

Tax Rules on Restricted Stock

In the restricted stock case as described above, Bob would not realize any taxable income on purchase of the shares, even though he was admittedly getting them at a bargain. The reason is that the shares are subject to a substantial risk of forfeiture: they are not really his until he has stayed on the job long enough for them to vest.

When the shares do vest, Bob realizes income at that point measured by the then value of the stock less what he paid for it. Table 14.2 provides an example.

At each vesting point the risk of forfeiture lapses as to 10,000 shares (20 percent of 50,000 shares) and Bob realizes taxable income based on the then value, less his cost for the same shares. The company is required to withhold on this income and report it on Bob's Form W-2.

However, to the extent Bob, the employee, realizes income, the Wolczk's corporation gets a deduction (assuming the overall amount is "reasonable" as compensation for Bob's efforts as employee). For example, Table 14.3 illustrates what happens in the tenth year. Here, Bob has incurred a $24,500 tax on his $70,000 income and the company has saved $28,000 in cash because of its equivalent deduction. Bob hasn't had a bad deal at all. He has been able to invest in the company on favorable terms. He invested in the future and made a profit. If the stock had not gone up in value he would have only paid $1.00 per share. Now those 10,000 shares are worth $8 per share and he has a market for them due to the buyout agreement.

The company has not had a bad deal either. It has secured the services and loyalty of a very valuable person. It has demonstrated appreciation for the fine job Bob has done. Would this work with the Wolczks' daughter, Molly Wolczk? Yes it would, provided her compensation is reasonable in

Table 14.2. Income on Vesting of Stock

Time	Shares Vesting	Then Value Per Share*	Value Total	Cost	Taxable Income
Now	0	$4	$ —		
2 years	10,000	$4	$40,000	$10,000	$30,000
4 years	10,000	$5	$50,000	$10,000	$40,000
6 years	10,000	$6	$60,000	$10,000	$50,000
8 years	10,000	$5	$50,000	$10,000	$40,000**
10 years	10,000	$8	$80,000	$10,000	$70,000

*This is the value at the time the restrictions expire and the stock vests in the employee.
**Note the value per share declined at this point.

Table 14.3. Example of Corporate Deduction

Risk of forfeiture expires on 10,000 shares @ $8	$80,000
Bob's cash cost for shares	10,000
Bob's taxable income on W-2	$70,000
Bob's tax @ 35%	24,500
Corporation's deduction	$70,000
Corporation tax saved @ 40%	$28,000
Net Cash benefit to Corporation when stock vests in 10th year	$28,000

amount and that she has the same deal as other, unrelated, employees. If the Wolczks gave Molly too good a deal, the IRS might properly claim a gift element was involved, and/or disallow part of the employer's deduction.

Can this be bettered? Yes, consider that Bob incurred a tax of $24,500 because he vested in his 10,000 shares in the tenth year. (See Table 14.3.) He pays tax in cash for paper income—paper in the sense that, although he has stock that went up in value, he can't spend that value now, and the value could later go down. However, the company has received a $28,000 cash benefit and has only parted with paper in the form of Bob's stock. Suppose the company uses part of its $28,000 and grants to Bob a $24,500 cash bonus to enable him to pay his tax? The company gets an additional deduction for Bob's $24,500 cash bonus. Bob, however, must pay tax on the bonus. (More on this subject in Chapter 15.)

Employee's Election When to Pay Tax

Bob realizes income when the risk of forfeiture expires, when ownership of the stock truly vests in him. The income is measured by the difference between what he paid for the restricted stock at the time he acquired it and the value of the stock at the time the risk of forfeiture expires. Unless the company plans to help Bob pay the tax when due, Bob has a significant triple risk:

- income could be realized at a time when he does not have the cash to pay the tax (especially if the stock is not marketable),
- the IRS might assign a very high value to the stock and leave it to be thrashed out, expensively, in audit procedures, and
- the stock value, on which he paid the tax, could decline before he gets a chance to sell it and pay the tax.

The tax law comes to the employee's aid here. It permits the employee to elect to have income taxed when the stock is issued, even though there is then a substantial risk of forfeiture of the stock. For example, in the case where stock worth $4.00 per share is issued to Bob for $1.00 per share the results would be as shown in Table 14.4.

Table 14.4. Effect of Election to Realize Income on Issue of Stock

When Issued	General Rule	Employee's Election
Stock value	$4.00	$4.00
Bob's cost per share	(1.00)	(1.00)
Taxable income	zero*	$3.00
Bob's cost per share for determining taxable gain in event of future sale	$1.00	$4.00

When Restriction Expires

	General Rule	Employee's Election
Stock value	$8.00	$8.00
Bob's cost	(1.00)	(4.00)
Bob's taxable income	$7.00	zero**
Bob's cost per share for determining taxable gain in event of future sale	$8.00	$4.00***

*General rule is that no income is realized on issuance of stock that is subject to restrictions. Rather, income is realized on the value when the restrictions expire.

**If a special election is made (within 30 days of the issuance), income is realized upon the issuance of the stock, and not later when the restrictions expire.

***If this employee's stock were repurchased after his death, his or her estate would get a new cost basis for the stock and there would be no income on its sale back to the company.

Thus the employee has a basic choice when the stock is issued:

- pay tax when restrictions expire based on the then value, be it higher or lower, or

- pay tax now based on current value and run the risk of never realizing on the stock, which may decline in value.

Generally, it makes sense to defer the realization of income and then pay a tax on the value at the time the restrictions expire and the stock vests. However, the risk of deferring is that the tax will be much higher when the restrictions do expire. A supposedly beneficial plan can put your valued employee on the horns of a tough dilemma.

How can we resolve this dilemma? Remember, the tax burden will probably be less when the stock is initially issued to the employee. Therefore, a good strategy is

- employee elects to recognize income on issuance of the stock, and

- the employer uses part of its own tax benefit to help the valued employee pay the tax.

The important principle here is that you, the employer, get a tax deduction equal to the amount the employee reports as income. If the employee pays $1.00 per share for stock worth $4.00, the employee has income of $3.00 *and* you have a deduction for $3.00. Chapter 15 tells how to use your tax deduction to hold the employee harmless of any income tax on issuance of the stock.

Offer Key Employees Stock Options

Another way to compensate, to reward, a key executive for achievement is the stock option. For example, instead of issuing stock to Bob Lewis now for $1.00 per share, you could give him a written option to buy 50,000 shares for that price at some time in the future. In comparison with the vesting schedule on Table 14.2 above, let us say the stock option is exercisable as follows:

Option Exercisable	No. of Shares
Now	0
2 years	10,000
4 years	10,000
6 years	10,000
8 years	10,000
10 years	10,000

After the tenth year, the employee can exercise the option for any of the 50,000 shares not already purchased.

Instead of paying $1.00 per share, $50,000, Bob lays out nothing now, but waits to see what the stock will do in the future. If the stock becomes more valuable, say $8 per share in year six, Bob pays $30,000 for 30,000 shares. He has purchased $240,000 worth of stock for $30,000 with a profit of $210,000.

He has to pay a tax on his gain which is $210,000, even if he has not resold the stock. Any time an employee, as part of a compensatory plan, receives property from the employer at less than fair value, the employee realizes income. Assuming the option agreement permits, the employee can pick and choose the best time to exercise the option. If the stock does not appreciate in value, the employee pays out no money and runs no risk of tax.

But when the option is exercised, there may be a big tax, and the lack of a market for the closely held stock may make it difficult for Bob to come up with the cash (by selling some shares) to pay the tax. Here is where the tax rules can help. If Bob realizes $210,000 of income (in our example), you (the employer) have a tax deduction of $210,000, saving $84,000 in its taxes. (Chapter 15 shows how you can use your company's tax deduction to help the employee pay his or her taxes.)

Why not always use the stock option?

For one thing, the tax situation is more controllable with restricted stock where the employee elects to pay the tax up front. The restricted stock can be appraised in advance so the value is a known quantity when it is issued and the employee recognizes income. You then know what your company's current income picture will be, so its ability to generate cash from a tax deduction is reasonably certain. The tax risk in any event is apt to be lower because the parties anticipate that the stock will rise in value.

Incentive Stock Option

We have been speaking in terms of what is called an "unqualified stock option" or "nonstatutory stock option." This is the type of option used in the context of the closely held or family company, because, absent a public market for the stock, there is no way to ascertain the precise value of the stock.

Public companies can use the Incentive Stock Option (ISO) which enables the employee to escape realizing income when the option is exercised. The ISO rules are set out by the IRS and as a practical matter they are of little use to a nonpublic company because they depend on accurate valuation when the ISO is issued.

The concept of value appears again and again in this book—value for gifts, value for estate taxes, value for freezes, value for qualifying for deferred estate tax payments, and value for division of assets among heirs.

In the employee compensation area, the value of the stock issued to key employees is again crucial. It governs the employees' compensation income and it governs the employer's tax deduction. Errors in reporting value can cost extra tax, interest, and even penalties.

We are dealing in an area where a definite tax is imposed on a nebulous concept, value. Go carefully and use independent appraisers wherever possible.

Offer Key Employees Phantom Stock

This discussion of restricted stock and stock options is a highly simplified presentation of a complex subject. The complexity results, not from the concepts as described, but from the great variability of results which depend on the value at the time income is realized by the employee.

With restricted stock, the employee can select the time to realize income, but how does he or she know what the stock value will be at time of sale, retirement, or death? Money is invested at one point and may or may not be recouped at a later point. Likewise, with an option the employee can also make a choice, exercise the option or don't, at any given time during the option period. But, the future value remains an unknown.

There is an alternative compensation method, one which dispenses with most of the complexity and risk. This is the use of so called phantom stock or shadow stock. To explain this, let us examine the essence of what we are doing with restricted stock and option stock. We are:

- issuing stock in our company to a key employee,
- with income tax consequences to the employee when the stock is acquired or vests, whichever is later,
- with a deduction by you, the business owner, at the time and in the amount that the employee realizes income,
- under conditions where value can only be estimated, with attendant appraisal costs and risks of tax penalties, and
- incurring the ultimate financial risk of eventually having to buy out the employee with nondeductible cash dollars.

The phantom stock concept alleviates these problems. Phantom stock is another word for a deferred compensation plan in which the compensatory amount is measured by hypothetical shares of the company set up in the employer's books of account.

Suppose that in 1993 we are going to set up an account of 50,000 "shares" of stock for Bob Lewis, the key employee of our prior illustrations. At that point the market value determined by appraisal is $4 per share. The stock vests 20 percent every two years. Ten years from now, in 2003, there are 50,000 vested shares in Bob's account and he is ready to retire. The company has the stock appraised and it comes out to $8.00 per share for the

Table 14.5. Robert Lewis, Phantom Stock Account

Year	No. of Shares	% Vested	No. Vested	Per Share Value	Total Value
2003	50,000	100%	50,000	$8.00	$400,000
1993	50,000	0	0	$4.00	$200,000
Increment in value over base value					$200,000

company. These are not actual shares, but fictional shares in Bob's account; hence the term phantom stock. Table 14.5 shows what Bob's account looks like after the ten years.

The increase, if any, in the vested shares overall value from 1993 to 2003 is the amount of deferred compensation due to Bob. Normally, this $200,000 would be paid over 5, 10, or 15 years with interest on the unpaid balance, starting at retirement.

Financial Matters; ERISA

These three kinds of compensatory plans may have an impact on your company's audited balance sheet and P&L statements. As of the time of this writing, an accrual on the books (not a tax accrual) is required to take into account the future cost of the option and phantom stock plans; no accrual is now required in the case of restricted stock (but this may change). In any event, you should check with your CPA to determine the effect, if any, on your company's financial statements.

Another thing to be considered is that some states make shareholders personally liable for unpaid compensation to employees. Could the payments due under such plans come within the definition of unpaid compensation in your state? Check with your company counsel.

This discussion has been about stock plans for key management employees, relatively highly paid. If a broad group of employees is to be included, your company will have to check into the ERISA rules (U.S. Dept. of Labor) enacted to protect interests of employees. Expert counsel in this area is desirable.

Summary

These stock-based plans can be a very good incentive device for key personnel. They do not require IRS approval, but may require shareholder approval in some states. Chapter 15 describes how an employer's tax deduction can help your employees finance their personal taxes on acquisition of stock.

Figure 14.1. Comparison of Stock Incentive Devices
(See Table 14.2)

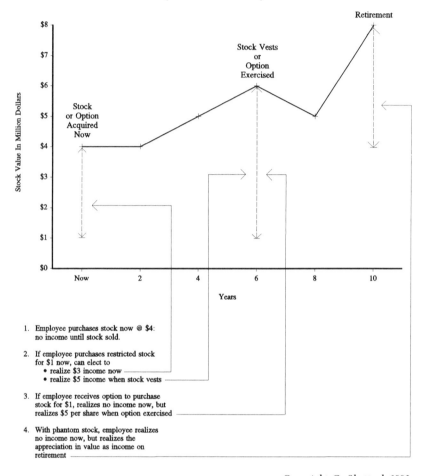

Figure 14.1 summarizes the tax effect on the employee of these four approaches to using stock incentives to retain key employees:

1. Employee purchases stock at current market value and realizes no income or loss. Transfer is restricted by agreement, but employee is now 100 percent vested.

2. Employee purchases "restricted stock" at a discount and can elect to realize income when the restriction expires, or now, on acquisition of the stock.

3. Employee receives an option to purchase the stock sometime in the future, at a price below its current value.

4. Employee receives an interest in phantom stock. At retirement he or she receives an amount equal to the increase in value, if any, from now.

Each of these devices has merit, a place of its own in the right circumstances. Chapter 15 shows how you can help your key employees acquire the stock on a tax-advantaged basis.

15

How Key Employees Can Acquire Stock Painlessly —Use the Bonus-Out

In Chapter 14, we pointed out how you, the business owner, get a tax deduction equal to the amount that your employee realizes as taxable income on receipt of stock. This chapter explains how you can use your tax deduction to help your employee pay his or her taxes and so acquire stock in a most advantageous way. A word of caution: the amount paid to an employee must always be "reasonable" in amount in order to be deductible for tax purposes. Transfers of stock to a family member are subject to extra scrutiny on this point.

This chapter discusses the cash-flow impact of alternate forms of (a) investment in employer stock by employees, and (b) reacquisition of such stock by the employer at retirement or death of employee. The premise is that you want some of your employees to own stock as an incentive, as a means of keeping the valuable ones as long as possible. The raising of capital for your company is very important, but this can be done by reinvesting earnings and by bank financing. You don't look to your key employees for capital, so you should think in terms of issuing stock to key employees at a discount or for no consideration.

To keep things simple, our illustrations assume that the applicable individual income-tax rate is 28 percent and the corporate rate is 34% percent. Further, there is no difference in tax on ordinary income and capital gain. These are just assumptions. One thing is certain: these rates will change. However, the use of a constant tax rate gives us a valid base to compare the alternatives available.

167

Using The Bonus-Out Concept to Reduce Taxes on Stock Issues

Where unrestricted stock is issued to an employee for less than full value, the differential is taxable to the employee as compensation. You, the employer, get a deduction for this compensation even if it represented a transfer of stock, not cash. But you may not want your key employees to have to shell out money for taxes. To alleviate their potential cash flow problem, the tax benefit your company derives from its deduction can be passed through to the employee as a bonus. Then the employee has the cash to pay the tax on the value of the stock received.

But the cash bonus is taxed too. The answer is that your company also gets a deduction for the bonus, which you then use to reimburse the employee for the tax on the bonus. And so on. And so on. And so on.

If you carry out the reimbursement process long enough, the employee gets the stock free and clear, with all tax costs completely reimbursed. You have realized your objective of getting company stock in the hands of a key employee and you have incurred no cash cost. This is all subject to the employee's overall compensation being reasonable in amount; with unrelated employees this is usually not a problem.

The following tables illustrate this process and assume that your company is a corporation taxed at 34 percent and the employee at 31 percent. Using a tax rate differential illustrates how the mechanics of the bonus out work, but we must keep in mind that

- the 34 percent and the 31 percent are assumed rates and in actuality the parties could be taxed at different effective rates,
- Congress can change the rate structure any time in the future, and
- if your company is an S Corporation, your shareholders' personal rates would be used instead of the 34 percent corporate rate.

Take a simple situation where your corporation transfers $100,000 worth of stock to Bob Lewis, an employee, as a reasonable bonus for work performed and as an incentive to stay with your company. Table 15.1 illustrates.

Thus, your employee has acquired $100,000 worth of stock for zero cash outlay. Your company, being in a higher bracket in our illustration, actually gets a small net cash benefit. The following tables condense much of the math shown above for illustration. Another assumption is that the employee realizes income when the stock is issued to him or her (i.e., the stock is not subject to forfeiture).

Figure 15.1 shows what happens in a condensed form:

- Step One: you give stock to your employee as a bonus and enjoy a tax benefit of $34,000. The employee has a detriment of $28,000 due to tax on the value of the stock.

Table 15.1. Illustration of Bonus-Out Concept

Step	Impact on Company	Impact on Bob Lewis
Issue stock to employee	($100,000)	$100,000
Tax benefit to company and employee	34,000	(28,000)
Reimburse employee for his Tax	(28,000)	28,000
Tax benefit to company and employee	9,520	(7,840)
Reimburse employee for his Tax	(7,840)	7,840
Tax Benefit to company and employee	2,666	(2,195)
Reimburse employee for his Tax	(2,195)	2,195
Tax benefit to company and employee	746	(614)
Reimburse employee for his Tax	(614)	614
Tax Benefit to Company of employee Tax	209	(172)
Etc, etc, etc . . .	—	—
Net all the *cash* impacts, including "etc."	$ 8,330	$ 0

- Step Two: you give your $34,000 tax benefit to your employee as an additional bonus so the employee can pay the income tax. Because of the deduction, your company has an additional benefit and the employee has a tax.

- Step Three: finally, the employee receives another $4,870 as a bonus so he or she is completely reimbursed for the taxes incurred.

The upshot of all this is that the employee has the stock free and clear, and in terms of cash, your company is a little ahead.

Six Ways to Transfer Stock to Employees

Having demonstrated the bonus out principle, we will describe 6 alternatives to getting $100,000 worth of company stock in the hands of your key employees at the least possible cash cost after taxes to both parties.

Sale of Stock to Employees

The first scenario is a simple sale of $100,000 worth of stock to the employees, to be paid for by the employees after tax out of $138,890 of salary or bonuses (the $138,890 is the before tax amount needed to arrive at the $100,000 purchase price) received from your company. The results are shown in Table 15.2. Here, you can see that given the current federal rate structure, your company comes out a little on the plus side as you furnish the money to purchase your own company's stock.

Figure 15.1. Tax Impact of Bonus-Out Arrangement, if Employer Gives Employee $100,000 of Stock as a Bonus

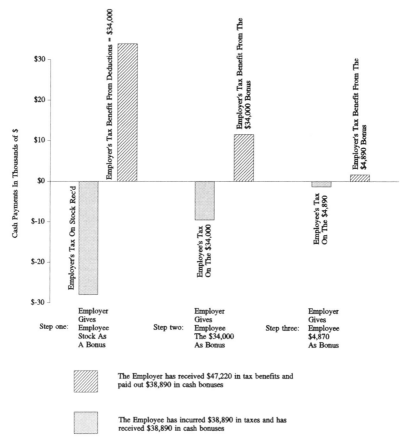

The Employer has received $47,220 in tax benefits and paid out $38,890 in cash bonuses

The Employee has incurred $38,890 in taxes and has received $38,890 in cash bonuses

Copyright G. Shattuck 1992

Table 15.2. Cash-Flow Cost: Sale of Stock for $100,000 by Corporation to Key Employees

	Corporation	Employees
Pay employees	($138,890)	$ 138,890
Tax benefit/(tax)	47,220	(38,890)
Payment for stock	100,000	(100,000)
Net cash flow	$ 8,330	$ 0

Give Stock to Employees as a Bonus

Strange as it may seem, you can just *give* the same value in stock to the employee and the cash cost comes out the same. Table 15.3 illustrates. As shown in Table 15.3, your company can use most of its cash tax benefit from the deduction to reimburse the key employees for taxes. (See Figure 15.1.) This "bonus out" procedure can be very handy where you wish to benefit key employees. Such transactions also have equity dilution as a cost, but this is not considered here because you would not transfer stock to an employee in any case unless you thought it worthwhile as a business transaction.

Table 15.3. Cash-Flow Cost: Issuance of $100,000 Stock to Key Employees as Bonus

	Corporation	Employees
Issue stock	($100,000)	$100,000
Tax benefit/(tax)	34,000	(28,000)
Pay tax benefit to Employees as bonus	(34,000)	34,000
Tax benefit/(tax)	11,560	(9,520)
Pay *part* of tax benefit to employees as bonus	(4,890)	4,890
Tax benefit/(tax)	1,660	(1,370)
Net cash flow now	$ 8,330	$ 0

Pay Employees Cash to Purchase Stock from Another Shareholder

By way of contrast, what if you arrange a purchase of $100,000 worth of stock by a key employee from another shareholder? Table 15.2 illustrated a sale *by the company* to the employee. Assume the cash sale price does not go to the company, but to an outsider. You have to pay the employee $138,890 so he or she can net $100,000 after 31 percent taxes. Here, your company is behind because you still have to supply the cash for the purchase price to the employee; yet, you did not get the cash back, as in the prior cases. This is illustrated in Table 15.4.

Use Qualified Plans

As a means of getting stock ownership out to employees, the ESOP, or Stock Bonus Plan is very effective at the outset. Either permits a transfer of stock from the company to the plan on a deductible basis and the employees

**Table 15.4. Cash-Flow Cost: Other Shareholder
Sells Stock for $100,000 to Key Employees**

	Corporation	Employees	Others
Pay employees	($138,890)	$ 138,890	—
Tax benefit/(tax)	47,220	(38,890)	—
Payment for stock	—	(100,000)	100,000
Net cash flow now	($91,670)	$ 0	100,000

do not have to pay a tax when the stock is transferred. Employees do, however, pay a tax when they receive their vested benefits in cash at retirement or termination, or when they sell the stock. An alternative is payment of cash (deductible) to the plan, which then uses the cash to purchase stock from a third party for the benefit of the employees. The drawbacks of such plans include the need for IRS approval and for coverage of a fairly large group of employees. In most cases, you want to use stock to give to *key* employees, not the broad coverage required in a qualified plan. Another drawback is that an ESOP or Stock Bonus Trust can cause loss of Subchapter S status because such a trust does not qualify as a shareholder. (See Chapter 16 for details on ESOPs.)

The current cash-flow effect of issuing actual shares in an ESOP or Stock Bonus Plan is illustrated in Table 15.5. Here, the larger positive cash flow results from a tax deduction for a noncash transfer of stock, plus the fact that the employees have no current tax under a qualified plan, and no need to reimburse them.

**Table 15.5. Cash-Flow Cost: Issue $100,000
of Stock to Stock Bonus Plan or ESOP**

	Corporation	Plan
Issue stock	"($100,000)"	"$100,000"
Tax benefit/(tax)	34,000	0
Net cash flow now	$ 34,000	$ 0

Offer Phantom Stock

A further alternative, not involving issuance of stock at all, is the so-called Phantom Stock Plan. Under this arrangement, you set up an account for each key employee and credit a certain number of shares of stock to the account. As the shares grow in value, the account grows in value by the same proportion. If dividends are paid on the real stock, a like amount per share is credited to the phantom shares in the account. In most cases, the "dividends" are reinvested in additional shares of phantom stock, so there's a compounding effect. Of course, you can assign a number of phantom shares to the account this year as incentive, a further number next year, and so on. In short, it's a very effective incentive device for key employees that does not involve the legal and other problems found in issuance of actual shares. At termination of employment, the value of all the "stock" accumulated in the account is established and the employee is paid the difference between the original value and the retirement date value over a period of years with interest. Table 15.6 illustrates how the phantom stock plan works.

The IRS is currently tinkering with regulations on when a company has "two classes of stock," that would disqualify it from Subchapter S status. From this standpoint the phantom stock plan has many advantages because no stock is actually issued; the stock is just a measuring device.

Table 15.6. Cash-Flow Cost: "Issue" $100,000 of Stock to a Phantom Stock Plan

	Corporation	Employees
Paper transaction:		
Issue stock	"($100,000)"	"$100,000"
Tax benefit/(tax)	0	0
Net cash flow now	$ 0	$ 0

Offer Non-Qualified Stock Options

Sometimes employers wish to give employees an option to purchase stock at a minimal price. Then the employees get the benefit of the original option spread plus future growth when they exercise the option. At the point of exercise, when an employee receives the stock, he or she realizes income on the spread. The impact of this is illustrated in Table 15.7 (page 174), assuming the spread is $100,000:

Summary of the Six Stock-Transfer Scenarios

In all the six cases above we have employed a "zero" cost to the employee for acquisition of stock and assumed that the money had to come from the company in one way or another. This holding to zero gives a basis for comparison of the dollar efficiency of the various alternatives from the company's standpoint. Viewed this way, a summary of the effect on net cash flow—leaving out equity dilution and other factors—is shown in Table 15.8 on the next page.

**Table 15.7. Cash-Flow Cost: Issue Employees
Options to Purchase $100,000 of Stock for $1.00**

	Corporation	Employees
Exercise of option	"($100,000)"	"$100,000"
Tax benefit/(tax)	34,000	(28,000)
Pay tax benefit to employees	(34,000)	34,000
Tax benefit/(tax)	11,560	(9,520)
Pay *part* of tax benefit to employees	(4,890)	4,890
Tax benefit/(Tax)	1,660	(1,370)
Net cash flow now	$ 8,330	$ 0

Table 15.8. Summary of Net Cash Outlays

Current cash-flow benefit/(cost)	Corporation	Employees
Sale of stock by corporation	$ 8,330	0
Give stock as bonus	$ 8,330	0
Other shareholder sells stock	$(91,670)	0
Issue stock to ESOP or stock bonus plan	$ 34,000	0
Issue "phantom" stock	$ 0	0
Use stock option	$ 8,330	0

Remember, this is a measure of *current* cash costs. The ESOP seems to be the most attractive on this basis, but there are other factors that may rule out this approach. The ESOP and Stock Bonus Plans are IRS qualified and thus present many costs and problems. Such plans require thorough economic analysis which should consider the owner's equity dilution as one of the costs of the plan. (See Chapter 16 for details on ESOPs.)

The sale to the employee by another shareholder, presumably also an employee, looks very negative at first blush, but the company will not have the burden of redeeming the selling shareholder's stock unless it agrees to do so. This is discussed in the next section.

Getting the Stock Back

When offering stock incentives to key employees, you must also consider how you will reacquire the stock when the employee dies, retires, or is terminated. Tables 15.9 through 15.12 show various scenarios for how a company can reacquire the stock and still give such employee an economic benefit measured by the performance of the stock over years.

Table 15.9. Cash-Flow Cost: Redemption by Corporation for $300,000 After 20 Years*

	Corporation	Employees
Cash payment for stock	($300,000)	$300,000
Tax benefit/(tax)	0	(56,000)
Net cash flow now	($300,000)	$244,000

*Indicates annual growth rate of 5.65%

Table 15.10. Cash-Flow Cost: Profit Sharing Plan or ESOP Purchases Stock from Employee for $300,000

	Corporation	Employees
Cash contribution to plan	($300,000)	
Cash received for stock from plan		$300,000
Tax benefit/(tax)	102,000	(84,000)
Net cash flow [20 years]	($198,000)	$216,000

Table 15.11. Cash-Flow Cost: Other Employees Purchase Stock for $300,000

	Corporation	Other Employees	Others
Pay other employees	($416,670)	$416,670	—
Tax benefit/(tax)	141,670	116,670	($ 56,000)*
Payment for stock	—	(300,000)	300,000
Net cash flow now	($275,000)	$ 0	$244,000

*This assumes that the employee paid a tax of $28,000 when originally receiving the stock worth $100,000.

In these tables, assume that over the years the stock originally acquired at $100,000 has increased in value and is now worth $300,000. Here is where the key employee is rewarded for good efforts. The employer now has a cash cost to require its stock and give the employee the promised benefit.

If the employee is to be put on a comparable basis to the other illustrations, he would have to net $244,000 after tax. This means that the em-

Table 15.12. Cash-Flow Cost: Corporation Pays $300,000 Under Phantom Stock Plan, at Retirement in 20 Years

	Corporation	Employees
Pay employees cash	($300,000)	$300,000
Tax benefit/(tax)	102,000	(84,000)
Net cash flow [20 years]	($198,000)	$216,000

ployer would have to pay $339,000 before tax, resulting in a net of $224,000 after tax as shown in Table 15.13.

Table 15.13. Cash-Flow Cost: Unrelated Party Purchases Stock for $300,000 in 20 Years

	Corporation	Employees
Employees receive price	—	$300,000
Tax benefit/(tax)	—	(56,000)
Net cash flow, 20 years	—	$244,000

To rank the alternate buy-back forms in terms of after-tax efficiency in reacquiring the stock to get $300,000 cash for the stock into the hands of the employee, see Table 15.14. From a purely economic standpoint, phantom stock is probably the best. It's foolproof and it's simple. However, that is not the whole picture. There is nothing like ownership, the feel of a nice green embossed stock certificate in your hands. In terms of real incentive for a valued person, we believe that the restricted stock best meets this "feel" test.

Table 15.14

Cash Flow Benefit/(Cost) in 20 Years	Corporation	Employees
Corporation redeems stock	($300,000)	$244,000
ESOP purchases stock	($198,000)	$216,000
Other employees purchase stock	($275,000)	$244,000
Payment under phantom stock plan	($224,000)	$216,000
Unrelated party purchase of stock	0	$244,000

So it is eminently possible to get a sizable block of stock in the key employee's hands to provide incentive and keep him or her on board with "golden handcuffs," as it were. This applies to any of a group of key people you select, not just executives, but scientists, programmers, sales personnel or a key secretary . . . the real movers are found right down the line and into the production groups or lines.

Where restricted stock and options are involved, there are very important decisions regarding the timing of the tax impact. If you get into this type of plan, you will have to advise your employees of their tax issues. The recipient of restricted stock can elect to pay tax on the value when the stock is issued, or at a later time when the restrictions lapse. The recipient of an option can control the tax impact by timing the date of exercise.

For a really broad-coverage stock-incentive plan, consider a stock bonus plan. This is a tax-qualified plan that invests almost wholly in stock of the employer. This lets all the employees share in the fortunes of the company. Initially, you contribute stock to the stock bonus plan for the benefit of the employees and deduct the current value of the stock for tax purposes. Eventually, though, you will have to contribute cash to the plan to enable it to buy out the employees at death. It's a nice incentive fringe benefit in the right circumstances.

The chief drawback of the stock bonus plan is that it must be "qualified" for federal tax purposes, and it generally must encompass significant percentage of the employees irrespective of their contribution to success. Some employers want all employees to share; some want to be more selective. You have a choice. Or you can do both, have a qualified stock bonus plan for all and an nonqualified incentive plan for a few key people.

Summary

Stock ownership by key employees, in one form or another, can be a great incentive. The tax rules, including the fact that the company can deduct the value of the stock and all tax reimbursements, make it very painless to get stock to employees. We prefer the "restricted stock" route as described above, but there are several other effective ways to get stock to the employees. In a Subchapter S corporation, restrictions on transfer must be very carefully handled in order to avoid loss of Subchapter S status.

In our context, employee stock ownership is not just an incentive; it is a very important factor in succession planning. It should be considered in that light.

16

The ESOP and
the Stock Bonus Plan

This chapter brings us into the realm of the tax-qualified plan. Chapters 14 and 15 deal with ways to give stock-based incentives to a chosen group of key employees. These plans, for giving restricted stock, stock options, or phantom stock, fill one need.

The tax-qualified plan to be discussed now fills another, different need. Here, the goal is not to benefit a select group of high-performing executives and managers. Rather, the assumed goal is to provide broad-based employee ownership and incentive. The discussion here will be in the context of a closely held business where ownership is usually limited to one family, perhaps two.

Why a Qualified Stock Plan?

Restricted stock and stock options can result in the employee realizing taxable income at untimely points. With restricted stock, income is realized either (i) when the stock is received and the special election is made, or (ii) when the restriction expires. With options, income is realized when the employee exercises the option. The bonus-out concept can alleviate the tax consequences raised by providing these incentives in certain cases, but the basic need to pay tax on acquisition of the stock creates complexity and possibly hardship.

The income tax problems for the employee can be solved by use of a tax-qualified employee trust. With such a trust the employee does not receive complete ownership of the stock initially, but rather the employee receives an interest in the employee trust. If the trust is determined by the IRS to be qualified, the employee realizes income only at retirement or death, when

179

he or she or the estate actually receive a cash distribution of his or her interest in the trust or sells the stock. This deferral of taxable income until retirement is of great benefit to the employee.

The company, the employer, also gets an upfront benefit. It can deduct currently the cash, or the value of stock, contributed to the qualified trust. Thus, the employer can get the incentive benefits of employee stock ownership *and* a deduction for the contribution and need not pay out the cash benefit up front because the employee does not have any tax at that point. In the bonus-out concept, discussed in Chapter 15, the employer does get a tax benefit via the deduction for the value of stock vested in the employee but must turn around and share the tax benefit with the employee in order to solve the employee's up-front tax problem.

In a qualified plan the employer gets an up-front deduction and the employee gets a deferred tax. This tax timing makes a big difference. It seems that everyone comes out ahead. But the benefits come at a cost, whose elements are:

- the qualified plan generally must cover a broad, representative group of employees. If you want to select a few persons who can really contribute to profit, or research, or quality, or whatever, the qualified plan does not fit this picture.

- If the qualified plan with its broad employee coverage does fit your needs, there is the further element of compliance with a skein of complex, technical rules and rules for reporting and disclosure to employees. This is the price paid for IRS approval of a qualified plan.

- The qualified plan must be designed and drafted by an expert, often an expensive process. Compliance with applicable administrative, reporting and disclosure rules, promulgated by the U.S. Labor Department, also can be expensive. Changes, amendments to suit your ongoing needs, also may be expensive because they often will require further IRS approval. The nonqualified plans described in Chapters 14 and 15 can be changed without great formality, but of course an agreement with an employee may not be changed unilaterally.

- Finally, as pointed out before, a qualified stock bonus plan or ESOP requires a trust. The existence of such a trust prevents an election to be taxed under Subchapter S.

Pointing out these disadvantages of a qualified plan does not mean that such plans are never suitable for the closely held company. On the contrary, a qualified plan can be the best answer to a company's needs. The bottom line is that all the pros and cons must be examined thoroughly.

The fact that an S Corporation cannot have a qualified stock plan is regrettable. We believe that ability to avoid the "double tax" at the corporate level is of extreme value to the closely held business. This is achieved by election to be taxed under Subchapter S of the Internal Revenue Code. Unfortunately, under current law, only natural persons and certain trusts can be shareholders in a corporation seeking Subchapter S treatment. A trust that holds the stock of such a corporation in connection with the corporation's tax-qualified plan is treated as a shareholder and, thus, precludes Subchapter S treatment. In addition to the trust problem, another qualification for Subchapter S is that there be no more than 35 shareholders. This also limits broad employee ownership. The following discussion, then, must be considered in the context of a corporation that is not taxed under Subchapter S and never intends to be so. The two basic types of stock plan are:

- the profit sharing stock bonus plan, and
- the ESOP

which are explained in the following sections.

The Profit Sharing Plan

Imagine that your corporation has a qualified profit-sharing plan. It covers most of your full time employees whose interests in the plan vest after a given number of years of service. The corporation contributes to the plan each year in cash a share of its profits and each employee has an account in the plan which receives a share of the contribution based on pro rated compensation or some other formula approved by the IRS.

The corporation contributes cash to a trust established in connection with the plan to hold and manage the plan's invested funds. The employer gets a deduction for the contribution in the year the contribution is accrued, subject to certain limits. The trust is IRS-approved so that contributions made to the trust are not taxed nor are the trust's investment income and gains earned on those contributions. Thus, the opportunity for tax-free compounding. The employees, who are the beneficiaries of the trust, do not realize taxable income when contributions for them are made to the trust by the corporation. At retirement or termination, the employees receive their vested interests in cash.

The employer benefits by letting the employees know that profits are important and that the employees are responsible for profits and share in them. The employees benefit by having a tax-free retirement account which invests and accumulates income for them. At retirement, the employee receives payment of his or her account in a lump sum or over a period of years; the payments are taxable income when received.

This, in essence, is the classic profit-sharing plan. It is a very valuable employee benefit for the right situation. The IRS rules are designed to keep it fair for the rank and file employees and to protect their interests. The employer has an incentive plan, which helps employees at retirement but does not bear the risks of a defined (or fixed) benefit pension plan. The employees will tend to think of this more as a retirement benefit than actually having a current piece of the corporate profits.

The Stock Bonus Plan

We emphasize that the context here is that of a family company or a closely held company where the individuals who can generally contribute to overall success, are not outnumbered by people who do their job but can't or don't affect end results. We are talking about a company where the Indians don't hopelessly outnumber the Chiefs.

Take this a step further. You, as the employer, want to ratchet up the incentive element, to make it clear to the covered employees that the future of the company impacts their future.

Provide more incentive element? Give employees a real stake in the business? How do we do that? One way is to use the garden variety profit sharing plan, described above, and let it invest in your company's stock instead of General Motors and AT&T. Is that legal? Yes, it is legal and a recognized, IRS-blessed, type of employee benefit plan. Here are the basic elements:

- Like the profit sharing plan, you need a trust set up for the benefit of the employees.
- The employer contributes cash or its stock to the trust and gets a current deduction. For the stock the deduction is measured by the then fair market value of the stock. If the employer is in a 40 percent bracket, a contribution of $100 worth of stock yields a $40 reduction in taxes, a current cash benefit.
- The employees do not recognize taxable income when cash or stock is contributed to the trust.
- The employee is paid at retirement in company stock, or cash, or other listed securities. At that point the employee realizes taxable income if paid in cash. Corporate stock or other securities are received tax free until they are sold.
- If the employee receives company stock at retirement, he or she has a "put" option to sell the corporate stock back to the corporation, or to the trust. If the employee sells to the trust, the employer can contribute deductible cash to the trust to enable it to repurchase from the employee.

In addition, if cash is contributed to the trust by the employer corporation, the trust can use the cash to purchase company stock from you and its other shareholders. The owners can sell stock on a capital gain basis paid for with money that the company can deduct. "Wait! Is there a catch here, somewhere? I get a capital gain selling my stock and the company deducts the payment." No, there really is not. But the sale transaction must be totally fair and at a price determined by an independent appraisal. *A corporation can contribute deductible cash to a profit sharing trust, which then uses the cash to buy part of your stock.*

If you have an estate liquidity problem, the stock sold during a lifetime or by your estate is replaced by the cash which can be used to pay taxes. If the stock is purchased by the trust from your estate, there will be no capital gain tax as the sale and the (deductible) cash is available to pay estate taxes.

"Why isn't this used more often?" the answer is that stock bonus plans are complex and costly to set up and require inclusion of a broad spectrum of employees. Most family companies are unwilling to take in rank and file employees as co-owners, even if the family members and trusted key employees can be the trustees of the trust. The stock bonus plan is great where it fits, but unattractive in many situations.

The ESOP

ESOP is short for Employee Stock Ownership Plan. This is a special kind of stock bonus plan. The ESOP has the following characteristics:

- The employer can contribute cash or stock on a deductible basis.
- The employees realize no income when the employer contributes and the trusts future earnings are tax deferred.
- The employee is paid at retirement in company stock, or cash, or other listed securities. At that point the employee realizes taxable income if paid in cash. A shareholder who sells his or her shares to an ESOP may defer tax further, if the shareholder can qualify for treatment under a special "rollover" rule. Corporate stock or other securities, even if unrelated listed companies, are received tax free until they are sold or invested in something else.
- The employee has a "put" option to sell the corporate stock back to the corporation, or to the trust. If the employee sells to the trust, the employer can contribute deductible cash to the trust to enable it to repurchase from the employee.
- If the trust wants to purchase a big block of stock, say from a shareholder or estate of a deceased shareholder, it can "leverage" the transaction by borrowing from a lender or from the employer. The employer makes tax deductible contributions to the trust to enable it to pay the debt service on the loan.

- In some cases the bank lending to the trust can exclude from income part of the interest on its loan to the trust.

This option presents a very attractive picture. But the same things that dissuade people from the stock bonus plan are at work here. The complexity, the cost, and the mystery discourage people. In the leveraged plan, where the trust borrows to buy out a shareholder, there is the added element of risk; risk that future adverse business conditions make it difficult to pay off the loan. Tax deductible contributions by the employer aren't much benefit if it is not making any money. The next two sections describe things that must be considered when evaluating the stock bonus plan or the ESOP.

Equity Dilution

The stock bonus plan and the ESOP lend themselves beautifully to analysis and printouts showing the almost magical benefits of being able to

- contribute stock to an employee trust on a tax deductible basis, thus generating cash after tax benefits, and
- sell your own stock to such a trust and having your corporation pay for it in deductible dollars.

These are not magic, they are very real benefits. But the other side of the coin must be examined with equal thoroughness: *as employees benefit from the plan, the original owners' equity is diluted.* You truly give away ownership to the extent your company contributes stock for the benefit of the employees. This is equally true of the restricted stock and stock option plans described in Chapter 15, but the scale is usually smaller.

The key here is, *when looking at the benefits of an ESOP or a stock bonus plan, also look at the cost in terms of your stock equity reduction.* What it comes down to is that all such stock-based plans have to be worth while in terms of employee incentive, of compensation. If they are, well and good. Go forward with the plan.

Assessing the Value of Your Company's Stock

The term "value" keeps sprouting up all over the pages of this book. At risk of boring the reader, let us repeat the reason. The estate tax and the gift tax are assessed, calculated, on the value of property. If the property is an interest in a closely held business, it is very difficult to be sure your value judgment accords with that of the IRS.

Now we have a new dimension. We are talking, in this part, about an employer taking *an income tax deduction* based on the value of stock transferred to employees (Chapter 15) or transferred to an employee trust (Chapter 16). The same concern is present, but the tables are turned. *When you contribute stock to an employee trust you want a high value to maximize the tax deduction. When you make gifts of other stocks to your children, you may want the same stock valued low.* Voila! The need for an independent, and sometimes costly, appraisal.

Now let us make things a bit more difficult. This whole Part, dealing with employee stock ownership, presumes that one day the company will be buying the stock back from the employees. Added to the need to be honest and fair with the IRS is the new duty of being honest and fair with employees and former employees who may need the cash proceeds of the sale for their retirement.

If you, or your estate, plan to sell stock to an employee trust as discussed above, the trustees (who may be family members or close associates) must ascertain and perhaps negotiate a value in the employees' behalf. If they pay too much they could be held liable to the trust; if the corporation funds the purchase the trustees could be held liable to the company creditors if they pay you too much. In such a case the use of 20/20 hindsight comes into play.

The IRS rules recognize these difficult problems and set up appraisal standards, but, as usual, there is complexity and areas where the rules are nebulous and confusing.

Summary

In Chapter 15, we show how stock ownership and phantom stock can be used to benefit a few key employees. Chapter 16 explains the additional tax and economic benefits of the stock bonus plan and the ESOP.

These benefits make the stock bonus and ESOP plans worth working at, but add serious complexities and costs. Even after the initial start up costs, the future cost of continued compliance with ever-changing IRS and Labor Department rules can seriously impact the benefits.

17

Comparing Stock-Based Incentive Plans

Chapters 15 and 16 describe the concepts behind these five devices: three types of nonqualified stock plans—restricted stock, stock options, and phantom stock—and two types of *qualified* incentive plans—stock bonus plans and ESOP plans. The concepts are few but the mix is complex. This chapter is devoted to a step-by-step comparison of the five alternatives.

The distinction between the Nonqualified and the Qualified arrangements is crucial. The Qualified plan confers certain very real tax benefits to employers and employees but at a cost: Part of the cost is that the plan must cover a broad spectrum of employees, those who contributed markedly to success and those who do not, and Labor Department requirements can be burdensome. The Nonqualified plan has no particular tax benefits for the employer (assuming the bonus-out concept is applied), but it can be selective.

Either concept can be very useful, but the distinction is very important as you explore company stock as a compensation and incentive device. Your choice must be informed and geared to your company's singular needs. The following sections compare the five devices listed above with respect to questions one could reasonably ask.

When Do Our Key Employees Actually Get the Stock Issued to Them?

- *Restricted Stock:* employees get stock at outset, but subject to risk of forfeiture.
- *Option Stock:* employees get stock on exercise of option, but subject to a risk of forfeiture if plan is so designed.
- *Phantom Stock:* no actual stock is issued, but employees' benefit is measured by increase in stock value.

187

- *Stock Bonus Plan:* initially stock is contributed to or purchased by employee trust but is distributed to employees or purchased from them at retirement.
- *ESOP:* same as stock bonus plan.

Can We Use Nonvoting Stock?

- *Restricted Stock:* Yes
- *Option Stock:* Yes
- *Phantom Stock:* N/A
- *Stock Bonus Plan:* Yes
- *ESOP:* No. Employee trust must get voting stock.

When Does the Employer Get a Tax Deduction?

- *Restricted Stock:* Employer gets a deduction when the employee realizes taxable income, i.e., when stock issued and election made, or when risk of forfeiture expires.
- *Option Stock:* Employer gets a deduction when option is exercised, stock is issued and employee realizes income.
- *Phantom Stock:* Employer gets a deduction when the cash benefit is paid out to employee.
- *Stock bonus Plan:* Deduction when stock or cash contributed to trust.
- *ESOP:* Same as Stock Bonus Plan.

How Is the Plan Treated on Our GAAP Audited Statement?

- *Restricted Stock:* If agreements require future repurchase after vesting, employer accrues charge as value of stock increases.
- *Stock Option:* Employer accrues charge as value of stock under option increases.
- *Phantom Stock:* Employer accrues charge as in (b) for the deferred compensation.
- *Stock Bonus Plan:* No accrual required. Expense charged when contribution to trust is made.
- *ESOP:* Same as Stock Bonus Plan.

When Does The Employee Realize Taxable Income?

- *Restricted Stock:* At employees election (i) when employee gets stock, or (ii) when risk of forfeiture expires.

- *Option Stock:* When employee get stock unless restricted as in restricted stock plan.
- *Phantom Stock:* When employee gets paid.
- *Stock Bonus Plan:* When employee gets cash from plan or cashes stock received.
- *ESOP:* Same as Stock Bonus Plan.

Must the Employer Repurchase the Stock?

- *Restricted Stock:* Depends on provisions of plan or agreement with employee.
- *Option Stock:* Same as Restricted Stock.
- *Phantom Stock:* N/A
- *Stock Bonus Plan:* Employer must purchase stock if there is no public market for it and employee timely "puts" stock to employer.
- *ESOP:* Same as Stock Bonus Plan.

What About Rigamarole And Complexity?

- *Restricted Stock:* Can be quite simple if only a few employees.
- *Option Stock:* Same.
- *Phantom Stock:* Simplest of all.
- *Stock Bonus Plan:* Complex. Beset by changing IRS and ERISA regulations.
- *ESOP:* Even worse than Stock Bonus Plan.

What About Personal Liability?

- *Restricted Stock:* Little risk.
- *Option Stock:* Little risk.
- *Phantom Stock:* Benefits are employee fringe benefits and some states make stockholders liable for payment.
- *Stock Bonus Plan:* Trustees and persons dealing with the plan undertake legal risks, especially in the area of valuing the stock purchased from owner shareholders.
- *ESOP:* Same as Stock Bonus Plan except that added complexity adds to the risk.

Does ERISA (Labor Dept.) Play a Part?

- Yes. Whenever you have a plan for employees, there are filing requirements.

Summary

For the average business owned by a family or by several stockholders, the restricted stock route seems best and phantom stock is a close second. Stock options rank about third. However, in some cases the stock bonus plan would make sense. Rarer still is the case where an ESOP makes sense for a family company—it ceases to be a family company.

Part Five

HOW TO ACHIEVE
A SMOOTH MANAGEMENT
TRANSITION

CHAPTER 18. Buy, Sell, and Redemption
            Agreements: Sale of Stock
            to Others
CHAPTER 19. Succession Planning for a Smooth
            Transition

Thus far, this book has used the terms "family company/family business" almost interchangeably with "closely held company/ closely held business." This is deliberate because most of the text is equally applicable to

–a business owned by one person or one family, and

–a business owned by several unrelated persons or families.

Indeed, most of what has been written up to this point could apply to a business with a dozen or more unrelated owners. As the number of owners increases, it is still possible to use the tax-saving and succession planning devices discussed above, but it becomes more difficult and complex as more interests are involved.

The fact of nonfamily co-owners, and often other considerations, render complex even the best succession plan. This is
not a book about probate and estate administration, but several
important elements of a smooth transition are covered in the
following chapters.

18

Buy, Sell, and Redemption Agreements: Sale of Stock to Others

Assume that we are dealing with multifamily ownership of a business. We speak here in terms of a corporation, but we could say virtually the same things about a partnership business. Here three families own the stock: the Abrams family 40 percent, the Bennet family 40 percent, and the Charles family 20 percent. The parents in each family are in their 50s and two of the families have a son or daughter in the business. The business has been very successful and the owners see good long-term growth prospects.

As they think about their retirement, estate planning, and their health, the owners are concerned about the usual things: estate taxes, voting control, good management, and security for the spouse and family. Continued viability of the business is required to provide retirement income to the owners. As we shall see later, the business may be the source of cash used to buy out a retiring (or deceased) owner's interest. What are their options?

- Have a stock restriction agreement among the owners that requires the shares to be kept within the three families. Start a program of gifts to children, using nonvoting stock, if desired.

- Use "freeze" techniques to leverage gifts and pass on future growth to children. Maintain a stock transfer restriction agreement.

- Provide for a buy out of a family interest at the death of the parent who is active in the business. If Mrs. Abrams is the spouse active in the business, all the Abrams stock could be bought out at her death, disability, or retirement. The buy out can be funded at least in part by insurance and may take two different forms:

–at Mrs. Abrams' death, her family's stock is purchased by the corporation (or partnership if the business is a partnership).

–at Mrs. Abrams' death, her family's stock is purchased by the other two families.

• Take key employees, including qualified children of the owners, into the business and arrange for a leveraged buy out now, or an agreement for them to buy each family's interest at death of the parent who is active in the business.

• Start now and plan for a sale of the whole company to outside parties. If this is the solution, don't wait until death of Mrs. Abrams or some other key person. Bargaining power is at its peak when none of the owners has any compulsion to sell in a hurry.

• Do something else. This is by no means an exhaustive list of possibilities. Other avenues are open. Combine some of the concepts described above.

• Do nothing? In the case described: good business, three unrelated middle-age, families thinking in terms of tax savings, retirement, estate planning, security. At the very least, they adopt a very simple first refusal agreement to prevent stock from going to outsiders.

These options are discussed in detail in the following sections.

Set Up a Restrictive Stock Agreement

The three families that own the business decide that they don't want to enter a buy-sell agreement or other options described above. They do want to start giving stock to their children to spread ownership and help control estate taxes. The answer here is to have a stock restrictive agreement, which inhibits transfer to persons outside the group. (See Exhibits 3.1 and 3.2 in Chapter 3.) For instance, the agreement provides that before any member of a group can transfer stock out of the group, the stock must be offered first to the members of the family group, then to the company, and then to the other groups of shareholders. This can be done with a minimum of fuss. (An absolute prohibition against any transfer may not stand up legally, nor should the parties agree to it.)

The parents should go one step further: recapitalize the company to issue 10 shares of new nonvoting stock for each share of voting stock. By retaining the voting stock and giving the nonvoting stock to their children, the parents keep control as long as they want, while being able to transfer partial ownership to their children.

Use the Estate Freeze to Limit Value in Owner's Estates

Suppose the Abrams', the Bennets and the Charles' want to freeze their current value so future growth can be given to the children. The freeze techniques described in Part Three can be used here. It may be mechanically more difficult because more people have to agree on what to do, but it can be done.

Suppose the Abrams' and the Charles' decide to freeze by selling part of their nonvoting stock to their children. (See Chapter 11.) The Bennets do not want to do this, they want to keep their stock for now. That should not present a problem except that the Bennets will have to concur in a dividend payout which enables the Abrams' and the Charles' children to pay their parents for the stock.

Establish a Stock Redemption Agreement

The Abrams', the Bennets, and the Charles' have had a meeting. They all acknowledge that they have dealt with each other in a fair and friendly manner for years and that their efforts have made the business a success. But none of them is interested in dealing with the spouse and family of a deceased co-owner, or co-partner. So, if Mrs. Abrams, Mrs. Bennet or Mr. Charles (the ones who have actively been in the business) dies, his or her family's whole interest shall be purchased at an agreed price. After careful consideration they decide that, in their case, it is best that the stock of a deceased party and that of her or his family shall be purchased and redeemed by the company. Here are the essentials of the deal:

- Transfer of stock henceforth is permitted only to the parties' children and spouses, or to trusts for them. An agreement is executed which restricts all stock transfer except pursuant to the agreement, which would include a lifetime transfer to another party to the agreement. A first refusal is not used here because the stock is sold at death.

- At death of a party who is active in the business (Mrs. Abrams, Mrs. Bennet or Mr. Charles) all of the stock of that person and his or her family must be purchased by the company within 90 days. Mrs. Abrams husband and the other spouses do not work in the business and his death would not trigger a buyout.

- The price is determined with the help of an expert from the company's CPA firm, the formula is an average of (i) book value as of the month prior to death, and (ii) eight times a five year average earning figure (insurance is valued at cash value).

- The company purchases key person life insurance on each of the three owners and agrees to pay the premiums when due and to keep the policies unencumbered. (Part of the insurance proceeds may be subject to the alternate minimum tax when received by the company.)
- The terms are: (i) down payment equal to the insurance proceeds on the life of the deceased party, and (ii) the balance amortized over 10 years at an appropriate interest rate. The stock sold is pledged until the note is paid in full.

Thus, upon the death of an owner, that family's interest is extinguished, subject to payment of the purchase price. If Mrs. Abrams died, the Bennets' and the Charles' would then own the remaining stock 2/3, 1/3. When one of them dies, the remaining family will own the whole company. The impact of the life insurance funding, which all three parties have paid for, should be considered here.

Very neat. Very nice. But will it really work? The answer is yes. Many, many corporations and partnerships have had similar agreements and things worked out just as planned. The concepts are simple but the implementation can be complex. Especially where you have multiple owners. Perfecting such a buy sell agreement takes careful thought and planning. The larger the company, the more difficult such a buy out. Problems of availability and cost of insurance can be encountered. And, very important, the impact of the buy out on the company's financing and its loan covenants must be considered.

What Happens if the Stock Buyout Heads to Financial Difficulties

Sometimes Things Do Not Go Right. What if a buy-sell agreement is carefully worked out today based on current business conditions and reasonable expectations for the future, *but the future does not come out quite right*? When Mrs. Abrams dies, the business is stumbling a little. There is little profit for the past year and it is losing money this year. The price formula, weighted to book value and an historic earnings average is based more on the past than on the present or the future. Mrs. Abrams has had a series of medical problems and the company has not kept the amount of insurance up to the buyout formula price. Thus, the down payment is relatively low and the 10 years' debt service on the balance becomes a burden.

The buy-sell agreement had provided that the *proceeds* of insurance shall be included in book value and that the real property will be appraised as a further adjustment to book value. These adjustments made the buy out price even higher.

The redemption payments for the Abrams' 40 percent stock interest have reduced the corporation's surplus to a low level. Four years after the buy out, losses continue and these reduce surplus further. The company can't make the payments to the Abrams estate, nor payments to other creditors. The company files Chapter 11 bankruptcy.

A creditor's committee for the company claims that the estate's stock was grossly overvalued at time of sale. Their position is that the Abrams's estate should repay part of the payments it received for the stock in order to restore surplus. In a bankruptcy, creditors come before shareholders. A corporation cannot distribute funds to its shareholders and thereby leave the corporation insolvent or without reasonably adequate capital for its ongoing operation and payments to creditors.

The estate has paid an estate tax based on the agreement's formula value. It could not defer the tax payments because the estate's stock was sold pursuant to the agreement. The insurance down payment was used to pay estate taxes. More than three years has passed by now and the estate cannot amend its estate tax returns to urge a lower value.

Is this a common scenario? No, it is not. Most buy sell arrangements work well.

Is this an impossible or implausible scenario? No, it is not implausible, and certainly not impossible. Things happen.

This bleak postscript to an otherwise rosy picture of a stock redemption buyout results from the application of the rule that a shareholder cannot remove property from a corporation when the corporation's legal capital is or would be impaired. Different states may express this in different ways but if the corporation's stock has a stated capital or par value of a given amount, the corporation cannot pay dividends or redeem stock except out of the surplus capital above that stated amount.

A related concept is that the shareholders of a corporation cannot impair the rights of its creditors by taking out property at a price that is less than fair value, where such taking would make the corporation insolvent or more insolvent. Further, even if there is a surplus on the books, a redemption of stock cannot leave the corporation with an unreasonably small capital. Creditors would contend that the failure of the business proves that the redemption left it with unreasonably small capital.

How can you ever have a stock redemption agreement that is totally safe? You can't. If the company sails along without troubles, then there is no problem. But if the company is in financial trouble at the time of a shareholder's death, or while installment payments for the stock are being made, there is no way to avoid potential trouble with a stock redemption agreement.

Use a Cross-Purchase Agreement

We have been speaking of a redemption agreement where the business (corporation or partnership or LLC) buys out, redeems, the interest of a deceased owner.

In a cross purchase agreement the other shareholders or partners buy out the interest of a deceased or retired partner. This is a very different sort of animal. Corporate insolvency is not directly relevant because the corporation is not making the payments to the deceased owner's estate. The other shareholders are personally making the payments.

Using Insurance to Fund a Buyout

The buy out of a deceased co-shareholder has long made sense. Equally, life insurance has been the perfect funding device. From a mechanical standpoint, buy outs can be accomplished by

- a stock redemption agreement, pursuant to which the decedent's stock is repurchased, redeemed, by the corporation, or
- a cross purchase agreement, pursuant to which the decedent's stock is purchased by the other shareholders.

In either case, premiums on life insurance are not deductible, by the corporation or by the shareholders. However, if the corporation owns the insurance, the proceeds may be subject to tax when received by the corporation.

In the not too distant past, the corporate income tax rate was 10 or 15 percentage points below the individual shareholder's tax rate. Moreover, use of the S Corporation (where the corporation is not taxed at all) was less common. If life insurance premiums on Mrs. Abrams, Mrs. Bennet, and Mr. Charles were $5,000 per year each, it made sense with the old tax rates to have the corporation own the insurance and pay the premiums.

	Corporation Owns Insurance	Stockholders Own Insurance
Before tax income	$25,000	$30,000
Less tax @ 40%	(10,000)	NA
Less tax @ 50%	NA	(15,000)
Required premiums	$15,000	$15,000

*These are the rates in effect prior to the 1986 legislation which reduced the individual rate to below the corporate rate (now 31% to 34%).

In this case, under the old tax rates, the three shareholders would have saved $5,000 per year by having the corporation own the premium rather than themselves.

Now, the corporation tax rate is higher than the individual rate, once corporate income exceeds $75,000 per year. Thus, from a pure tax standpoint, it makes sense for the shareholders to own the policies and pay the premiums. Within reasonable limits, the corporation can increase their (deductible) salary to enable them to do this.

What we are leading to is that the cross-purchase agreement, described above, is preferable to the redemption agreement from these standpoints:

- the premiums on the funding life insurance can be paid for with fewer after-tax dollars; and
- the policy proceeds may be subject to a corporate tax; and
- the shareholders have a much lower risk of the creditor problems (discussed above) where the corporation gets into financial trouble;
- with a cross-purchase agreement, the purchasing party gets a new basis for that stock.

How, is the redemption agreement better than the cross-purchase? There is one very important factor: simplicity. A funded buy-sell agreement is more complex than a redemption agreement.

Let us go back to the scenario in the prior section and assume that Mrs. Abram was a party to a cross purchase agreement, not a redemption agreement. In this case, the three insurance policies, one on each shareholder, would be held by a trustee or an escrow agent. The policies are owned by the shareholders, not the corporation. The premiums have been paid by the shareholders out of their salaries. When Mrs. Abrams dies the escrow agent would collect the proceeds of the policy and pay it over to the estate as a down payment on the purchase price. Mrs. Bennet and Mr. Charles would give their personal notes for the balance of the price in the ratio of 2/3:1/3. No cash has come into or been removed from the corporation except the salary used in the past to pay the premiums, which was compensation for services rendered. No creditor of the corporation has been damaged by any removal of funds or alleged overpayment for the stock because the corporation did not buy the stock; no funds came out of the corporation to purchase the stock.

Thus, if the corporation gets into financial trouble four years hence, Mrs. Bennet and Mr. Charles won't get distributions from the corporation to enable them to pay the estate. The estate may not get all the money due it under the price formula in the agreement, but neither will the estate have to pay back any money to the corporation. To some extent, Mrs. Abrams's estate may have a loss here but that is not due to the structure of the agreement. It would be due to (i) the price formula was not fairly reflective of value, or (ii) the insurance amount was not kept up-to-date.

Insurance funding is a matter real insurance experts. For instance, it is possible to obtain "first to die" joint insurance on two parties to an agreement. Then you pay lower premiums than if you had two individual policies.

Financing the Deferred Buy Out Payments

As we have envisioned it, the insurance on the life of Mrs. Abrams provided the down payment on her estate's sale of stock. In the redemption agreement, the corporation (a partnership if it were a partnership agreement) would pay the deferred payments out of future income. The interest would be deductible as a corporate expense.

In a cross purchase agreement, the remaining shareholders make the deferred payments. They can get this money from:

- salary from the corporation if reasonable in amount,
- dividends, that are subject to an additional tax in a C Corporation,
- dividends, that are *not* subject to additional tax in an S Corporation, and/or
- other financial resources of their own.

As pointed out, the corporation can deduct the interest on the deferred payments. The interest paid by the shareholders of a C Corporation is investment interest and may only be deducted against investment income, e.g., dividends, but could not be deducted against salary income. By contrast, in an S corporation, the interest on debt to acquire stock may be deducted against the Subchapter S income of that corporation.

How a Buy-Sell Agreement Can Control Estate Tax Value

Assume A and B, unrelated persons, are 50-50 owners of a business corporation or partnership. They have an agreement that, if one dies, the other buys out the estate's interest at a specified price or a formula price.

A dies. Pursuant to the agreement, the sale price is $700,000. The sale closes and As executor reports a $700,000 value on the estate tax return. The IRS audits the return and asserts a value of $1,900,000. In effect, the IRS agent is substituting his judgment for that of A and B. On this much increase the tax deficiency and penalties could easily amount to over $300,000. Who wins?

This is a potentially serious problem. If B, the other party to the buy-sell agreement, were a son or daughter of A, the IRS might well contend that the agreement was a sham designed to pass on the business interest at a low tax value to a child.

What about the case where the other party was unrelated and the agreement demonstrably negotiated in good faith as a business arrangement? Should such an arms' length agreement be controlling as to value? The answer here is yes, such an agreement controls value for estate tax purposes.

The IRS, backed by the courts, says that a buy sell agreement controls the price only if:

- the parties during their life cannot sell at a price higher than specified in the agreement—it must bind as to lifetime transfers as well as at death,
- they must be bound to sell at the agreed price at death,
- the price and terms of the agreement must be comparable to other agreements of the same kind, and
- all bets are off if the other party is related, the natural object of your bounty.

In 1990, these rules were enacted into law. So it is possible for you to negotiate a buy-sell agreement (redemption or cross-purchase) with an unrelated party that will be binding for estate tax value purposes, but such an agreement with a child or other heir will not.

The typical first refusal agreement, such as the one illustrated in Chapter 3, will not serve to bind as to value. The IRS reasons this way:

> If you, as a party, have to give the other party a first refusal, you can negotiate a high, medium, or low price with a potential buyer. Then you have to offer it to your partner at the negotiated price: this is the so-called first refusal. Your partner has to pay that price, or you can sell it to the party at that figure. So the agreement does not control the value at all.

Even an agreement which binds to sell at a given price at death will not control value, if during lifetime the owners can sell at any price subject to a first refusal.

Who Pays the Estate Tax?

In the case of A and B, assume the final IRS value was $1,100,000 and the estate received only $700,000 for the stock. B, got the benefit of a discount price. As estate has been assessed an extra tax. Is it fair for the estate to pay the tax on the unanticipated benefit going to B? What happens here? The laws of the states may vary on this point and, here, the business owner should definitely check with legal counsel. One thing is very clear: if your will directs that all estate taxes be paid out of your residuary estate, then *your estate, not the other owner, will bear the tax.* If that is what you want to happen, then that's fine.

New York state has a rule which would permit an estate to seek contribution for part of the estate tax where a buy-sell agreement causes a sale below estate tax value. This rule may also apply in your state. If it does, consider having a clause which *directs* the executor to seek contribution for taxes if the buy-sell agreement does not work to control estate tax value.

Sale of Stock to Key Employees

We have discussed how to transfer stock, as an incentive, to key employees. We have discussed the stock bonus plan and the ESOP in terms of an incentive device.

Whether there be one owner, or two or more owners, current employers are a logical market for the stock. In Chapters 14, 15, and 16 the thrust is use of stock as an incentive bonus, a form of compensation for good work. In this section, the motive is to secure a market for your stock. Let us go back to our friends at A, B, C Company. Things did work out financially following the death of Mrs. Abrams and Mrs. Bennet and Mr. Charles, now in their early 60s are wondering what to do next. Neither of them has a child in the business now; neither feels like going on if the other should die or be disabled. Both would like to retire in a few years, but who will mind the store? Again, the viability of the business is important because the retired owner's consider the business as the source of cash for the payment of their interests.

Six key employees now own stock under a restricted stock plan installed when the company got in trouble (after Mrs. Abrams's death). But all told it's only 18 percent, and all subject to a corporate buy back when the six retire.

This particular company has a high percentage of Chiefs in relation to Indians. Thus, a higher percentage of employees, as key persons, are purchasers. It does not manufacture but rather designs and services products in the electronics field. All told there are 60 professionals (in addition to the six key persons) and 32 clerical, accounting, and secretarial persons. Let us illustrate two alternate plans to show how the concepts in Chapters 14, 15, and 16 can be applied to create a market for Mrs. Bennet's and Mr. Charles's stock:

Plan A: LBO by Key Employees (Including Family Members)

Objective. To create a market for stock of current owners. To save the company as a going entity after owners retire.

Method. Company will issue restricted stock to three additional key persons, bringing the total employee ownership up to 27 percent by nine persons. Bennet and Charles will then sell their stock back to the company at an agreed price which will not exceed the value in an independent appraisal.

Security. The company will make a down payment consisting of excess liquid assets and the proceeds of a bank loan. The balance of the price will be paid with a long-term corporate note which will be subordinate to the bank loan. There will be a loan agreement, similar to a bank's, which will place certain restrictions on the employees' salary and on corporate operations. The stock sold will be pledged as security.

Guaranty. The nine employees will guaranty their pro rata shares of the corporate note.

Interest. The corporation can deduct the interest payments to the sellers.

Result. When the sale closes, the stock of the original owners is cancelled (subject to the security interest) and the nine key employees own the business. Good management will hopefully continue and Mrs. Bennet and Mr. Charles will realize the value of their stock.

The stock will be paid for, as to the principal amount, with after-tax dollars. The note interest is deductible.

Plan B: Sell to ESOP

Objective. To create a market for stock of current owners. To save the company as a going entity after the owners retire.

Method. Corporation sets up an ESOP plan in which all permanent employees participate pro rata based on compensation. The six key employees who have restricted stock get to keep it and additional restricted stock is issued to the three other key persons. Mrs. Bennet and Mr. Charles have their stock appraised by two independent appraisers and then sell it to the qualified employer trust at the lower value. The trust gives them a 10-year note in payment. Alternatively, the ESOP could borrow the repurchase price from a bank or other lender and pay the full repurchase price to the selling shareholders at once. (In this way, the selling shareholders do not have to be concerned about the continued viability of the business—they have their cash and essentially are out of the picture.) Periodically, the corporation makes deductible cash contributions to the trust which are used by it to make the note payments to the former shareholders (or loan payments to the lender).

Security. The note is secured by a pledge of the stock, by a guaranty of the corporation, and by limited personal guaranty of the nine key employee stockholders.

Interest. The trust pays interest to the sellers (or lenders). Deductibility is immaterial because the trust is tax exempt.

Result. When the sale closes, the trust owns 73 percent of the stock for the benefit of the employees who participate in the plan and the nine key employees own the other 27 percent.

The payments by the corporation to the trust are deductible within limits. Thus, it is paying for the stock in before tax dollars. With Plan A it is paying for the stock in after tax dollars. The burden on the company is less, and the security of the sellers' notes is therefore greater in Plan B than in Plan A.

Sale of Business to Unrelated Parties

This book is devoted to succession of ownership of the business by transfer to family members, key employees, or partners. It tells how to facilitate such transfers and how, by reducing the estate tax burden, to make them possible. Sometimes there are no family members able to run the business, no partners to buy, no key employees who have the ability and financial resources to accomplish a buy out.

Here, we examine briefly the pros and cons of a sale to outside interests. The subject of sale of a family business is worth a book or two in and of itself. This question breaks down into two sub questions:

- Under what conditions should an owner sell to outsiders rather than take one of the other courses described in this book?
- What is the best timing for such a sale?

Let us consider the simpler question first: timing. It is human nature to want to hold on. It is the nature of business owners, the kind of person who can innovate, lead, build, and above all, work to want to keep what he/she has done. That desire leads to succession planning and is the fuel that drives this book. Assume that the owner (or owners) conclude that the business must be sold, that internal succession is not feasible.

If the current owner is at retirement age or in poor health, and comes to the conclusions that the business must be sold to outsiders, the best time to do it is now. Now, while the business is doing well; now, while the owner is in good health; now, while bargaining power is at a maximum. To illustrate, take the other extreme, a clause in the owner's will that reads as follows:

> I hereby direct that my business be sold by my executor after my death as expeditiously as possible.

This clause in a will puts the executor in a poor bargaining position. Every potential buyer will know that the business must be sold. Even if there is no such clause in the will, the fact that the estate has no logical choice but to sell will tend to depress bargaining power. So, to repeat, the best time to sell is at the peak when bargaining power is evident to the potential buyer and you, the owner, are here to negotiate.

Under what conditions should the owner consider sale to outside interests. This is subjective, but the first condition is a *mindset*, "I don't want to do this anymore. I want to retire, to go sit on the beach and enjoy life."

The second condition is more measurable. Lack of a market, or a recipient, for internal succession. We have discussed transferring the business to the children, sale to key employees or employee trust, and buy-sell agreements with other shareholders. If none of these means of succession are available, then the only choice is a sale to outsiders.

What Are the Options in a Sale?

Let us list the options, with brief comments on each. Each assumes a desire to do something now.

Liquidate. Sometimes a business should be liquidated. Where personal involvement, talent, reputation are major factors, there may be nothing to sell. Perhaps the owner could have transferred by taking in a partner years ago. But it's too late now. Most successful businesses do not liquidate but the possibility belongs in this list.

Merge. There are really two kinds of mergers:

* join with a similar privately held business and take back stock (or a partnership interest) in the new entity, or
* be acquired by a publicly held company in exchange for its stock, a marketable asset. Such transactions are usually free of tax; but the owner still has a major investment in the new entity.

Sell Business Assets but Keep the Company. Sometimes the owner has a huge potential gains tax on sale of stock and a lesser gain on sale of assets by the corporate business. It is possible to sell off the corporate assets, pay the corporate tax, and then keep the corporation going as an investment company. At the owner's death, when the stock requires a new cost basis in the hands of the owner's heirs, the corporation would be liquidated. If the corporation is an S Corporation and always has been, the future investment income will pass through to the owner without corporate tax. If the corporation is a C Corporation there is a double tax on the future investment income; this must be factored into the decision whether to continue the corporation as an investment company.

Sell Business Assets and Liquidate the Corporation. Here, we have a real problem with a C Corporation: two taxes to pay. One by the corporation on its sale of assets. One by the owner on receipt of what is left. It may be the best thing to do but at least you should know the cost in taxes. With an S Corporation, the double tax may be reduced or even completely liquidated.

Sell Stock to Another Company or to Investors. For openers, this might eliminate the double tax incurred if you sell business assets and liquidate because here, the corporate assets are not being sold. But there are two problems here. First, most purchasers want to buy assets, not stock, because they are concerned about unknown corporate liabilities (environmental, product liability, taxes, etc.). Second, buyers want to get a new basis for the assets purchased and the only way to achieve this is by having someone pay a tax on the value increase in corporate property.

Set Up an ESOP. We have discussed sale to an ESOP, but it is worth mentioning this option again.

Go Public. In some cases a very successful company in an attractive industry can go public. In our context, this probably involves a secondary offering of some of the owner's shares to the public. There are many ramifications here which should not even attempt to address in this book.

The S Corporation Excels

The S corporation has many virtues from a tax standpoint but it really stands out where a sale or liquidation of a business is considered. The way the tax law has been structured since 1986 is that a liquidation or sale transaction involving a C corporation incurs a double tax. First, there is a tax at the corporate level on the difference between the current value of corporate assets and the assets' current book value. Once this tax has been paid, and it could be as much as 40 percent of the corporate gain, the net balance goes to the selling shareholders. Then, they pay another tax based on the difference between what they receive and their cost for the stock. With an S corporation there is no double tax. Moreover, the shareholders receive an increase in their cost basis for all the income they have left in the corporation. The difference between the tax on a C Corporation and an S Corporation can be dramatic. As usual, there are some qualifications to this and your professional tax adviser can explain them.

19

Succession Planning for a Smooth Transition

We have written in great detail about saving taxes, deferring taxes, freezes, employee stock ownership, value, insurance, and other assorted topics. Up to this chapter, you have been led through a tax maze, hopefully with benefit. Let's assume your estate won't pay a nickel more tax, a day sooner, than the absolute minimum. Is there more?

Yes, because business succession is about more than taxes. Sometimes it seems like taxes are the tail that wags the dog. This chapter brings out other elements of a successful transition of business ownership on the death of an owner, who had been a driving force in the business. It shows how the human element must be considered. Let us start with a short fable of how things can go wrong.

Case Study: What Happens When There Is No Business Succession Plan

All those present listened intently to find out how the estate would be divided. As lawyer Crumbly's voice droned on, intoning the last words of Jimmy Clyde's will, the eyes of Jimmy's daughter, Sarah Clyde Roberts, and his son, Malcolm (Mal) Clyde, locked in better hatred.

"He left Sarah all the voting stock, and made her executor, did he? Well, we will see about that." Mal turned to his lawyer, Frederick D. Jarndyce III, Esq., who, flanked by two associates, sat behind Mal. "That will is 20 years old and hopelessly out-of-date. I run Clyde Agribusiness and I want that voting stock, which Dad promised to me. File suit today."

Phil Crumbly, the lawyer who had just read the will, said "Mal, I know that will is a little old, but it's what your Dad always wanted. He felt that

Sarah was the more stable of you two and—." Fred Jarndyce, Esq. leaped to his feet. "Hold it right there Crumbly, you'll get yourself into a slander suit. Be careful."

Sarah, flanked by a gray pinstriped lawyer on one side and a blue pinstriped investment banker on the other. "Mal, I want to let you know that Mr. Crumbly and I, as the remaining two directors of Clyde Agribusiness, Inc., have had a meeting at which your services as Vice President and General Manager were terminated effective today. Your salary of $650,000 a year will continue for two years. After that you an live on your dividends, if any. We then elected Mr. Raeder here as director replacing Dad." She nodded to Mr. Raeder (blue pinstripes), the banker, by way of introduction.

Phil Crumbly, age 76, and an old friend of the deceased Jimmy Clyde, sighed and said "Well, I may as well go over to the courthouse and file this will. It's a good thing your mother isn't alive to see this mess."

"Not so fast, Crumbly." said Jarndyce handing him a paper, "here is a restraining order which forbids you to probate the will." *Exeunt all.*

The Elements of Transition

Of course, this case study is an exaggerated, over dramatized fable, right? Well, yes, maybe a bit, but the Clyde situation has in it all the elements found in many business succession situations:

- A large, successful company worth, in the Clydes' case, about $10,000,000.
- Jane Clyde predeceased her husband, Jimmy. Therefore, there is no marital deduction and the estate tax bill will be $5 million plus.
- Children who have different talents, perspectives, and economic interests. Sarah, who is married to a nephew of Phil Crumbly's, has been acting President of the family business for several years and did, in fact, enjoy her father's confidence. Mal is perhaps more talented than Sarah, but likes his fun, his alcohol, and a few other things. He never got along with Jimmy, who paid him $650,000 a year as "General Manager" with the understanding he would stay away.
- Directors who have a personal interest in the situation and act accordingly: Sarah and her uncle-in-law, Phil, are the remaining directors. They elect Sarah's newly retained Mr. Raeder as the third director. Mr. Raeder hails from New York City, which is 1,583 miles, as the crow flies, from the office of Clyde Agribusiness, Inc.
- Sarah has the voting stock, 1,000 shares, which gives her the "right to elect directors." Under the corporate charter, all the stock, including Mal's 1,000 shares of non-voting stock, gets to vote on merger, dissolution or sale of the business.

- The will is silent on which stock, if any, is to be redeemed to pay estate taxes. It does not direct who is to bear the burden of taxes.
- The will named Jimmy's wife, Jane Clyde, as executor and empowered Phil Crumbly to name the executor if Jane predeceased.
- Some years ago, Jimmy and Jane had taken out two $5 million joint life insurance policies to pay estate taxes at the death of their survivor. They gave one to Sarah as trustee for herself and one to Mal as trustee for himself, with the understanding that the $10,000,000 total would be used to pay estate taxes.

Presence of some of the above elements is fairly common in family situations. The difference in the Clyde family is the jealousy and enmity that exists between the steelyeyed Sarah and the dissolute Mal. There's always a Jarndyce and a Raeder around to take advantage of a bad situation. How can one avoid such a situation? The following sections discuss the need for an independent board of directors and the great benefits of the living trust.

The Value of Independent Directors

Let us go back to basic corporation rules. The stockholders own the corporation and elect directors, as their representatives, to oversee the business and set broad policy. The directors, in turn, elect the officers who actively manage and conduct operations. In closely held corporations, these roles are often blurred and confused. The "one-person show" is great as long as you are there to direct it. The problem comes up when you are not there.

In this author's view one of the best estate planning tools you can have is an informed and independent board of directors. If old Jimmy Clyde had several additional persons on the board, Sarah would have still wound up in charge, but not with the problems attendant with having herself elected by Phil Crumbly, the estate's lawyer, and Mr. Blue Pinstripe, her investment banker. These independent directors need not meet often, quarterly is fine, nor should they get into the day-to-day workings of the business. They are there to provide judgment, stability, confidence as the business makes the difficult transition from founder to successor. It may take a while to get these people in place, and it may take some effort, but the effort is worthwhile. Start now.

Should the family lawyer, banker, and CPA be on the board? Normally, no. Serving on the board makes a participant out of someone whom you value and pay for independent counsel and judgment. It may be difficult to attract really qualified people to be directors of a family business. Two things can help: pay them a generous fee, plus expenses, for attending meetings and use agreements and charter provisions to assure that they will be indemnified by the corporation in case someone decides to sue them. What if the business is a partnership? The partnership's legal structure does not call for directors, but there is no reason you can't build in an advisory committee which has the same practical effect as directors. Pay them and indemnify them as suggested above.

The transition of a business from founder, owner, to successor can be fraught with problems. Having an independent board of directors or advisor can alleviate if not solve such problems.

Ensure a Smooth Management Transition by Using a Living Trust

Probate rules vary from state to state. In some it is a simple procedure to get the will filed and an executor or personal representative appointed. In others, it is more difficult, more legalistic. But always there is a chance for an unhappy heir, a Mal Clyde, a would-be spouse, or a live-in "friend" to disrupt and cause trouble, to delay the transition of the management and ownership of the business. The best way to avoid all this, and perhaps to reduce probate costs as well, is to use what is called a living trust, an inter vivos trust, or sometimes a revocable trust and other names. All describe a concept which may be described by telling what Jimmy Clyde and his wife, Jane, could have done back in 1973 when the will was signed.

Instead of using a will to effect transfer and succession of the business at his death, Jimmy could have executed a living trust instrument whereby he, Jane, Sarah, and Phil Crumbly are appointed trustees. Perhaps a friend, one of the business directors, is also appointed a trustee. Jimmy then transfers to the trust all of his stock in Clyde Agribusiness plus all of his other investment assets; only the personal residence and certain affects are not transferred to the trust. As long as Jimmy is alive he is the only active trustee. The others are on a standby basis in case Jimmy becomes too ill to act as trustee. Jimmy can revoke and amend the trust any time, vote the stock, and receives all trust income.

At Jimmy's death the trust becomes irrevocable and acts just like his will. The marital deduction and bypass trust are used for Jane, if she survives. At Jane's death, the voting stock is distributed to Sarah, the nonvoting stock to Mal. There is no probate; the trust just sails on as it had since 1973. There is nothing for Mal to contest. Perhaps he's named as a trustee for his shares and executed the trust too. The will contest promised by Mr. Jarndyce won't happen because the will doesn't control the stock or the business. It only disposes of the residence and whatever else that wasn't put in the trust.

If Jimmy became very ill, or incompetent during his lifetime, the trust would just sail on because named trustees are already in place. All in all a very excellent transition device in the right situation.

Transition of Employee Benefits

Owners of a successful business often have very substantial benefits from qualified plans. These can be a major part of the liquid estate, available for the support and security of the spouse. The planning for such benefits is not within the scope of this book, but keep in mind the following:

- Such benefits may be disposed of in accordance with numerous options. It is very important that the settlement options tie in with the owners wishes as to economic division, the marital deduction, and liability for estate taxes.

- Employee benefits are, for the most part, subject to estate tax at the employee's death and to income taxes when the employee's spouse or other beneficiary receives them. A limited income tax deduction is available for the estate tax paid on the benefits.

- Employee benefits, when paid to the employee's estate or other beneficiary, may be subject to a 15 percent estate excise tax (in addition to other estate and income taxes) if the amount exceeds certain size limits. Careful planning by experts in the employee benefit field is needed to keep the double and triple (estate + income + excise) taxation to a minimum.

Succession Planning When the Business Is a Partnership

The Clyde family saga was told as though Jimmy was the sole owner of Clyde Agribusiness, Inc. What if Jimmy had a partner, his brother, Ben Clyde? Would that alter things? Yes. It would make things even more complex. The company would still need the independent directors. A living trust would still be advisable for Jimmy's situation. In fact, Ben Clyde probably needs a living trust too. This way transition and succession are all set up in advance. Certainly the owner in Ben's position does not want to get in the midst of a battle royale between Sarah and Mal, and their phalanxes of lawyers whose artfulness is exceeded only by their greed.

Perhaps, on exploration, Jimmy and Ben found that individual living trusts for their respective families did not quite solve the potential problems. They could consider a voting trust to hold all their stock, each family retaining its separate beneficial ownership. For the duration of the voting trust (up to 15 years in some states) the voting trustees vote the stock irrespective of who owns it. Even though 15 years be the maximum duration of such a trust, Jimmy and Ben can extend it each year, so that there is always a running 15-year period of protection in case one of them dies or becomes incompetent.

Living Wills and Health Care Proxies

Here we have a sector of law that is in rapid evolution, the law of the terminally ill person. Medical science has given many of us prolonged life, but does not necessarily prolong our mental capacity at the same time. Every business owner should execute power of attorney, have a living will, and appoint a health care proxy.

Power of Attorney. The owner of a business, 55 years old, has a serious stroke. A living trust and capable directors can hold the fort at the business until the owner recovers or dies. But what about personal financial matters: bills, tuition, investments, tax returns, and so on? The trustees of the living trust can do a lot here, if there is one.

Each owner of a business should execute a power of attorney giving to a spouse or some other trusted person the power to manage financial matters. Some states allow a "Springing Power of Attorney" which becomes effective only if the grantor of the power is certified by his/her personal physician as being incapable of handling financial matters.

Living Will. This is not to be confused with a living trust. A living will is simply a statement of the person's wishes governing where he or she is in a physical health situation where the issue is to "pull the plug" or not. The living will is applicable where the person has no reasonable hope of medical recovery and a normal life, and is and will be so mentally impaired that communication of his/her wishes to the physician is impossible. If this happens, the living will speaks for you. The typical living will states that in such a case the person does not want life to be prolonged by artificial means. It is not a request for euthanasia, but rather, a peaceful death. If you do want life prolonged by every possible means, at whatever cost, you can say that too. But few do. The living will is recognized by many states.

Health Care Proxy. The health care proxy is to health matters what a power of attorney is as to financial matters. Having expressed your personal philosophy in a living will, you need someone to implement your wishes, to make medical decisions in your behalf when you cannot do so. The health care proxy empowers someone, typically a spouse or child, to act for you. It is a necessary companion to the power of attorney and living will.

Dealing with Professional Advisors

Most every estate planning symposium, course, or book will emphasize the "team" approach, the efficient use of your lawyer, CPA, insurance expert, investments expert, appraiser, and trust officers. Were you trained to be an orchestra conductor? Unfortunately, the client can get so involved in an unwieldy team of would-be superstars that he or she runs out of patience or out of money. It is well to have one member of the team as a sort of quarterback; it could be any of the several disciplines mentioned. Or, if there be such a person on hand, delegate a corporate financial person or in-house counsel to relate to the team in your behalf. The final judgments have to be yours and your spouse's, but someone else can do the leg work.

People can validly have different ideas about the value of a given service. Have it understood in advance what the costs are. Attorneys should, on request, give you estimates, or at least explain their methods of billing, for both estate planning and probate (estate administration) services. Don't let them low ball the planning with the idea of signing off from the estate at the end (your end). (Any major insurance investment should be bid out by your insurance agent or advisor to at least three highly rated companies. Insist that the bids be comparable; don't try to compare apples and oranges.)

In most states, the only one of these advisors with whom confidences are privileged is the attorney. The privilege only attaches to *confidential* communication. A letter sent to your attorney, with copies to CPA and CLU is not privileged. A conference with these advisors present is not privileged. An appraisal ordered by *you* is not privileged. It can be subpoenaed by the IRS in a valuation trial, even if you believe the value was way too high. The opinion of an expert, including a valuation expert retained by your attorney to help the attorney counsel you, will in some states be privileged.

Your Spouse Is Your Best Advisor

Your spouse is probably the most valuable member on your team. The number crunchers come up with numbers, the scriveners with documents and the experts with their reports. Your spouse is your best independent guide to the human factors, and probably to the overall common sense of your plan. He or she should be involved in the whole process, not necessarily a participant in every meeting nor copied in every letter, but in a position to discuss, consider, critique, question. Most importantly the spouse should be involved in the decisions.

Part Six

CASE STUDY:
ESTATE PLANNING FOR
KAYJIM ELECTRONIC DEVICES, INC.

CHAPTER 20. **Building a Successful Business**
CHAPTER 21. **The Business as "Star Performer": 10 Years Later**
CHAPTER 22. **The "Colossus": Estate Planning for the $25-30 Million Business**

This Part shows how the rules work in actual practice. It relates the story of Jim and Kate Wolczk, founders of a very successful electronics company. Their estate planning is reviewed in three stages, 10 years apart. Each stage presents different facts and problems as the business prospers and the estate tax bills grow ever higher.

The overall theme is *the crushing burden that estate taxes levy on American business.* Unfortunately, as it turns out, the estate tax laws in effect in the 1990s exact a toll on our family businesses resembling the one President Franklin D. Roosevelt envisioned for huge business trusts in the 1930s. The current estate tax laws have such a serious impact that the closely held business cannot survive the impact of estate taxes on each succeeding generation unless active steps are taken to reduce these taxes. Using the principles described in the text, the case study leads you through a series of the steps that can be taken.

20

Building a Successful Business

Jim Wolczk's first and only job was with General Electric Company at Schenectady, New York. He was moved along the fast track to fortune. His intense drive and sparkling personality made it easy to single him out for the choicest jobs. He was no slouch at the books either. The master's degree at nearby Union University came easily.

Jim always said, "The smartest thing I ever did was to go skiing and break a leg." That's because, when he woke after the leg-setting operation, the first person he saw was his nurse, Kate Ryan. Jim had been at GE about a year then, and Kate was finishing up her masters in nursing administration. A year later they were married, and a year after that along came their daughter Molly, followed by Jim Jr. and Maureen.

When Jim was 34, he received a big promotion, a bonus, and a raise. The only problem was that he did not want to move to Oklahoma. With regret, he decided it was time to leave GE, his second family. Jim secured licenses on two electronic products, leased machinery and a small building, and set up shop.

The rest is history, as they say. Five years later, KayJim Electronic Devices ("KJ") earned $523,000 net profit before tax. Kate could no longer keep the books at home; instead, she supervised two bookkeepers and a part-time accountant. The two products had grown to eight, six licensed and two developed in-house. KJ made no claim to be the sole producer of a product nor the least costly; its success was based on quality of product and quality of service. A promise made was a promise kept. It was that simple. But wondering competitors never did learn why the customers preferred KJ every time.

It all began to cost, though. After celebrating his fortieth birthday with a five-mile jog, two sets of tennis, and a steak dinner, Jim decided he didn't feel well. His left arm hurt and he had "indigestion in my chest." Early next morning, Kate herself canceled all his appointments and marched him off to the family doctor. A series of tests disclosed that Jim had suffered a mild heart attack and, given the state of his body, that the next one might be his last.

Joe Warren, CLU, had his luckiest day when he popped in at KJ on the first full day that Jim returned to work. Joe and Jim had met several times at the tennis club, and, building on this slender reed, Joe hoped to sell Jim some life insurance or, as he termed it, "review Jim's estate and family financial plan." Now, he found a very attentive ear. Up to this point, Jim, believing himself immortal, had acquired no life insurance except a $300,000 group policy at KJ. But now he was having second thoughts.

As a matter of routine, Joe asked for a copy of Jim's will. It was a one-pager drawn up 15 years earlier by a next door neighbor who worked as a lawyer for a state agency. The will left all to a family trust for Kate and any children they might have. Kate was executor, trustee, and guardian for any children of theirs. No substitute guardian or trustee was appointed. Joe sighed when he saw this and said, "Jim, you'd better see your lawyer about your will. This is hopelessly inadequate."

Jim had long equated lawyers, doctors, and hospitals (in that order) as things to be avoided. Ongoing experiences as a business person and as a patient only confirmed his basic instincts. "Joe, I thought you were my friend. Is your brother-in-law a lawyer, or something?"

Joe only sighed again. "Jim, I know how you feel. I have seen your symptoms too many times before. You're especially repelled by lawyers who use 'decedent,' 'probate,' 'estate taxes,' and other nasty words, right?"

"Right!" said Jim, "a thousand times."

"But Jim, you know you have to."

"Yes, I suppose so. I guess I can stand a lawyer for a meeting or two."

Joe hesitated over that "meeting or two" but made no comment. Instead, he wrote out the names of several law firms and handed it to Jim. "Here are several I could recommend. Call and check them out."

Assessing the Value of the Estate and the Business

Kate and Jim's first meeting was with lawyer Claibourne C. Hannon, "Clay" for short. Clay got right down to business. "Jim, we've heard of your company and are delighted to have you as clients. . . ."

"Well, I'm delighted to meet you, too," interrupted Jim, "but before we begin, I'd like to know how you charge for this estate-planning service. Joe Warren said we would have no problem about that, but I would like to know now. Do you charge a percentage of our property?"

"Percentage of your property? Wow! I wish we could," said Clay. "But let me put your mind at rest. We charge, essentially, an hourly rate which is very often reduced on a case-to-case basis, frankly, because we sometimes feel our usual rate just won't 'look right' to the client. If you want, we can furnish you with a detailed bill showing date, attorney, time spent, and service performed."

"Fine!" said Kate. "Jim can relax now, so, Clay, why don't you start? Now that we are embarked on this, we want it done right, and basically we don't care what it costs.

"Clay said, "Let me start then. The most important element in the estate plan is what you personally want to happen with your property in the event one of you should die, or if both of you should die. The personal element is the key, but let me pass over that for a while so I can set up a framework of tax and legal considerations. Then we can come back and see how your wishes fit into the framework. In the event they don't fit our framework, then we change the framework."

"Jim, you have given me a detailed personal financial statement and also filled out our family tree questionnaire. So let me summarize your family's assets." He showed the Wolczks a simple table he had prepared. (See Table 20.1.)

"KJ is growing very fast. It is not incorporated, and its earnings last year were $523,000 before tax; its book value is $1,110,000. Since most businesses are valued on an after-tax corporate basis, I have converted KJ's earnings for the past five years to an after-tax basis, and they came up to a $167,000 weighted average. At six times this weighted earnings average, we come up with a value of $1,000,000 for the business."

"What weighting did you use?" said Jim.

"I weight the latest year at 5 and the prior four at 4,3,2,1, respectively. This gives recent earnings the most weight but takes the past into account, too. Actually, a $1,000,000 value for your business is very conservative, but the plan we will recommend will take future growth into account."

Clay had previously reviewed financial and personal information sent him by Jim and was able to launch right off. "Okay, let's go. Here is the framework that I can see right now. Let me preface it with a summary of the

Table 20.1. Assets of Wolczks' Estate

	Jim	Kate	Total
Business: d/b/a KJ Electronics	$1,000,000		$1,000,000
House, net of mortgage (jointly owned)	50,000	50,000	100,000
Securities and bank accounts	40,000	60,000	100,000
Group life insurance (to estate)	300,000		300,000
Cars & miscellaneous personal property	20,000	30,000	50,000
Totals	$1,410,000	$140,000	$1,550,000

tax situation. On the basis of assumed values of $1.5 million for your combined property, the total of that belonging to each of you, *there would be no estate tax if Kate died first and almost $300,000 at Jim's death if he died first.*"

"That would be a total disaster," said Kate. "The group life insurance would just cover that amount."

"Kate, keep in mind that he said 'on the basis of assumed values . . .'," said Jim defensively.

"Right," Clay said, "we have to start somewhere. But two things are likely to happen to my value assumption. The IRS may challenge the value and hold that the business is worth more than my value. Or, more likely, the value will grow anyway before someone dies.

The Tripod of Estate Planning

"What I plan to review today are three concepts: The marital deduction, the insurance trust, and the effect of gifts to your children. This is the basic and very simple framework I propose for you." Clay continued. "What I propose is a conceptual framework like a tripod, a very secure footing, consisting of

- the correct use of the estate-tax marital deduction,
- a safe program of gifts of growth assets to your children, and
- a tax-free insurance trust to provide cash to the estate.

Clay took a piece of blank paper and sketched out his "tripod". (See Figure 20.1.) "These tripod concepts are as secure a base for your estate planning as is a tripod used for a camera. My goal for estate planning is this: Do not let the tail wag the dog. Reduce taxes if possible, but not at the cost of undue complexity and turning the clients' lives upside down." Kate and Jim nodded their vigorous assent.

"When we have all that down, we need to talk about more specific planning for the succession of your business in the event of Jim's death. This will involve setting up a survivable management structure, attracting and keeping key management, and preparing for the eventuality of a sale of the business if that is needed to maintain values. But let's go back now and discuss the three legs of the basic tripod plan."

Correct Use of the Marital Deduction

"Jim, the will prepared for you many years ago may have made sense then, but it is the worst thing you could have now. What your will does is to leave all your assets to Kate as trustee for herself and your children. At the time your will was drawn up, your GE life insurance and generous employee

Figure 20.1

The Tripod

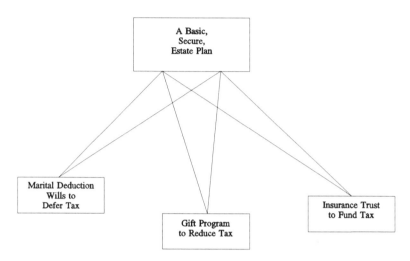

benefit programs, then the bulk of your estate, all would have gone to Kate outright and tax free. But now things have changed; now, most of your estate would go to the trust for the children and Kate, and not just to Kate. *That* spells disaster. That is why you would be paying a huge estate tax."

Squirming uncomfortably, Jim said, "What are you talking about? The lawyer, 15 years ago, assured me it was okay." "Yes, it was okay—when you were 25 years old and had minimal assets," replied Clay. "Here's what is wrong with it today. Under current law, there is an unlimited marital deduction for property left to a surviving spouse, which goes to the spouse either outright, or in a trust where she or he receives all the income plus any principal that is distributed."

Clay was ready with an illustration: "If you had a $20-million-dollar estate and left it solely to Kate—or to a trust where she received all the income for life—it would pass completely free of estate taxes. However, the trust under your current will includes the children as beneficiaries. Therefore, it does *not* qualify for the marital deduction, and it is *all* taxable. As we see it, your estate is at least $1.4 million and the only items that qualify for the marital deduction are your interest in the house, and the cars and other tangible property, which do qualify because they pass only to Kate. This leaves you with an estate of $1,340,000, and the federal and state tax on that would be about the $300,000 mentioned before." He paused for effect, and then pointed out: "Your tax could be zero if your will were correct."

"Fix *that* in a hurry," exclaimed Jim.

"I'll do just that," said Clay. "Stop in here at nine tomorrow morning, and I will have interim wills ready for you both. In addition, call your company before you leave here and tell them that you want your $300,000 group policy changed so that Kate and not your estate is the sole beneficiary, as you now have it. Sign the new form today. That $300,000 will then qualify for the marital deduction because it goes to Kate, and you save about $120,000 in estate tax on that, if you do nothing else."

"Done!" said Jim and Kate in unison.

"Now tell me," asked Jim, "what is going to be in this will we are going to sign tomorrow?

"Yes, I'll tell you right now," said Clay. "Your current will is all wrong, Jim, because it leaves your estate to a trust for Kate and the children. Since Kate is not the sole lifetime beneficiary, it does not qualify for the marital deduction. The result is no marital deduction and, hence, a large tax. The will I suggest as a temporary expedient gives to Kate, outright, your entire estate less $600,000.

"The amount that goes to Kate outright will be tax-free in your estate because it qualifies for the estate-tax marital deduction. The other $600,000 will also be tax-free because you have a tax credit that is the equivalent of a $600,000 'exemption.' I say 'exemption' because that is a convenient way to express the concept of the tax-free credit.

"Jim, if there were any reason to do so, you could also get the marital deduction by way of a trust for Kate, a trust where she would be entitled to all of the income for her life, with no principal distributions to anyone but her. But at this point I see no reason why there should be a trust for Kate."

"Nor do I!" interjected Kate, looking at Jim. "If I'd known you had a trust in your will, you'd have changed it a long time ago."

Clay said, "Kate, you will be pleased to know that I am suggesting a trust for you, consisting of the $600,000 tax-free exempt amount."

Kate was puzzled. "Why, may I ask, are you putting almost half of Jim's estate in a trust for me? I thought you said trusts were no good."

The Bypass Trust. Clay explained, "The reason for the $600,000 trust is that it skips Jim's estate for tax purposes because that is the amount of the 'exemption' I mentioned. Kate, it also skips your estate because it is in a trust that enables you, as trustee, to distribute assets to the children. That is why it is sometimes called a *bypass trust*, it bypasses your estate." Once again, an example was in order.

"Let's go back a step, and I'll show you how this works. Assume your estates are $1,410,000 and $140,000, as shown on the summary I gave you, and that Jim dies first. Under your current will, only the home and contents qualify for the marital deduction, and the balance of Jim's estate is taxable, resulting in a tax of $300,000 after allowing for his $600,000 exemption. Kate's own assets, at her subsequent death, would be the house and her securities, totaling $160,000. Your trust for Kate and the children is not taxed in her estate. Thus, no federal tax on Kate because of her own $600,000 exemption and the fact that a large tax was paid in the first estate."

"We've already decided we don't want Jim's current will," said Kate, "but why any trust?"

"If Jim leaves you his entire estate outright, then you own it all, plus your property. Then at your death it is all taxed in your estate. Assuming no growth in value, the tax on your $1,550,000 would then be about $380,000 at your subsequent death.

"If Jim leaves the $600,000 in a bypass trust for you instead of outright, your estate is only $950,000 and the tax on that is $140,000 instead of the $380,000 if he leaves everything to you outright. *This is a significant saving—$240,000.* Kate, I know you do not like the very idea of a trust but here is what is involved." He ticked off his points on his fingers as he talked.

"You are the sole trustee, you keep the books, invest the assets, make the investment decisions, pay yourself the income. If you want tax-exempt income, you invest in tax exempts. If you want a high income rate, you invest in appropriate securities. If you want growth, you invest in growth stocks. In short, you are the practical owner of the property with one exception: You can withdraw principal only up to 5 percent per year."

"Well, that's no problem," said Kate. "I'd never spend the principal anyway."

"You might need it, Kate, and if you do, you can appoint one of your children, or a bank, as co-trustee, and they can invade principal for you over the 5 percent. If you alone have the power to invade principal over 5 percent, the trust accomplishes little because part will be taxed in your estate."

"Let me show you in dollars and cents how this works." With that, Clay pulled out some sheets of figures he had prepared in anticipation of the meeting. He had worked out three cases to illustrate his point.

Table 20.2 shows how a tax of $296,000 is paid, upfront, at Jim's death. Kate and the children lose the income this amount could have earned them. In contrast, Table 20.3 shows how the payment of the tax is deferred until the death of the survivor (i.e., Kate) and *so that Kate and the children have $296,000 more capital during Kate's lifetime.* A substantial tax is paid at Kate's death even assuming no growth in assets.

In Table 20.4, a formula clause gives Kate outright everything over $600,000 and the $600,000 goes into a tax-free bypass trust for Kate and the children. Table 20.5 compares the three case scenarios.

After studying the figures, Jim nodded in comprehension. "I see what you mean. Just a few different words on a piece of paper and you get a very different tax result. Kate, I think we are almost impelled to accept what Clay says."

Kate nodded in agreement, saying, "Yes, but I want to see that trust, how you have it worded."

Clay replied, "We'll have them ready tomorrow morning, and we can

Table 20.2. Case I: Current Will, Trust for Kate
and Children—Jim Dies First

At Jim's death

Jim's total estate	$1,410,000
Less marital deduction	(70,000)
Taxable	1,340,000
Less exemption	(600,000)
Balance	740,000
Tax	$ 296,000

Later, at Kate's death

Trust for Kate and children ($1,340,000 minus $296,000). This trust *not* taxable in Kate's estate	$1,044,000
Kate's total taxable estate (her assets plus house and personal property)	210,000
Less marital deduction	(0)
Balance	$ 210,000
Less exemption	(600,000)
Balance	0
Tax	$ 0

go over the wording in great detail. Let me say that there is a great deal of flexibility here. We can adapt these principles to almost any specific wording you want."

"It's settled then," said Jim. "We will be here at nine o'clock sharp tomorrow to read and sign. Is there anything else we should discuss?", he asked, looking at his watch.

"Yes, we have to discuss the other two legs of that tripod I spoke about."

Gifts to Children

"The first leg of the tripod was getting your wills in shape. That we will do tomorrow morning. The second leg is a program of gifting growth assets to your children. Your business is expanding very rapidly. The numbers we used reflect current values, but if your principal asset, KJ, is expanding at 15 percent per year, its estate tax value is going to expand at about 15 percent,

Table 20.3. Case II: All to Kate—Jim Dies First

At Jim's death

Jim's total estate	$1,410,000
Less marital deduction (whole estate goes to Kate)	(1,410,000)
Balance	0
Less exemption (not used)	(600,000)
Balance	0
Tax	$ 0

At Kate's death

Kate's total estate (her assets plus Jim's)	$1,550,000
Less marital deduction	(0)
Balance	1,550,000
Less exemption	(600,000)
Balance	950,000
Tax	$ 380,000

Table 20.4. Case III: Proposed Will—$600,000 Bypass Trust for Kate

At Jim's death

Jim's total estate	$1,410,000
Less marital deduction	(810,000)
Balance to bypass trust	600,000
Less exemption	(600,000)
Balance	0
Tax	$ 0

At Kate's death

Kate's own property	$ 140,000
Marital deduction property	810,000
Total estate	950,000
Less marital deduction	(0)
Balance	950,000
Less exemption	(600,000)
Balance	350,000
Tax	$ 140,000

Table 20.5. Summary: Cases I, II, III

	Tax	When paid
Tax with Case I, current will, all in trust for Kate and Children	$296,000	at Jim's death
Tax with Case II, will leaves all to Kate, no trust	$380,000	at Kate's death
Tax with Case III, proposed will, $600,000 bypass trust for Kate, and balance to Kate outright	$140,000	at Kate's death

or more. That means a doubling every five years or so, all of which will eventually be subject to estate taxes before it goes to the next generation. *You are talking about tax rates in the range of 50 percent and up as the business value increases.* Thus, Uncle Sam is a senior partner in your future growth, like it or not."

"Well, I *don't* like it," said Kate. "We are working our butts off to generate income, we pay an income tax on it, and then we have to pay an estate tax, too, on what's left?"

"That's right, Kate. That's why I suggest that gifts to the children start now."

"That's the $10,000 per year we've heard about," said Jim.

"Right, $10,000 per year per child, and you, Jim, can use Kate's $10,000 to give away a total of $20,000 per year to each of your three children. *Thus, over a period of 10 years, you could give away, totally tax-free, a total of $600,000.* Moreover, the increase in value of the gifts, the amount removed from your estate, would far exceed the $600,000.

"If you gave your children $60,000 worth of the KJ business today and it grows at 15 percent per year, the value of their $60,000 interest would be $243,000 in 10 years. Your estate at that point would have been reduced by the $243,000 and thus the potential tax by at least $120,000. That is why a program of consistent giving over a period of years will have a marked estate-tax advantage. As I figure it, if you start with a value of $1 million now and have 15 percent growth, in 10 years you will have given to the children a major share of the company at the rate of $60,000 of gifts per year. Clearly, you should start the annual gift program early on."

Kate never stops thinking, "Then why doesn't Jim give me stock every year, too?"

"That would be a good idea, Kate, but for a different reason. As shown by the examples, the total property belonging to both of you is eventually taxed with one exception. It really does not make any difference which spouse owns it. It is taxed at the death of the survivor in any event.

"The exception I mentioned is the reason why gifts of KJ ownership to Kate would be a good idea. If she dies first, her estate is only $140,000; thus, $460,000 of her $600,000 exemption is 'wasted,' in a sense. If you give her enough to bring her estate up to $600,000, then she can use her $600,000 and create a tax-free trust for you in her will—just like the one I hope you'll have created for her. In summary:

- The gift goes to Kate tax-free because of an unlimited gift-tax marital deduction.

- Similarly, if she dies first, the $600,000 is tax-free in her estate because of the exemption and then skips tax in Jim's estate because it will be in a tax-free trust.

- Moreover, *it is not just the $460,000 which is tax free in the second estate, it is whatever the value of the asset has then grown to; it could be several million dollars.*"

"I like that," said Jim. "That is a real shelter."

Kate said with a wink at Clay, "By the way, what if we should get divorced at some point? Is the stock still mine?"

Clay decided to change the subject so he brought up a little complication. "Your company, KayJim Electronic Devices, is just a proprietorship, at this point. Jim has nothing to split up and give away. He could form a partnership with the children, but that is not very feasible since they are teenagers." Jim admitted that his CPA had many times urged him to incorporate to limit his personal liability and agreed that he would incorporate the business right away so he could start his gift program.

Tax Free Life Insurance Trust

Clay continued, "Bear with me a while longer. I want to put the third part of my tripod framework in place so you can both think about it in the current context.

"If we were talking about a constant value for $1,000,000 for KJ, then the marital-deduction wills plus a program of gifts to the children would be all you need. But that will not be the case if KJ keeps on expanding and prospering. Ten years from now, KJ could easily be worth $5 million or more, and the tax on the survivor's estate would be up in the 50 percent bracket. If you were both to die then the tax on the survivor's estate could easily be in the $3-million range."

"What would happen to our dream of a family company in that case?" asked Kate. "There's no way the business could provide that kind of cash to pay taxes. The children would be forced to sell."

"How do we handle that?" asked Jim.

Clay replied, "The answer is the third leg of my tripod. Let us review the marital deduction rules: If Jim dies first, there is no tax burden because of the marital deduction. Likewise, no tax if Kate dies first because her will will be virtually identical to Jim's. The tax is always going to be on the second estate."

"Yes, I can see that," said Jim, "but what do we do about it?"

"What you do is obtain a policy of joint life, or 'last to die,' life insurance. The policy pays off at the death of the survivor of you two, when the tax is due. Because you have two life expectancies, you get a lower premium rate on the coverage. At your age, forty, the joint life insurance on a straight life basis should cost about $7,300 per year for each million dollars of joint coverage. This would protect the business when it needs it, at the death of whoever dies last. The $7,300 per year is based on a policy that is paid up in 13 years, with no premiums due after that."

"That is really different," said Jim, "but I understand it and like the concept. If I buy the insurance just on my life, I'm overinsuring because my life is not the risk if Kate survives. The risk is if Kate then dies. If Kate dies first, there is no tax either, and the risk is my death. Joe Warren said something about the concept when we discussed my life insurance policy, but he did not want to get into it deeply until he had more facts."

"Now," said Clay, "go one step further with me. If you or Kate, or the company, owns the policy, it will be an asset of your estate, only making the tax problem worse because the proceeds of the policy are taxed in your estate too. What you need is a way to have the policy there and available, but not owned by either of you."

"Then let the children own the policy," said Kate. "We can give them the money to pay the premiums."

"Right on!" said Clay. "That's precisely the idea. I have just one variation on that. Since the children are all minors at this point, I suggest you purchase the policies in irrevocable trusts for the benefit of the children. The trusts are the applicants for the policies and the owners. You contribute to the trusts cash equal to the premiums. The trustee pays the premiums, and the trust is the owner of the policy.

"The beauty of this is that you have a fund of insurance when you need it, free of income tax and estate-tax, and available to the estate of your survivor to pay estate-taxes. The trustee collects the insurance money and either lends it to the estate or buys assets from the estate. For instance, in your case, the trustee would probably buy an interest in KJ from the estate.

"There is only one catch in all this: When you make a gift to the trust to pay the insurance premium, the beneficiary has a right to withdraw it within, say, forty-five days. If not withdrawn in that period, the money stays there forever. What the withdrawal right does is to permit use of your $20,000 annual gift tax exclusions."

"That's not a risk," said Kate. "So forget that, and tell us specifically what you propose."

The Tripod Step-by-Step

Clay said, "Okay, here is my specific proposal for the framework, the plan, I promised:

- "Step One: Each of you sign the marital deduction wills I will prepare for tomorrow. We can meet later and explore the nuances, make changes if need be. But let's not delay in getting the basic wills done.

- "Step Two: Set up three insurance trusts, one for each child. Contribute $7,300 to each trust as a tax-free gift to the child. The trustee will immediately apply for a joint life policy, $1,000,000 of insurance, for each trust. The premium on the policies is $7,300 per year per $1,000,000. This will provide a total of $3,000,000 to pay estate-taxes in the second estate. At the end of about 13 years, under current earning assumption, the policies are all paid up.

- "Step Three: Adopt a program, right now, of giving $12,700 ($20,000 exclusion minus the $7,300 insurance premium) worth of KJ to each child each year. You could put it in the trust, but I'd rather have the stock gifts to the children outright. I say 'stock gifts' because you should incorporate KJ to make giving easier, as well as to limit personal liability. When making a gift of stock, the donee should always sign an agreement restricting the transfer of it, keeping it in the family. But since your children are minors, they can't sign an agreement. A bylaw restriction will have the same effect as an agreement. Thus, the stock can never be transferred out of the family unless you concur."

Jim, Kate, you are a great couple. You have done it right, I can see that. Kay Jim Electronic Devices has been a great success, and you want it to go on. Unfortunately, you have a partner, Uncle Sam, who wants a large cut of the income each year plus at least a 50 percent share of your wealth at each generation. Your business cannot bear that cost. My charts and graphs show that.

"To show you how to handle the problem of family succession of your business, I have mentioned the analogy of a tripod. One leg of the tripod is a correctly drawn marital-deduction will for each of you. This ensures that the 50 percent tax on wealth and value will not be collected until the death of the survivor of the two of you. We did not save the tax on your wealth, but we did postpone it. You have signed the wills I prepared for you. The cost of postponement is that the tax may ultimately be based on a higher value, after years of growth.

"The second leg of the tripod is giving value and growth to the next generation, your children, so it will skip tax in both your estates. You can't give the children shares in the proprietorship business you now have. So you form a corporation with a large enough number of shares so you can give the shares in easily divisible units. Then, if you wish, you and Kate can give each child $20,000 per year of the stock. I have a corporate charter here for you to sign, together with a Subchapter S election form. When you sign this, I'll confer with your CPA about the mechanics of transferring the business to the corporation.

"Finally, the third leg of the tripod: Unless you dispose of KJ at Jim's death, which I don't recommend, you will surely need some cash to pay taxes at the death of the survivor of the two of you. Joint life insurance pays on the death of the second person and is a perfect fit for the situation. You can keep the insurance out of both of your estates by forming tax free insurance trusts for the children. Let's discuss that now."

"I feel better already," said Jim. "That is a simple, coherent plan I can comprehend. Do the documents, and we will be here tomorrow."

That afternoon Clay prepared the required documents: wills for Jim and Kate and three insurance trusts, one for each child. The next morning they reviewed and signed the proposed wills and took home the insurance trusts to study. Jim called Joe Warren, who allowed he just might be able to fit them into his schedule and obtain the $3,000,000 of insurance.

Projecting the Impact of Increasing Business Value

After the meeting to sign the wills, Clay got out his trusty calculator and speculated to himself. "Now let's see. Assume $167,000 of average after-tax income at this point and capitalize that at six times to arrive at a value of $1,000,000 for the business. If you have an earnings record of a 15 percent annual increase for 10 years, the price/earnings ratio will surely be at least 8 to one and if you go on another 10 years at that rate, the price/earnings ratio will be at least 10 to one. Let's see what that does to the value of the business."

So Clay fiddled around with his calculator a while and came up with projections of future values. Then he figured estate-taxes using a 40 percent estate tax rate for the current estate size and a 50 percent rate for the projected larger estate. (Table 20.6 shows his calculations.)

"There," said Clay to himself, "that will explain to Jim why his business won't survive his death unless he does some pretty serious tax and business planning." Then Clay assembled the figures on a graph and gave it all to his secretary to key in and print out for him on the word processor. The graph of future growth and the impact of estate-taxes shows clearly that Uncle Sam is a more than equal partner in Jim and Kate's future success. Uncle Sam not only takes a percentage of increased book value, but of market value based on an increasing earnings multiple. Clay faxed Table 20.6 to Jim and Kate so they could review it before the next meeting.

The start of the Tuesday meeting was not a pleasant one for Jim Wolczk. It was then he reviewed Clay's figures and became really aware of his

Table 20.6. Wolczk Family Tax Projections

	Now	10 Years	20 Years	30 Years
Average income* after tax	$ 167,000	$ 930,000	$ 3,760,000	$ 15,200,000
Price/earnings** multiple	6	8	10	12
Tentative estate tax value	$1,000,000	$7,440,000	$37,600,000	$182,400,000
Estate-tax rate	40%	50%	50%	50%
Estimate of estate tax liability	$ 400,000	$3,720,000	$18,800,000	$ 91,200,000
Years of income to pay tax	2.4 years	4.0 years	5.0 years	6.0 years

*Average income, after corporate tax on a weighted (5,4,3,2,1) basis.
**Note that this multiple increases with the history of earnings growth.

partnership with Uncle Sam. "You mean to tell me that every after-tax dollar of value that I create is going to be taxed at over 50 percent? Why am I working so hard, only to hand it all over to the government? There's no way the company could devote four or five years of earnings to pay estate taxes. Reinvestment would stop. Growth would stop. We'd be eating next year's seed corn." His voice rose as he talked.

Kate thought she had better pour some oil on the troubled waters. "Jim, I want you to sit here and hear Clay out. Clay, it's clear to me that the Wolczk family has a problem, and we need your help to solve it. So please tell us what to do."

"Okay. Let's back up," said Clay. "For KJ Electronics, as you look at it over the long term, estate taxes are a cost of operations, just like inventory use, utilities, research, income taxes, and the like. Suppose your annual income statement looked like Table 20.7. You would certainly deal with that $90,000 tax item as a very important cost."

"I sure would," said Jim. "Anything that lops off half of my after-tax profit is a big item. But to be fair, shouldn't you use the present value of the future estate-tax cost? Realistically the figure is much smaller, though I appreciate your outlook on this."

"You are right, Jim. The income tax cost of $120,000 is right there because you incur it now, and we certainly hope the estate tax won't be due for decades. If you were an insurance company, you would present-value the estate tax, based on the joint life expectancy of yourself and Kate. But let's go back to the chart and graph I faxed to your office. They represent the personal balance sheet of you both at the moment of death of your survivor.

Table 20.7. Sample Annual Income Statement

Net sales	$1,000,000
Cost of sales	(500,000)
Gross profit	500,000
Other expenses	(200,000)
Profit before tax	300,000
Income tax	(120,000)
Profit after income tax	180,000
Estimated amount of estate tax on the growth in your estate	(90,000)
Net income benefit after all taxes	$ 90,000

You don't know when that moment will occur. An insurance company that has tens of thousands of lives to consider can afford to spread risks over a given life expectancy.

"But you, deeply concerned with the succession of your business, cannot afford to think like actuaries. Since you don't know when death will occur, you have to be prepared for it at this instant, next month, next year, and 20 years from now. Conversely, you also have to think in terms of 30 or 40 years from now as being a reasonable life expectancy of your survivor, of a couple in their early forties."

Assessing the Cost of Tax-Sheltered Life Insurance

"We would like to know how much the joint insurance costs," said Kate. "Right now, all our spare cash is being reinvested in the business."

"I have some figures on that, which I received yesterday from your insurance agent, Joe Warren." Clay handed each of them a sheet of paper showing the current cost per $1,000,000 of last to die life insurance at varying ages:

Age	Annual Premiums
40	$ 7,300
45	$ 9,600
50	$12,600
55	$16,600
60	$22,100

"These figures assume you are about the same age and in good heath. I have given you extended data because you can keep adding insurance as the projected value of the business goes up. Joe Warren tells me that the rates quoted assume that the insurance will be all paid up in 13 years or so. This fits right in with adding more insurance as time goes on."

"Aha!" said Jim. "What you are saying is that we can get $3,000,000 of insurance now at a cost of $21,900 per year for 13 years. Then, when that's paid up, add another $3,000,000 at a cost of about $40,000 per year for a further 13 years. This gives us a total of $6,000,000 cash for estate-taxes which is not in our estate."

"Exactly," said Clay, feeling he was at least making some headway.

"Do we have to deal just with Joe Warren's company?" asked Kate.

"No, of course not," said Clay. "Joe is your insurance broker, and a good one, but that doesn't mean you have to buy only through his company. You should ask him to get quotes from two other companies—but be sure that the quoted terms are exactly comparable. A small change in assumptions or policy provisions can make a big difference. There's a lot of judgment involved here. That's why you need someone like Joe; life insurance is not a commodity you can buy off the rack. In effect, you need a tailor-made suit."

They conferred for the next hour, reading the draft insurance trust line-by-line. Clay proposed three separate trusts, one for each child. Each trust would purchase $1,000,000 of insurance on the lives of Kate and Jim. They would contribute $7,300 per year to each trust to pay the premium. In order to use the annual gift tax exclusions, the child would have a forty-five-day option to withdraw the $7,300. (If a child did actually do that, Jim and Kate would simply stop any gifts thereafter.)

Since Jim and Kate have a total of $20,000 they can give to each child each year, the remaining $12,700 can be used to make annual gifts of KJ stock to each child.

The trust really remains dormant, except for the premium transactions, until Jim and Kate both die. At that point, the trustees may collect the insurance proceeds and use the money to provide liquid cash to the estate to pay taxes. This could be accomplished by purchasing assets from the estate at the value arrived at for estate-tax purposes, or by lending funds to the estate to pay taxes.

"The beauty of all this is that the premiums paid and the policy proceeds are free of gift or estate-tax for both of you." Clay pointed out. "We started with the objective of planning for the *succession* of your business in the event of death. No one tool will achieve that. Hence my reference to a tripod needed to solve the tax and liquidity problem that might result in a forced sale of the business." "All right, let's do it," said Jim, convinced at last.

Clay decided to bring up another subject. "Now that you have accepted my tripod, there are some nontax aspects of business succession that I have to discuss with you. Let's get together again next week."

Determining Business Management Succession

On Monday morning Jim, Kate, and Clay met to continue their discussions. Jim started by giving a complete and accurate résumé of all Clay's advice. He recounted why they each had signed marital-deduction wills, carving out $600,000 tax-free trusts. He handed Clay a signed and notarized charter of the proposed Kay Jim Electronic Devices, Inc. for immediate filing. He signed Clay's form stock power assigning 60,000 nonvoting shares, out of 1,000,000 total shares, to the children.

Clay and Kate had just assumed that the balance of the 1,000,000 shares would be assigned to Jim, who had owned KJ as a sole proprietor. Instead, Jim produced his own typed stock power, assigning half the remaining voting and nonvoting stock to Kate. Table 20.8 shows assignment of starting stock ownership.

Kate arched an eyebrow as she looked at Jim. "Thanks for the present, Jim."

"Thanks, nothing." said Jim. "This was yours from the start. We are fifty-fifty partners and always will be."

"Ahem!" said Clay. "Jim, you were giving a very good summary of the planning tripod. Why don't you continue."

"Well, the third leg of your tripod is the insurance trust. That, to me, is a good idea. Pay the premiums free of gift tax, then the proceeds skip both our estates for estate-tax purposes. Yet the money is available for estate needs at the right time. By the way, Clay, can we deduct the premiums in any way?" Jim asked.

"Nope. Sorry." said Clay. "Premiums on life insurance are not deductible even if paid by the corporation. That is one loophole Congress closed years ago."

"Well, we have our tripod now, said Kate. "What next?"

"As Jim has reminded me, our purpose here is succession planning, not tax avoidance. The tripod is based on tax principles: saving taxes through

Table 20.8. Assignment of Stock Ownership in KayJim Electronic Devices, Inc.

	Class A Voting Shares	Class B Nonvoting Shares
Jim	50,000	420,000
Kate	50,000	420,000
Molly	0	20,000
Jim, Jr.	0	20,000
Maureen	0	20,000
	100,000	900,000

correct wills, and by a gift program, and providing tax liquidity by means of last to die life insurance in a tax-free trust. That is part of succession planning, but not the whole of it. The other part is what happens to the business when the leader dies or is disabled. Without that leader, a good business will tick on for a while under its own momentum—but eventually it will stray off course or lose speed or even stagger drunkenly. I've seen it happen."

"So have I," said Jim. "Several of my best competitors lost their founders recently and it wasn't pleasant to see what happened. Without any initiative on my part, customers started switching over to KJ. They even called me to ask what was going on at the other companies." He paused, almost imperceptibly. "Frankly, I have always considered myself to be immortal, but some things have happened that have called that into question. Clay, what should we do? What if I die?"

Clay started, "Well, there are three basic procedures that I . . ."

"Another tripod?" Jim asked, "Do you think only in threes?" They all had a laugh at this, but Clay responded, "I really didn't think in terms of another tripod, but I guess you're right," said Clay. Here is my second tripod, if you want to call it that. It is less dramatic, in terms of dollars, than my first tripod but no less important:

- A succession plan for top executive management if Jim should die;
- An effective board of directors, comprised in large part of independent people who are not family or employees; and
- Provision for the disability of Jim or successive top management.

Succession Planning. "Obviously, the first line of defense is backup leadership. That's nice for a lawyer to say, but more difficult for a business to achieve."

Jim nodded in agreement. "I know I can't run a one-person show forever, and I've been talking to a headhunter as well as looking into the ranks. Kate and I need help even now."

"Thanks, Clay," said Kate, "for bringing this into focus for us. KJ is so much a part of our lives now that I want it to go on beyond us. I used to write the checks and keep the books, such as they were, but now it's all being done by computers—computers even sign the checks for us. Now I help some with the personnel, but sometimes I wish I was back keeping the books again." Clay was beginning to see that the loss of Kate would be as traumatic to the business as the loss of Jim. If something happened to Kate, Jim would be there physically, but not the same Jim that sat before him. Clay began to feel his three points were rather trite but continued nevertheless. "Well, anyway, the first point is that succession is based on having the right personnel there in case something happens to one of you."

Establishing an Effective Board of Directors. "I've been speaking about management leadership, but there's another thing that you bring to

KJ, and that's policy guidance, direction. The best insurance against an untimely death of one or both of you is a good independent board of directors who know the business in general and would be available to continue its direction, provide stability. Someone needs to appoint a new CEO, make major decisions as to the form succession is to take. Will that form be a continuation of the business stand-alone with family ownership and nonrelated management? Or a continuation by means of a sale or merger, combining with another business? A new CEO or president can't make that decision for the family and run the business at the same time.

"For openers, Kate and you, Jim, must be on the board of directors. Then you should select, say, three good experienced business people to serve with you. Get them on board now. Get them oriented. Pay them $500, or $1,000, or whatever, for periodic meetings. I'd say bimonthly at first. Later you can go to quarterly meetings, but no less frequent than that."

"Aren't directors concerned about liability?" said Jim. "Yes, they are," said Clay, "and that's why the corporate charter you just signed, and the bylaws you just approved, contain provisions that exonerate and indemnify the directors against liability except for out-and-out stealing or something like that."

"You may have some trouble getting good directors, but start now. A year from now, or two or three, and you'll have things in place. That's succession planning. Plan long for the long term."

Kate spoke at once, "Clay, you are our first choice for director, and you're elected right now," she said.

Jim concurred. "Yes, that's a given. Clay, I have a feeling right now that you are a friend of mine, and I want you on our board."

After a long moment, then Clay answered. "This is very difficult to say. As your lawyer, I should not be on the board. I can't have both jobs at once and do right for you, my friends." His eyes met Jim's. "While it's unlikely ever to happen, there could come a day when as a lawyer I would have to give you advice that a director, as a participant, could not. I might have to tell you and Kate that you are absolutely wrong or that you cannot do this or that. As your lawyer, I'd do it and damn the consequences. As a director, I might be impelled in the other direction, I'd be part of the problem."

Jim looked unconvinced, so Clay elaborated.

"Jim, you need my independence. You need your ability to fire me in an instant. I need the ability to resign in an instant. Believe me, I am more valuable to you, if at all, in that capacity. If you insist on my being a director, I'll do it, but you will then have to get another lawyer."

"I see, I see," relented Jim. "You're right, of course."

Kate nodded. "We understand," she said. "We'll get the directors."

Planning for the Disability of the Company Principals. "Let's move on from that one" said Clay. "There is one final thing you need to do. If one of you becomes totally disabled, physically or mentally, the other needs to take over. The way to do this is with a Power of Attorney, Living Wills, and a Health Care Proxy." Clay handed them forms to look at. "In the Power of Attorney, each of you gives the other the right to handle financial transactions. In the Health Care Proxies you give the power to make medical decisions if the other is incapable of doing so. The living will is a statement of your wishes for care if you should become incurably mentally incapacitated."

Jim wanted to sign them, then and there, but Kate, more cautious, wanted to take them back to the office and read them carefully. Kate won.

Summary of the Succession Plan's Impact

In terms of succession planning, what have Jim and Kate accomplished?

Clay liked to use for himself a 10- or 15-year span to measure the value of estate-planning measures. In other words, he would assume that both spouses had died by the end of that period. Allowing for anticipated growth in values, he would then ask what the estate-tax then would be with his recommendation and then without. Table 20.9 shows his calculations in the Wolczk's case.

It is easy to see that Clay's tripod program "works" in the sense of reducing tax and providing enough cash within the reasonably forecast boundaries used. The limitation here is, of course, time. When will the survivor of Jim and Kate die? The longer the growth period, the greater the tax burden.

As shown by the preceding data, the earnings of the business with 15 percent growth double in a little over five years. (Use the "rule of 72": Divide the percentage growth rate into 72; the resulting figure in years is the time it takes the original amount of value to double.) Not only would earnings be doubling, but an appraiser would surely use a higher price/earnings ratio to value the business.

Conceivably, Clay would now "plan" for a whole generation of growth, but does that make sense? Is the starting data that good? Forecasting the state of facts and tax law even 10 years from now is very tenuous; beyond that, it is almost impossible.

Clay had done a good job for his new clients, new friends. The financial context had been addressed with

- correct marital deduction wills,
- start of a lifetime gift program, and
- the double tax-free insurance trust.

The management and personal needs of business succession had not been "solved" in several short meetings, but

- the installation of an expert board of directors was under way,

Table 20.9. Calculation of Estimated Benefit on Death of Survivor of Jim and Kate, at End of Ten Years, First Spouse Having Died after Five Years

	No Gifts to Children, No Insurance Trust	With Gifts to Children of Stock, and Insurance Trust
Total value of business after ten years growth at 15% growth rate	$ 7,400,000	$7,400,000
Estimated value of other assets	1,500,000	1,500,000
Total	8,900,000	8,900,000
Less $600,000 bypass trust and growth thereon in first spouse's estate	(1,200,000)	(1,200,000)
Balance	7,700,000	7,700,000
Less value of stock given to children	(0)	(2,560,000)
Total estate, second spouse	7,700,000	5,140,000
Less exemption, second spouse	(600,000)	(600,000)
Balance of second spouse's estate	7,100,000	4,540,000
Tax, second spouse	$ 3,550,000	$2,270,000
Cash available in insurance trust	$ 0	$3,000,000
Other assets if liquidated to raise cash	1,500,000	1,500,000
Total assets available for tax needs*	$ 1,500,000	$4,500,000
Total taxes (see above)	(3,550,000)	(2,270,000)
(Deficit)/excess of other than KJ assets	$(2,050,000)	$2,230,000

*Excluding the KJ business.

- a policy of management continuation had been adopted and its implementation had been started, and
- the disability eventuality had been addressed by health care proxies, powers of attorney, and a review of the Wolczk family's medical and disability insurance coverage.

These are the two "tripods" that were subject of the friendly jokes between Clay, Jim, and Kate.

21

The Business as "Star Performer": 10 Years Later

We now meet Kate and Jim 10 years later. They are 50 years old and the business value has increased greatly. "Well, here we go again, Clay. What do you have in store for us this time around?" said Jim. Ten years ago a rather tense stranger, Clay was now a relaxed old friend of Jim and Kate.

"Here is where we are. You know it all generally, but this will bring you right up to date. KJ's earnings on an after-tax basis were $1,100,000 last year, and the weighted five-year average you like comes to $930,000 per year. Since we are still an S corporation, our comptroller reduced $1,840,000 of before-tax profits by an assumed corporate tax of 40 percent to arrive at those after-tax figures."

"Our book value was $7,170,000 last December 31 . . . but that's a joke. We recently had two computer giants bidding to acquire us, but we turned them down."

"Your darn right we did," said Kate. "We turned down $15 million cash for the plain and simple reason that I don't want Jim around under my feet at home all day. Besides, we both love the company and all it means. We have brought KJ to the point where we feel comfortable going away two successive weekends. We want to have our cake and eat it, too. In short, we want to continue to possess KJ and, in addition, enjoy ourselves."

Jim chimed in. "We are here because we still want KJ to stay in the family in case something happens to Kate and me. Actually, the only reason I even talked to the two computer companies was to get an idea of what we were really worth . . . not the depressing figures Clay uses."

"Jim," Clay interrupted, "*please* don't bandy those sales figures around too much. If we ever have a valuation problem for tax purposes, the IRS would have a field day with that information."

"Don't worry, pal, it was all verbal. Those guys understood when I told them I didn't want anything in writing. Both company CEOs said they understood why I want to keep the business, but that if we ever have an estate-tax problem you could call on them."

"Yes, that's right now," said Clay. "At this particular point, KJ may be a very desirable acquisition for them. A special-situation value. But estate-tax and gift-tax value is something quite different. It presupposes a willing buyer having no compulsion to buy and a willing seller having no compulsion to sell. Not a special situation. The tax law and regulations do not ask us to hypothesize a special-circumstance sale of the whole company to a buyer in the same business. Rather, valuation is done by analogy to the value of comparable companies that have a public market for their stock. This gives a more fair and predictable basis for valuation than what some CEO told you on a given day last month, reflecting the needs and policies of his or her company at that time.

"Furthermore, my friend, you will usually come up with a lower value using the IRS-approved valuation procedures. You'll notice that the figures I use are a lot lower than the $15 million you mention. I don't want to unduly flatter you, but that offering figure also includes you. If you are deceased, we have a different ball game."

Assessing the Assets of the Wolczk Estate
After 10 Years' Growth

"Let's turn to assets, now," said Clay. "You indicated that your weighted five-year average earnings comes to $930,000, which spells an incredible success story. But, as we have discussed many times, the downside is the taxes owed at the death of your survivor. For purposes of this discussion we will work with current values, but always keep in mind that we are really talking about the additional tax on future growth.

"Let's assume KJ overall is worth eight times average earnings, for openers. We could talk about premiums and discounts, but I'd rather err on the side of a high value. Eight times earnings yields a value of $7,440,000 for KJ. How much have you given away to the children?"

"Not that much, I'm afraid," said Jim. "The annual gift program you recommended ten years ago kind of fell by the wayside. Remember, we were putting $7,300 cash every year into each child's insurance trust? I guess, emotionally, I felt that was enough."

I understand," said Clay. "And as a matter of fact, if you had to choose between gifts of stock or the insurance trust, you selected the right one. In terms of estate-tax liquidity, the joint life insurance in a trust has a much higher leverage factor than gifts of stock.

"But now the stock is worth, say, $7.44 per share, which means that this year you could give away only 8,065 shares to the three children ($60,000 divided by $7.44 per share). This is only 0.8 percent of the company. The greatest value of the annual gift program was in the very early stages." He pauses, then switched tacks. "Just to fill out the picture, can you give me approximate values of your other assets?"

Jim and Kate were prepared for this question and produced a prepared schedule. The overall value of their estate is shown in Table 21.1.

Clay pointed out that even allowing for the two $600,000 exemptions, *the total estate tax would be in the order of $3,900,000*, assuming no further growth in the company's value. Kate and Jim quickly grasped that this was more than the tax-free insurance proceeds that would be available to the three childrens' trusts!

"Now, let's get down to work," said Clay. "I have some recommendations for you, plus some options. I am going to keep to our agreed focus: your wish that if Jim dies, the business will remain in the family as long as Kate or the children want. No forced sale to pay taxes.

"The wills you have are perfectly adequate. They each incorporate the $600,000 double exempt bypass trust and leave the balance of the estate to the other spouse. This means, Jim, that *if you die now, your entire $4,560,000 estate goes virtually tax free*. The first $600,000 goes to the bypass trust, which skips tax in your estate as well as Kate's, and the balance of $3,960,000 goes to Kate outright. You could use a marital trust for Kate's share, but I see no need for that here."

"Okay," said Jim, "What next? If I die, I do not want the business sold because of lack of management. If something happens to me and Kate, I don't want the business sold because of taxes. Period."

Table 21.1. Jim and Kate: Assets Ten Years Later

Asset	Jim	Kate	Joint	Total
KJ stock	$3,700,000	$3,700,000	$ 0	$7,400,000
Residence (net)			200,000	200,000
Summer residence (net)			150,000	150,000
Securities & cash	50,000	150,000	200,000	400,000
Life insurance-term	400,000			400,000
Life insurance-split dollar	100,000			100,000
Cars & other assets	10,000	40,000		50,000
Employee benefit plans	300,000	100,000		400,000
Totals	$4,560,000	$3,990,000	$550,000	$9,100,000

"At least," said Kate, "we don't want me or the children to be forced to sell for one of the reasons Jim mentioned. At some point it might be sold or merged because that was the right business judgment at the time. But we don't want the decision forced on us."

"As usual, Kate said it best," said Jim. "Now that we have the issue before us, tell us what to do."

Clay knew he had their full attention at this point. "Let's go back to our first meeting or two."

Clay reminded them how the marital deduction works:

- There is no tax on the estate of the first to die.

- All the remaining property, except the first spouse's bypass trust, is subject to tax in the second estate.

- The estate is taxed at the then value, including all growth in value to the second death.

Understanding the Need for Additional Insurance— to Pay Estate Taxes

"Since the tax needs occur at the death of the surviving spouse, you need insurance to cover that event: last-to-die insurance. This is the $3,000,000 policy that you decided to get 10 years ago. You put the insurance in three tax-free trusts, one for each child. Thus, when the insurance proceeds are needed to pay taxes, they are available tax-free." Clay pointed out that the insurance had "cost" Jim and Kate $21,900 per year for ten years and was now almost fully paid up (besting their insurance broker's original projection of being paid up in thirteen years). "Cost" for the insurance is a relative word. Actually, the three paid-up policies now had a total paid-up cash value well in excess of the $219,000 laid out over the past ten years. So the "cost" was really an investment, assuming care was taken to select a financially sound insurance company.

"Now," Clay said, "since the business is doing well and you have the money, I recommend that you purchase three new policies. Since you are now 10 years older, three additional one-million-dollar policies would cost you about $39,000 per year, or $12,600 per million, on the basis that the policy will be all paid for in about 13 years. *Then your estates will have a total of $6 million of tax-free cash to pay estate taxes.*"

"The next thing you need to do is have an agreement that the company will redeem stock from your estate, if need be, to pay estate taxes and administration expenses. . . ."

"Whoa!" said Jim. "Clay, you have been telling me for all of 10 years that I can't redeem stock, go back to my own company no less, without being taxed on part of the proceeds. You always said, 'Take it out as a deductible bonus, instead.' Now you're telling me just the opposite."

"If you die and need big money for estate taxes, you cannot take it out as compensation because you're dead at that point." Clay smiled at his own joke.

He went on. "If you die, remember that your estate gets a new tax basis for the stock equal to its estate-tax value. Let's assume that is $7.44 per share. The estate can sell stock back to the company to raise funds for federal and state estate taxes and administration expenses. There is no taxable gain because the cost basis equals the sales price. If the cash needed for taxes and expenses were, say, $3,000,000, the estate could redeem back 403,000 shares at $7.44 and pay no income tax. In addition, because KJ is an S Corporation, it could declare a large tax-free dividend up to the amount of your share of corporate earned surplus (your AAA account)."

"Why are we paying for all that insurance if it's as easy as that?" said Kate. "I don't mind spending $39,000 a year for our children and the company, but only if it is necessary. The company could generate the $3,000,000 if need be."

"The answer is," said Clay, "that we are here using figures as illustrations, but we have no idea, really, of how good the figures are. We can't rely on my illustrations to set a policy. The $7.4 million value, based on eight times average earnings, is probably in the ballpark now, and either the redemption, or the tax-free dividend, or the insurance would fund the taxes. If Jim died now and you died five years later, the tax figure could be much greater due to growth, but then the company could be in a financial bind because of Jim's absence from the helm or some other reason. The redemption might cause real financing problems to the company. *The present $3 million of insurance might be inadequate at the time and the company might be unable to pay out the cash needed for taxes and expenses.*

"We are now talking about increasing your insurance from $3 million to $6 million, and, on the basis of current value, that seems to be more than enough. But, we must continually monitor things to keep the insurance amount up to date, adequate."

"I get the drift," said Kate. "We are dealing here with uncertainty. The business, now, is worth $7.4 million, give or take 2 or 3 million each way at the extreme. If Jim and I were considerate enough to die right now, the $6 million in the trust would take care of the problem under even an extreme assumption as to value.

Kate continued, "But the estate-tax is on the last to die. That could be next week, in some kind of common disaster, or it could be thirty or forty years from now when the last of us totters off to our maker, or it could be anywhere in between. The business is worth a couple of million now, could be worth zillions then."

"Yes, Kate," said practical Jim, "and it could be worth zip, too."

Clay broke back into his own sermon. "Yes, Jim, and if it is worth zip, the paid up insurance trust will provide a substantial estate for your children. So, really, the insurance provides for a couple of risks, doesn't it?" Jim had to nod agreement.

"Now, let us go back and recap what we have discovered. You need some minor changes to your wills. You need to have agreements and a change of corporate by-laws to provide for the redemption of stock, if needed, to pay estate-taxes.

"Finally, you have decided to increase the insurance in the children's trusts from $3 million to $6 million total. This will cost you $17,000 a year more than you are now paying to the trusts."

Jim broke in at this point. "I have to say I'm bothered, in principle, by the extra insurance. Paying $39,000 a year for 10 to 12 years to get an extra $3 million of insurance seems okay, but where does it all end? As Kate and I get older, two things are going to happen. The first is that insurance will get more expensive and the second is that the business grows more valuable. Let's say we do all this again when we are 60 and the business is then worth $20 million and rising (we hope).

"According to Joe Warren's figures, at age 60, the insurance would cost $22,000 per million of coverage. So that's $66,000 per year for another $3 million. But our own figures show that won't cover the taxes on the projected future increases. Furthermore, I or both of us may not be insurable . . . or else insurable only at extra high rates. In short, why don't I just give KJ to the insurance company now and save everyone a lot of time and effort? I know this is a rhetorical question and I am going to get the extra insurance now, but I have to ask the question."

"That is a perfectly fair and valid question," said Clay. "The fact is that any technique I can talk about today has serious limitations if we are talking about long-distance estate taxes on a rapidly expanding business—a moving target. The $39,000 per year for another $3 million of insurance is based on the fact that the insurance will be entirely paid for in about 13 years. Even if your survivor lives to be 100 years old, after 13 years there is no further payment. That is a conservative, prudent way to do things at this time."

How to Reduce the Cost of Survivor Insurance

Clay added: "If you want pure insurance protection on a joint life basis you can use insurance that never becomes paid up, where the premiums go on year after year until both of you die. On this basis, you could get $10 million of joint life coverage for about $45,000 per year. Here are some schedules Joe Warren sent me. Before you jump at the bargain, though, be sure to talk to Joe about it."

Table 21.2 showed Jim and Kate that they could, at this point, purchase

Table 21.2. Compare Types of Insurance

Policy	When Paid Up	Premium per Year	Assume Paid Over	Assumed Total Payments of Premium	Assumed Total Payments with Interest
$ 3,000,000	13 years	$39,000	13 years	$ 507,000	$ 7,332,000*
$10,000,000	Never	$45,000	40 years	$1,800,000	$12,590,000

*Assume premium payments for thirteen years, after which the amount accumulates at 8 percent for 27 additional years.

a "last to die" insurance policy for $10 million at a cost of about $45,000 per year if the cost would go on until Jim and Kate both died. By contrast, the $3 million policy they had been discussing would cost $39,000 per year and would be all paid up at the end of about 13 years. If the survivor of Jim and Kate as of age 50 lives another 40 years (a likely possibility), the total payments on each policy, assuming earnings at 8 percent, would have accumulated considerably over 27 additional years.

Jim studied the figures carefully. "What this illustrates is that in terms of protection, it is better to pay $45,000 per year over 40 years for $10 million of insurance than $39,000 per year over 13 years for $3 million of insurance if you have the resources to pay every year for a long, long time. I will have to see Joe Warren about this."

Clay nodded in agreement. "Yes, be sure to see Joe. My calculations are very simplistic, and actual insurance results are based on dividend and earnings rates and other economic factors. For instance, dividends on the $3 million policy can be used to purchase more insurance coverage, and at death the value of that policy could well be in excess of the $3 million. It's a judgment matter for expert insurance professionals. All I want to do now is alert you to the fact that the premiums on the "last to die" insurance can be reduced if the payments are made over a longer period. This, in concept, allows you to purchase more insurance now for the same dollars. It also allows you to cram more premium gifts within the allowable $20,000 per year per child. So your next stop is a visit to Joe Warren."

How to Retain Key Employees to Facilitate Management Succession Planning

"Now," said Clay, "is there anything you have on your minds that we should discuss?"

Jim replied, "Well, yes, there is. Remember Bob Lewis, who came on board about 10 years ago as sales manager? He is now our executive vice president and manager of operations, production, and sales. Last year, he made over $400,000 in salary and bonuses, and well worth all of it. One of the computer companies I mentioned has been talking to Bob (with my permission). They have offered him a starting salary and guaranteed bonuses of $300,000 per year, plus incentive stock plans that could make him millions in a few years—if all goes well.

"Bob has already declined the offer. He said he did not want to move to Irvine, California, in any event. But he was frank to tell me his fondest dream was to own a piece of KJ, even if he could never sell it publicly. I think he was quite sincere about it. I told him he could set his own salary to any level he wants, make more than Kate and me, and that's okay. His answer was that he had more than enough money now for a bachelor, and he wanted a piece of KJ, which he would of course agree to sell back at his termination, retirement, disability, or death. He had it all thought out, as Bob would. That's him. A rare combination, thinker and doer and nice guy. I would like to meet his request if at all possible."

Fortunately Clay was familiar with the concepts of making stock available to key employees. He summarized the basic rules:

- If stock is issued to an employee at less than full value, the difference between the value and what the employee paid is income to the employee. If the stock is just "given" to the employee for no consideration, the whole value is income to the employee.

- The employer, KJ, has a deduction in the same amount that the employee reports as income. The employer thus gets a real tax deduction for just transferring "paper" (equity stock) to the employee.

- The employer's cash tax benefit from this tax deduction enables it to reimburse the employee for his or her tax, and still come out ahead.

To illustrate, suppose KJ issues $100,000 worth of its stock to Bob Lewis as compensation, a bonus. Bob reports $100,000 as income and pays a tax of $28,000. The employer, KJ, deducts the value of the stock and has a cash tax benefit of $34,000. Then the employer, instead of pocketing the $34,000 cash benefit, gives it to Bob Lewis as a bonus so he can pay his $28,000 tax. (This assumes for illustration that the employer is at a 34 percent tax rate and the employee 28 percent.)

But Bob also owes a tax on the $34,000, and the employer has a further deduction for the $34,000 paid out. If they keep doing this until they reach zero, the ultimate result is that Bob can own the shares tax-free and the company is a little ahead in cash (given the assumed tax bracket).

What has this to do with succession planning? Answer: Everything! If the founder-CEO dies or is disabled, excellent people are needed if the business is to continue. The best way to attract and bind these people is to give them an equity interest contingent on their staying aboard. Thus, some employers use options or plans that vest the stock ratably over a period of 5 to 10 years. And they keep issuing more stock each year so that the vesting period always is running as to some stock. (*Two warnings here:* the compensation must be "reasonable" in amount by IRS rules and, with a Subchapter S corporation, care must be taken that the stock options or restrictions do not cause loss of Subchapter S status. Further, the income tax impact on Bob and the Company has to be carefully worked out.)

Planning an Estate "Freeze" for KJ

"Let's go on to another tax-saving device, the so-called freeze," said Clay. "The need for a freeze concept," he continued, "is well demonstrated by the discussion of increasing future values. You have a company with a 15-year history of growth that averages out to about 15 percent per year compounded. Thus, it doubles in value about every five years. Over your joint life expectancy you are talking about a huge value and a totally unpayable tax. The company may not be able to support it if all trends continue.

"Over the years, the so-called freeze evolved as an important tool to rectify this kind of situation. It went like this: Take a company worth $5 million owned by one person. The owner would have the company recapitalize and issue new stock (tax-free) as follows:

8% noncumulative, nonvoting preferred stock, par value of	$4,900,000
9,000 shares of $10 par nonvoting common stock, class B	90,000
1,000 shares of $10 par voting common stock, class A	10,000
Total Value of Stock	$5,000,000

"Then the owner would give all of the 9,000 shares of class B nonvoting common and 490 shares of the class A voting stock to his children or trust for his issue. He would keep all the preferred and 510 shares (51 percent) of the voting class A common. A gift tax return would be filed reporting the $94,900 gift, which the IRS would probably never audit.

"Demonstrably, most of the future growth of that company would be reflected in the equity value of the 9000 shares of B common and the 490 shares of A common that were given away. The original owner would retain the control through his 51 percent of the A stock. Then over the years he could chip away at the preferred stock, reducing it by further gifts to his descendants. A dividend would never be paid on the preferred. Eventually, most of the preferred stock would be redeemed to pay estate-taxes.

"Truly, the owner had frozen, or locked in, the $4,900,000 value of the preferred plus whatever the few shares of A common were worth. The future gift of even a few shares of the A common would bring ownership below 50 percent and eliminate any IRS argument of a 'control premium'."

"Say, I like that," said Jim, so excited he couldn't sit still. "Let's do that right now."

"Sorry," said Clay, "I was telling you ancient history to bring out the concept of a freeze. The laws and rulings now tell us we can't do just that, but there are some things you can do, using the same concept. Let me list five freeze possibilities, and then I'll talk about them in detail." He handed Kate and Jim copies of the following list:

(1) Preferred stock, if dividends are paid

(2) Sale of S Corporation stock to children

(3) Gift of $1.2 million stock now

(4) Leasing partnership for children

(5) Family ownership of new ventures

Issue Preferred Stock if Dividends Are Paid

"Before you sign on the dotted line, Jim, let me tell you that you can still do a form of preferred-stock freeze—with benefit—but the cost is that you lose your Subchapter S status. You can't elect Subchapter S if you have preferred stock.

"Let me explain how the preferred-stock freeze works now. In the illustration I gave you a minute ago, in the good old days the owner of the business would never pay a dividend on the preferred stock. Under the old rules, the freeze was thus based on an artificially high value for the retained preferred and resulting low value of the gifted common. Now, under the new rules, the tax law says that the preferred stock is valued on the basis of the dividends to be paid. The preferred-stock value is subtracted from the overall value of the company, which is established by expert appraisal; the balance is the value of the common stock, part of which is given to the children. Moreover, the dividends must be paid or a penalty is exacted.

"Let me show you how this works: Assume that an appraisal by an expert confirms that KJ is worth $7,400,000, and KJ issues 68 percent of that value in new 10 percent cumulative preferred stock, which the expert values at par for tax purposes. That represents $5,000,000 of the total value. The remaining $2,400,000 of value, one million shares at $2.40 per share, remains in the common stock, as follows:

Total company appraised value	$7,400,000
Less appraised value of preferred stock	(5,000,000)
Common stock balance, 1 million shares	$2,400,000

You then give common stock to your three children, shown in Table 21.3.

Table 21.3. Illustration of Preferred Stock Freeze/Gift

	Scenario #1	Scenario #2
Total gift of common stock	$2,400,000	$1,260,000
Less annual exclusions	(60,000)	(60,000)
	2,340,000	1,200,000
Less use of "exemptions"	(1,200,000)	(1,200,000)
Taxable gift	1,140,000	0
Federal tax at 50%	570,000	0
Future growth owned by children	100%	53%

Thus, in one fell swoop, you would have given to the children all or a large share of the future growth of the company because value growth is all in the common stock. The $5,000,000 of preferred stock does not grow in value; it's "frozen" because, except to the extent of dividends, it does not share in future profits or growth of KJ. The preferred stock dividend is fixed and it must be paid at all costs. If you are willing to pay a large gift tax upfront, you can give away all future growth.

"Clay, what are you talking about? You told me a few minutes ago that the law has been changed so you can't do that with preferred stock now."

"The catch is this, Jim," said Clay. "Prior to 1988, people would issue the preferred stock and then, somewhere along the line, stop paying the dividends. Thus, they could "freeze" their estate at little or no cost. Now the rule is that the preferred stock must receive a dividend each year, or the IRS will include the sum of the unpaid dividend plus interest in the owner's estate. If KJ were a C Corporation, *the extra income tax cost on your receiving the preferred stock dividend would be a tax at 35 percent.* You would have to balance that current cost detriment against the future estate-tax benefit."

"It is very difficult for me to get a grip on that," said Kate. "If we had a C corporation and did that, we would have an extra tax cost every year until Jim and I both died—no estate tax till then, as you have so often explained to us. But we don't know how long we are going to live. If Jim and I both die in 10 years, we would have incurred current income tax costs of a certain amount, and our estate-tax saving would have to be more than that to justify the transaction."

"Kate, you have pointed out the crucial point here. There is no clear answer; there are many imponderables, many variables. Here," he said, handing each of them a computer printout, "is the best way I can explain it." (See Table 21.4.)

"This assumes your business grows at 10 percent. Section I, Estate-Tax Savings, projects the estate-tax your family will save, year by year, by the

Table 21.4. Illustration of Preferred Stock Freeze: Assuming 10% Business Value Growth Rate

	Year One	Year Two	Year Five	Year Ten
I. Estate-Tax Savings				
Company value, beginning of year	$7,400,000	$8,140,000	$10,834,000	$17,449,000
Company value, end of year	8,140,000	8,954,000	11,918,000	19,194,000
Company value in estate without recap.	8,140,000	8,954,000	11,918,000	19,194,000
Company value in estate with recap.	5,000,000	5,000,000	5,000,000	5,000,000
Estate-tax without recap.	4,070,000	4,477,000	5,959,000	9,597,000
Estate-tax with recap.	2,500,000	2,500,000	2,500,000	2,500,000
Estate-tax savings	1,570,000	1,977,000	3,458,000	7,096,000
II. Income-Tax Cost				
Preferred dividend	$ 639,000	$ 639,000	$ 639,000	$ 639,000
Extra tax cost of dividend	224,000	224,000	224,000	224,000
Cumulative extra tax cost	224,000	447,000	1,118,000	2,236,000
Cumulative extra tax and interest cost	224,000	465,000	1,312,000	3,240,000
III. Net Benefit (Detriment)	$1,346,000	$1,512,000	$ 2,147,000	$ 3,856,000
IV. Accumulated Preferred Dividend, After Tax	$ 415,000	$ 831,000	$ 2,077,000	$ 4,154,000

use of the preferred stock to freeze your interest and transfer all of the future growth to your children and grandchildren. I am assuming a gift of all the common stock, but you probably would not want to make such a large gift as it would incur a gift tax in your case.

"One more thing: my table does not show the after-tax amount of the preferred dividend, which itself is an asset taxable in your estate. You could spend it, invest it, or give it away but if you do invest it, it will be an asset taxable in your estate. However, it will be a liquid asset, able to pay estate-taxes on itself. In actual practice, most people would reduce their compensation from the company and live on the preferred stock dividends."

"Section II, Income-Tax Cost, shows the cumulative amount of that annual $224,000 tax cost I pointed out. In addition, I have built in an interest factor of 8 percent to represent the lost income on the $224,000 per year. So, if you both died at the end of the tenth year, *the estate tax saved would be $7,096,000* as against an accumulated income-tax cost of $3,240,000. *This yields a net saving of $3,856,000*, as shown in Section III, but also remember that the after-tax dividends have also contributed to your wealth if not spent. Also, any up front gift tax paid would reduce the benefit."

"That sounds great," said Jim, "but you are building assumption upon assumption. In my business that's a great way to go bankrupt. However, I'd like a copy of your program, and I'll have one of my computer experts play with it a bit so I can get a better feel for it."

"No problem at all," said Clay. "I'll ask my secretary to run off a copy of my program disk for you and also to print out a copy of the program. I think that you will find the really sensitive factor is the growth rate of the business. This printout assumes a growth rate of 10 percent per year, which is just an assumption. That is one reason why I would not recommend a preferred stock freeze in the vast majority of cases, certainly not in yours, because issuance of preferred stock would cause a loss of Subchapter S status."

"Hmmm! I see what you mean," said Kate. "The business better be growing faster than the cumulative cost of $224,000 per year, or we lose. Now, Clay, I know you have figured that."

"Yes, of course I have." Clay handed them two more printout sheets. "The first sheet shows a business growth rate of 5 percent; the others, growth rates of 10 percent and 15 percent, which approximates KJ's growth. These projections clearly show that a preferred stock freeze makes sense, if ever, only at a very high projected growth rate."

"How does a business owner ever know what the growth rate will be?" asked Kate.

"You don't, and there is a further clouding factor. Even if an owner considering a preferred stock freeze, can project or reasonably assume business and profit growth of a certain percentage, there is no way to project what the *value* will be at date of death. Many other variables and judgments enter into that. For instance, I have valued KJ at ten times weighted average earnings for purposes of this illustration. But if profit growth really keeps up at 15 percent for another twenty years, do you think the IRS or courts will settle for 10 times as a capitalization rate—after a history of twenty or thirty years of 15 percent growth?"

"Not very likely," said Jim. "More like 20 or 25 times earnings, depending on the stock market."

"Yes, that's it," said Clay. "The higher price-earnings ratio gives you a double kind of compounding of value doesn't it?"

"Clay, you paint such a rosy picture. I wonder why KJ doesn't issue preferred stock. I think we are willing to take a chance on the growth rate and value." Kate looked very thoughtful. "I think the company can afford $224,000 per year, if that is what it takes to avoid the huge estate-taxes on our future growth. Jim and I would reduce our compensation to partly offset the cost of the preferred dividends. What do you think, Jim?"

Jim was thoughtful, too. "I think that Clay has something more to tell us. Let's hear him out. Remember, he emphasized at the start that he was talking about a C corporation, which has a different tax structure than KJ. Clay, why don't you go on."

"Well, let me continue. I gave you the illustration of a C corporation and the use of preferred stock so you could get the feel of how it works. If you convert your S corporation to a C corporation, there will be some additional tax cost. I certainly do not recommend that. If KJ were a real estate partnership or a valuable farm property, I would certainly consider a similar freeze using a preferred partnership interest for you two. But now let me describe another variant of the freeze concept."

Sell S Corporation Stock to "Freeze" the Estate

"Another variant of the freeze is a sale of a major part of your stock to your children. Here, also, you have the stock valued by an expert appraiser and then sell to your children part of your nonvoting stock with a long-term payout. This way, the current value of the stock sold is frozen because you hold a promissory note and not the stock. Your children own the future growth embodied in the stock sold to them. Like the preferred-stock device which entails a tax on the preferred stock dividend, this also has a cost. The cost of a sale to the children is your potential capital-gain tax paid on the sale. This may be largely wiped out in your case because your cost basis for your stock is increased by the amount of your accumulated Subchapter S earnings (the AAA account)."

"I can see that," said Kate, "and I bet you have a printout to illustrate that, but the question I have is, where do the children get the money to pay us for the stock?"

"They get it from the Subchapter S dividends, which will be paid in the future to cover their interest and principal obligation. That's illustrated in the printouts I have here. If you sell 80 percent of your stock to the children, they get 80 percent of the dividends and you get the other 20 percent. In effect, you and Jim receive all the dividends because the children use their entire after-tax amount to pay you."

"Good, Clay, now you're warming up. But right now KJ can't afford to pay that amount of dividends. Could Kate and I lend back to the company part or all of the cash we receive?"

"Yes, under the current tax rules, but let's see how it pans out," replied Clay. "Assume again that the company is worth the $7,400,000 we used above, and that you and Kate want to freeze $5,000,000 of your current value and thus let the children have 68 percent of the future growth. You and Kate together own 100,000 shares of voting A common and 900,000 shares of nonvoting B.

"Currently the company earns $1,840,000 before tax, and we have valued the company at $7,440,000 overall. (Of course you would have this verified by an expert appraisal.) You decide to *sell* to your children about 68 percent of the equity of the company, 612,000 shares of nonvoting B stock, which I assume to be worth $5,000,000.

"Thanks, Clay, for the great idea. Now, where do you expect our children to get $5,000,000?" said Jim.

"Jim, you know exactly where," said Clay. "They are going to pay it over time, with interest, and the source is dividends from the company."

"That is what Jim was afraid you were going to say," said Kate.

"Let's follow it through," said Clay. "Assume the children pay you amortized over 16 years, with interest at 10% like a bank mortgage. Looking at my little book, I see that the constant annual payment on that debt is 12.8 percent, or $639,000 per year—part of which is interest and part principal. Now, the childrens' before-tax earnings on the 612,000 purchased shares come to $1,243,000 ($1,840,000 times 68 percent). In other words, the children have a potential $1,243,000 per year dividends before tax to pay you a total of $639,000 per year. As is the case of the dividends on the preferred stock freeze, you could reduce your salary, if you want, to boost earnings. You'll have plenty of cash."

"How does this work from a tax standpoint?" asked Jim.

"Yes, *there* is a difference. You may have to pay some tax on your gain on the stock, but this would be extended as you receive principal over 16 years. "What is our gain if we sell the stock now?" said Jim, clearly concerned about paying a tax on stock sold within the family.

"Well," said Clay, "your gain on the sale should be very small because you have increased the cost basis for your stock by the amount of undistributed Subchapter S earnings, your AAA account. We'll have to check that out with your accountant, but the transfer to the children should be essentially free of tax on your gain. You do, of course, have to pay a tax on the interest received from the children—but they can deduct it. One other thing to remember is that the law inhibits deferring gain to the extent that the installment note exceeds $5,000,000. If your accountant advises that you

Table 21.5

Earnings before tax, Subchapter S income, total earnings	$1,840,000
Childrens' 68% of Sub S income	$1,243,000
Deduction for interest on note (1st year)	$ (500,000)
Taxable income	$ 743,000
Tax at 35%	$ 260,000
Add debt service on note to Jim & Kate	$ 639,000
Dividends needed from KJ to enable children to buy 68% of stock	$ 899,000

do have a large gain, we will have to take this installment sale rule into account."

We also have to look at it from the childrens' standpoint. In the first year, the interest on the amortization would be $500,000 out of total payments of $639,000. The remaining $119,000 would be payment of principal. Table 21.5 shows what your childrens' tax picture in the first year would look like:

"Now, that is very interesting," said Kate. "Are you sure that interest is deductible by the children?"

"Yes, I am," said Clay, "but that is one of the risks in any of these transactions. The tax law or regulations could be changed at any time. According to recent IRS pronouncements, the note interest would be passive activity interest which is deductible against the Subchapter S income, which is passive activity income to the children because they are not participating in the Company. But the IRS can issue other regulations which change that rule. This is a gray area."

"Yes, I saw that when I lost so much with my tax shelters," said Jim. "Uncle Sam really zapped me when he changed the rules in the middle of that game."

"You are right about the IRS changing the rules in the middle of the game. There is a high risk factor in planning of this type, but I don't know how to avoid it. The interest is a big part of it," said Clay. "And, as you know, the interest element in each payment diminishes over time. Thus, the large interest deduction in the first year dwindles greatly by the sixteenth and final year. Please note that my illustration of a sale of stock assumes a sixteen-year payment schedule. If that put too much burden on the company, you could easily go out to twenty years on the payment schedule; this postpones your tax on the gains also.

"Let me illustrate with a printout which compares to the ones I gave you on the preferred stock freeze." Clay handed them another computerized projection. (See Table 21.6.)

"Thus, said Clay, "using the values and income projections we are talking about, a sale of a major part of your stock to the children is entirely feasible. The key to this kind of transaction is the Company's growth rate in taxable market value. At a low growth rate, don't bother. But remember the net cash after tax you receive each year during the payout period. This cash, if not consumed or given away, will remain an additional asset of your estate. It will then bear its own tax."

"Where do we go from here, Clay?" asked Jim. "I see what you are telling us, and I want to study your tables very carefully, but it seems to hang together. In short, what do we do now?"

Clay paused a moment, "What I am telling you as friends and clients is that you should definitely sell some of your KJ stock to the children. My illustrations are for $5,000,000 worth, payable over 16 years, to show you what the outside parameter looks like. But you don't have to go all the way. You can sell less than that and still get good results. If there is much gain on your part, you will want to limit the sale to $5 million due to the installment sale rules."

"In addition, due to the possible inability of KJ to pay large dividends in the future, I would limit the sale amount to what the children can pay for with reduced dividends. Take a conservative approach. The sale is a good way to eliminate taxes on future growth, but it is only one part of an overall strategy or policy."

"What about the preferred stock deal?" asked Kate. "That seems less risky, somehow."

"If KJ were a C corporation, I might possibly suggest the use of a preferred-stock freeze. But not with an S corporation, because the minute you issue preferred stock, you lose your S corporation status. The preferred-stock freeze is really not less risky. You must commit to paying that preferred stock dividend, or else the IRS will tax your estate as though you received it, plus compound interest, anyway. In fact, because of the extra income tax cost, the preferred-stock freeze is really more risky than the freeze by selling Subchapter S stock to the family. Only in exceptional cases does the corporate preferred stock freeze make any sense. However, in case of a partnership, a similar freeze can be done very effectively by structuring different kinds of partnership income interests. To summarize, I do think you should have an independent appraisal of KJ made, and, if the value comes out anywhere near the figures we have been using, sell some of your nonvoting B stock to the children. As to amount, we will have to confer with your accountant about the details when the appraisal is complete.

"Let's now go on to some other things to think about."

Table 21.6. Illustration of Sale of S Corporation Stock: Assuming 10% Business Value Growth Rate

	Year One	Year Two	Year Five	Year Ten	Year Fifteen
Children's 68% share of Subchapter S Income	$1,243,000	$1,368,000	$1,820,000	$2,931,000	$4,721,000
Interest deduction on note to pay for stock	(500,000)	(486,000)	(435,000)	(311,000)	(110,000)
Taxable income	743,000	882,000	1,384,000	2,620,000	4,610,000
Tax at 35%	260,000	309,000	484,000	917,000	1,614,000
Add debt service (principal plus interest) on note	639,000	639,000	639,000	639,000	639,000
Total Subchapter S dividends needed after tax to buy 68% of stock	899,000	948,000	1,123,000	1,556,000	2,253,000
Percentage of children's Subchapter S Income needed	72%	69%	62%	53%	48%

Give $1.2 Million as a Freeze

Clay launched his explanation of the third way to freeze Kate and Jim's estate. "Let me go one step further along this route. We have been talking about nifty tax-reduction devices. Clients love them. It intrigues them. Lawyers love them because the devices take legal work to set up and administer.

"Because we are such good friends, I'm going to let you in on a little secret: At your stage in life and in company growth, the most effective freeze is a plain and simple gift of $1.2 million worth of stock to the children or to trusts for them."

"I smell a bargain here," said Kate. "Proceed."

Clay smiled. "I knew you'd like that, Kate. Here's how it works: Remember that $600,000 exemption we used to set up a tax-free trust in each of your wills? Well, let's use it now for a one-shot gift to the children. Get an appraisal of the company and specifically of your nonvoting common stock. Just give a total of $1.2 million worth of nonvoting now and eliminate the exempt trusts from your wills. Use the exemption now before inflation eats it all up.

"In fact, use part of your $1.2 million as a gift of stock in connection with the sale to the children. That way, they won't have to pay you so much: They'll own more stock as a basis for the note payments; all would be pledged as security for the notes."

"Hmmm," said Kate, "I like that! The thought of that trust for me never appealed much even though I understand why it was a good idea from a tax standpoint. Why didn't you have us do this 10 years ago?"

"Ten years ago your company was not worth as much as now, and there's no way I would have let you and Jim give away such a large chunk of your estate and your security. I'm very protective of my clients' long-term interests."

"And *that* is why we are paying you these exorbitant fees!" said the ever-irrepressible Jim. "I told you a long time ago I did not want a lot of fancy footwork just to ease taxes. Remember?"

"Yes, I do remember," said Clay, "and that's why I'm discussing these particular options now, and not 5 or 10 years ago. Furthermore, some of them won't be of much use 10 years from now."

"If you are really interested in succession, you might consider a gift of part of the stock to a generation-skipping trust, which would ultimately go to your grandchildren without taxes in the childrens' estates. Having planted that little idea, I'll now go on and tell you about some more freeze devices."

Set Up a Family Partnership as a Freeze

"You use a lot of equipment and buildings in KJ. Most of it is paid for in cash, out of earnings. For future acquisition of such assets, you can form a family leasing partnership with the children as partners. You make an initial contribution to the partnership for seed money, which is of course reportable as a gift to the children.

"Then the partnership purchases equipment to be leased to KJ. It finances its purchases on the basis of the strength of the KJ leases. The lease arrangements between the partnership and KJ have to be fair and reasonable. In short, the children own a leasing company that builds up cash flow, equity, and value externally to KJ, instead of having the value build up within KJ."

"Who runs the partnership?" asked Kate.

"You do," said Clay. "You each own a 5 percent interest in the partnership and are designated as the managing partners. The children own the other 90 percent, 30 percent each. Thus, 90 percent of the growth is out of your estate. As you would expect, such a partnership has to be very carefully prepared to comply with all the IRS rules on family partnerships. And remember, there is little if any income tax benefit from such a partnership; all the loopholes have been plugged."

"Of course, you can do that with all kinds of property—real property, computers, terminals, salespersons' cars, and so forth."

"Clay, I'm going to buy your lunch," said Jim. "You are getting more and more practical as the day goes on. Do you have any more goodies?"

Encourage Family Ownership of New Ventures

Clay, ignoring Jim's jab, smoothly continued. "Take the leasing partnership concept one step further. Suppose you decide to develop an entirely new product or invention. Do you really want to work hard so you can give half of it to the IRS when you die?"

"The answer is no," said Kate. "Go ahead, because this is very important to us. What about new enterprises? Are you suggesting a partnership there, too?"

"Yes, in effect," said Clay, "some kind of entity, be it a family partnership or Subchapter S corporation, I don't know. The point is that new enterprises, new products, acquisitions should be initiated in entities owned mainly by the children, with you two as managers for the time being. Later, management succession will have to be a factor, just as with KJ. If the product or venture is one originally owned by KJ, the new entity will have to pay a fair price for it. But, if the venture prospers, the initial cost will be more than balanced by the eventual estate tax savings."

"That sounds great," said Jim. "Let's discuss it at lunch. I have an option to buy a small software company, and maybe that's a good place to start. I could lend the children the money to buy it and Molly could manage it."

22

The "Colossus": Estate Planning for the $25-30 Million Business

We now meet Jim and Kate at age 60? By this time their estate has a value in the range of $25 to $30 million. Jim is slowing down, and Kate wants him to stop. She would like the next phase of their life to be one that allows them to enjoy the fruits of their joint efforts; they could focus on travel, companionship, leisure, physical conditioning—the quality of life rather than the quantity of money.

Jim agrees with Kate but sees one task he must finish, the last act of the drama of K.J. Electronic Devices, Inc. Who will run it over the long term? How can Jim step aside now and be sure that KJ will survive his retirement and his eventual death?

To put this in perspective, we need to fill out the picture of a very successful, very wealthy couple who are now looking to retirement. Here are Clay's words at a meeting with the Wolczks.

Assessing the Growth and Management of KayJim Electronics

"We agreed many years ago to do a major update of your estate plans every 10 years, and now is the time. Let's review the salient facts as I know them.

"First of all, the central fact is the astounding growth of KJ Electronics, Inc. in the past few years. Its book value is $32,946,000, but that hardly reflects its value in view of the fact that its weighted five-year average earnings after tax is $3,761,000. Public companies in a business like KJ are selling at very high earning multiples right now so, provisionally, I'd capitalize your earnings at 10 X to arrive at a conservative value of around $37 million for the company. Your 57 percent interest is worth $21,000,000 on that basis. Expert appraisals might arrive at more or less value, but the point is that you are talking in the range of at least $21 million for your controlling interest.

"Second, You have given and sold a major value in stock to your children and continue to do so, but future gifts will have little impact from an estate standpoint. The overall growth in value will far exceed the $20,000 per year that you can give away to each child.

"Third, only one of your children, Molly, has shown any interest in working for KJ, and despite her MBA, she is years away from any kind of command position. Bob Lewis is now COO and could take over the business if you want to go that route. Jim, Jr. is doing well at his medical specialty, but his passion is helping sick people and not management of a business. Maureen is fully occupied and supremely happy with her home and three children.

"Fourth, Your health is excellent, both of you, but once you turn 60, certain creaks and groans are heard in our bodies and the doctors are more likely to say "Tsk, tsk" about something.

"Fifth, your wills, your gifting program, your insurance trust, all are in good shape, but as I think about the compounding value of KJ, I am very concerned about where it's all headed. We have to address the cost of estate taxes at the death of the survivor of the two of you. Because of the liberal marital-deduction rules, there will be no estate tax when the first of you dies. However, the cost of this is that the entire property belonging to both of you will be taxed at the death of the survivor. *This tax could be as high as about 60 percent of the total value*, including New York State taxes, but in our calculations I use 50 percent as an example. On a $25 million business value, that would be $13 million. If the payment is deferred, up to a maximum of 14 years, the interest factor raises the total cost to about 75 percent of value over the 14 years.

"It is not adequate just to give you a figure for tax on my estimate of current value. In addition, you have to figure that Uncle Sam is your "partner" for more than 50 percent of all future value increases—truly a senior partner. Since you live in New York State, the figure is more like 60 percent.

"What else can be done to (1) maintain at an acceptable level the cash drain caused by estate taxes, and (2) ensure that your company will endure the other stresses that will be caused by Jim's death? This seems to be a time for some very deep thinking by you both. I can't do the thinking, but I can help formulate the issues and list some of the options available to you to address each of the issues I've outlined. Let's discuss each issue in greater detail."

Assessing the Value of the Estate

"Normally, I discuss the facts in terms of the client's personal situation and the size and composition of the estate. In your case, a bit of philosophy is also in order: The fact is that your creation, Kay Jim Electronic Devices, Inc. has grown and prospered beyond any expectation at the time I first incorporated you, over 20 years ago. It is, in fact, a colossus of its kind.

"Owning a colossus is rather like having a wild Bengal tiger by the tail. What do yo do with it now that you have it? The KJ business has grown at a rate of about 15 percent per year, compounded. Book value was $32,945,000 last December 31, and a weighted (5,4,3,2,1) average of the last five years' earnings is $3,761,000 after tax. Since KJ is an S corporation, earnings have been recast to put them on a C corporation basis because valuation techniques are geared to a C corporation, but your S corporation earnings last year were $7,440,000 before your personal income taxes.

"In preparing this analysis, we wanted to take all bias out of our judgment as to value, so we retained an investment banker to give us a confidential appraisal. He reports that, on a conservative basis, KJ has a market value of about $37 million, but, depending on the kind of sale involved, it could be worth $40 million, or even as much as $50 million, if just the right purchaser came along. Companies of a similar nature that have a public market for their stock sell in the range of 15 to 20 times earnings. Remember that we can think in terms of $37 million, but the IRS can get its own appraisal and often seeks to increase the value used to compute estate taxes.

"Allowing for Bob Lewis's 15 percent and the stock given and sold to your children over the years, you own 57 percent of KJ, which would have a value of at least $21.6 million for estate-tax purposes. Thus, your total assets are roughly as shown on this sheet. (See Table 22.1.)

"In addition, your insurance trusts, set up when you were 40, now have $6 million of life insurance on the last of the two of you to die. For example, if Jim dies, the insurance pays nothing, but at Kate's later death the whole proceeds are paid. This trust is not taxed as part of your estate, but the $6 million will be available to help pay estate-taxes."

"This does not tell the whole tale. Assuming a conservative 10 percent annual growth in value of the business from now on, it will be worth the following at future dates:

	Whole Business	Your 57%
Now	$37 million	$21 million
5 years	$60 million	$34 million
10 years	$96 million	$55 million

"As I have many times pointed out to you, if Jim dies before Kate, his whole estate—be it $25 million or $55 million, or whatever—would pass tax-

Table 22.1. The Wolczks' Estate at Age Sixty

Stock in KJ	$21,600,000
Residence (joint)	500,000
Summer residence (joint)	200,000
Condo, Florida (joint)	300,000
Securities and bank deposits	800,000
Life insurance, term	500,000
Life insurance, split dollar	500,000
Cars and other assets	200,000
Interest in qualified employee plans	800,000
Approximate total estate	$25,400,000

free to Kate because of the unlimited marital deduction for property passing to a spouse. However, at Kate's subsequent death the entire property, including her half of the company, is taxed in her estate at a rate of about 50 percent. Here the growth factor is very important. If Jim died now and Kate survived to age 70, 10 years, *her estate at 10 percent growth would be on the order of $55 million and the tax about $28 million.* This is what I meant by having a Bengal tiger by the tail.

Determining Management Succession

"The deep thinking has to start with a grasp of what would happen to the business if one or both of you died. Although Jim has tried to build a management team and a set of informed, expert, outside directors, the fact is that, except for Bob Lewis, you have no one on hand qualified to be CEO of a hi-tech company with sales of $30 million and growing fast.

"Bob Lewis' 15 percent interest is worth over $5 million, and he has indicated to me that he would like to liquidate some of his value now so that he can diversify. At the very least, Bob would like some kind of buy-out arrangement on his death or retirement. This would be in the company's interest, too.

"You made a very smart move, two years ago, in naming Bob Lewis as president and CEO, retaining the office of co-chairperson for each of you. But we both know that Bob as a bachelor has three great passions: (1) the welfare of KJ, (2) fly fishing for Atlantic salmon in New Brunswick, and (3) fly fishing for bonefish in the Keys. Up to now KJ has always had first call on his time and his energies. He has made it clear that sometime as he approaches his late fifties, he is going to want more time for his other interests, or to develop new interests. Goodness knows, he has earned it."

"The company has $3 million of key-person insurance on Bob's life, but that does not solve the long-term issue of backup management. We need to discuss strengthening your board of directors as well as a plan to recruit and groom likely prospects to succeed Bob.

The Personal Facts. "The facts about your family and your personal goals and wishes rank with financial data as your long-term planning is considered. Note: In the past our reviews at age 40 and age 50 concentrated on the eventuality of death of one or both of you. Now, in addition, we need to focus on retirement planning for both of you and, I hate to say it, on the possibility that one of you may suffer a debilitating illness."

"You are both, at age 60, in excellent health. Jim's weight is back down to younger-than-forty status, and his heart, blood pressure, and cholesterol are normal. Kate, you have never lost your slim figure, and I understand your health is excellent. Likewise, the children. Let me list them now to make sure I have their status correct."

"Mary ("Molly") R. Wolczk–Age 35; divorced; no children; BA and MBA degrees; good health; works for KJ as vice president for foreign sales. Molly is doing very well at her job in sales but has no electronic engineering background nor any experience in hands-on operational management. Molly would like to advance in management but does not envision herself as being a contender for the top job in the foreseeable future."

"James ("Jim") Wolczk, Jr.–Age 32; married; two children; BS and MD degrees; good health. Unlike Molly and Maureen, Jim never had any interest in working for KJ and never did so. It seems to us that Jim has unconsciously steered away from anything that might put him in a competitive or conflicting situation with Jim, Sr. You can be very proud of Jim. He may wind up dean of a medical school some day, but never a CEO of a business."

"Maureen W. Osborn–Age 29; married to Frank Osborne, MD; three children; BS in computer science; worked for KJ during and after college. By talent and education Maureen would be highly qualified to work at KJ in an executive position, but at this point she has no interest in doing so. She and Frank live in Phoenix, Arizona, where he has an internship at the Forman Hospital."

"You can be proud of your children. They are self-sufficient and resourceful. Great wealth will not "turn their heads" nor deter them from pursuing their own course in life—wealth or no wealth. If they do have great wealth some day, I feel sure they will use it to the best advantage of themselves, their families, and their communities. Not every couple in your financial position can say that.

"In terms of the personal situation, there is no compelling reason why KJ needs to remain in the family, nor, on the other hand, why it would have to be sold at Jim's death. The answer to this vital question, rather, lies in your answer to the economic problems engendered by estate taxes. Management succession is an issue, too, but not an issue that depends on your family's situation for an answer.

Estimating the Loss of Estate Taxes: Impact and Options

"We need to discuss the impact of estate taxes. Remember that, if Jim dies, the marital deduction permits Jim to pass his entire estate to Kate tax-free. It is only on the death of the survivor of you both that estate tax is imposed. In very rough terms, and on the basis of the assumptions stated above, estate taxes on the KJ stock at the survivor's death would be as follows:

Time	KJ value	Value of Your Stock	Approximate Tax at 50%*
Survivor dies now	$37 million	$21 million	$11 million
Survivor dies 5 years	$60 million	$34 million	$17 million
Survivor dies 10 years	$96 million	$55 million	$28 million

* Tax is that on the presumed value of the stock with future growth at 10% per annum from now. Other assets would also be taxed at the same rate, 50%. Jim and Kate own 57% of KJ."

"This tax is due and payable nine months after the survivor's death!

"As a practical matter, KJ cannot afford to pay such a tax on its value. Its current net worth is just under $32.9 million, and there's no way it can generate a cash distribution of $11 million in nine months. Unfortunately, growth is not the solution because the tax grows apace with value. In fact, growth is the problem, because it is the historic rapid growth that justifies increasing price:earnings ratios and a value so far in excess of net worth.

"Let me mention various options that you, as owners of a colossus, have for meeting estate-tax needs. We will discuss them in more detail later.

The Options:

- Redeem stock or pay dividend, tax-free, to get cash from company.
- Pay tax in 14 annual installments; or in ten installments.
- Have the insurance trusts purchase more insurance.
- Pay part of tax at first death to save tax on value increases.
- Have the company sold after your deaths.
- Sell the balance of the company now to the children.
- Sell the company to Employee Stock Option Plan (ESOP) or Stock Bonus Plan.
- Make a public offering to create a market.
- Make charitable gifts.
- Change residency to a state with lower estate taxes.
- Create new enterprises owned by the children.

"You will note that gifts to the children are not listed as an option. Gifts of stock to children and grandchildren are certainly very advisable, and you have been doing this for many years. However, gifts do not solve the estate-tax problem in your case because the annual increment in value now far exceeds the amount you can give away tax-free. So keep up the annual gifts, but don't look to them as anything but a minor part of the solution."

Jim, Kate, and Clay spent the better part of two hours discussing his portrayal of their situation. It was agreed that real, in-depth discussion was in order. Accordingly, Clay invited them for a weekend at his summer home.

Planning the Future of KayJim Electronics

By agreement, two hours Saturday morning, three hours Saturday afternoon, and two hours Sunday morning were to be devoted to discussing the future of Kay Jim Electronic Devices, Inc. The initial meeting started as follows.

"Okay, Clay, begin. "I have thought a lot about your initial report and, after 20 years of kicking this succession stuff around with you, I think I understand, most of it. But so what? I don't have a clue what to do now."

"Then let me speak to that," said Kate. "I know about now. Jim and I are each 60 years old. To hear you tell it, Clay, we are worth about $30 million between us. But that is just a number. We have our home in Cazenovia, New York, and the place in Naples, Florida. For all other practical purposes, we live about the same as we did when we were 40. Unless you are nuts, or a jetsetter, you can only spend so much money. Our happiness is in each other, our children, and our grandchildren. After 25 years devoted to KJ, Jim will agree with that."

"Yes, I surely will," said Jim. "But KJ is very much part of my life, too. It represents our accomplishment, Kate's and mine. We can't eat it, we can't wear it, but we take great pride in what we have done. I know most of our four hundred employees by their first names. This includes the one hundred in our Hong Kong plant.

"When Kate and I go, what is going to happen to that? Will it wither and die after a few years? Will it succumb to the huge bite of estate-taxes? These are rhetorical questions, but they are also very real questions. Over the years, Clay, we have listened to you and done some, but not all, of the things you suggested. Now we look at our situation, and we face very much the same issues you showed us twenty years ago."

Clay replied, "Twenty years ago, or ten, no one could have forecast what KJ has done. Any options I posed in the past were tempered by the basic questions of how much of the future you should give away. Always the prudent answer was that your basic security, well-being, and sense of ownership outweigh the impact of taxes that may not be payable for decades to come."

"Let me try to sum up where we are. First of all, for the business to succeed after you retire, you have to have a management team in place. I don't think you need a whole line-up of CEO candidates sitting around till you decide to go. The central strength of KJ is, first, that you have in place a very strong board of independent directors who are capable of conducting a search and selecting a CEO. Second, you have built up an infrastructure of a fine Chief Operating Officer and several very excellent division presidents who can sustain the company if need be until the new CEO is on board.

"Also, you have a very strong stock incentive plan so that a really successful CEO can wind up a millionaire, too. The kind of person you need can't be expected to work on just a salary basis. He or she will want to be an owner as well."

"And don't forget Bob Lewis," said Jim. "Bob's plenty capable of running the whole show right nowin fact he's pretty much doing it."

"I know that," said Clay, "but Bob's not young either and lately he has been talking about cashing in—his stock is now 100 percent vested—and moving to North Carolina, or someplace. So, even with Bob, you need the directors to be able to fill his place if you are not here."

"Anyhow, one way or another, we have management succession pretty well in hand," said Jim. "What we don't have in hand is the impact of estate-taxes if something happens to me and Kate. The underwriter, customers, joint-venture partners, and even your hot-shot CEO recruit are all going to wonder what the hell happens if KJ has to come up with tens of millions of dollars, someday, for estate taxes, when our partner, Uncle Sam, wants to cash his 50 percent share and get paid."

"Okay, let's talk about that first," said Clay. "I'll make this as painless as possible. After 30 years, taxes have lost some of their appeal for me, too. But bear with me. We have to talk about Uncle Sam's taxes, just as you would have to talk to a real 50 percent partner, if you had one.

How to Pay the Estate Taxes

"First of all, let me point out once again, that the tax burden falls at the death of the second spouse. If either of you dies and leaves your assets to the other, the marital deduction reduces your taxable estate to zero: no taxes. But then the spouse has all the property, and eventually when she or he dies, the taxes are due at the then current value."

"At the death of the survivor of the both of you, *the value of your interest in the business plus your other assets will bear an estate-tax of at least 50 percent*. There are two basic approaches to solving this problem. The first in effectiveness is to reduce or limit the amount of estate that is subject to tax. I plan to get into this topic this afternoon. So let us put it aside for the moment.

"The second approach is to provide beforehand for payment of the tax that is due. This is not an alternative to reducing the tax but rather a necessity at any event—especially in your case.

"You do not have a very liquid estate. Apart from what you spend, you have always reinvested your profits in KJ, so that is the first source of funds for taxes. When the survivor dies and the taxes come due, the estate can sell part of your estate back to KJ. The sale back to KJ will be free of income tax because (1) the stock acquired a higher basis at your death, and (2) where stock is sold to pay estate-taxes and administration expenses, the law says that such sale to your own company is not a dividend. The upshot of this is that KJ can be one source for the case to pay the tax on its value."

"Then why don't we set up a reserve account and put a million dollars a year in it, then let the fund invest and accumulate? In a few years we'd have a huge fund," said Jim.

"You can do that, since KJ's an S corporation. (Of course, you couldn't with a regular C corporation because of the danger of the accumulated earnings surtax, a penalty tax on accumulating unneeded cash at the corporate level.) But you can also do the same thing another way: Declare extra tax-free dividends now and build up the funds in your own pockets. Those funds come out to you tax-free because, as an S corporation shareholder, you have already paid the tax on that money."

"There's one catch, here," said Kate. "We own 57 percent of the stock, so if we declare an extra dividend of $1 million, we get only $570,000. The children and Bob Lewis get the rest."

"We'll cover that," said Jim, "by telling the kids this is part of a plan to save ultimate taxes. So they just put their extra money in special 'tax accounts' to be accumulated until needed. I like that idea from a tax standpoint, but not from KJ's standpoint. It needs all the cash now it can get for Bob Lewis's expansion plans."

"Speaking of Bob Lewis, he owns 15 percent of the stock, so he'd get $150,000 out of that $1 million extra dividend, but now I think on it, that would be a good idea. Bob clearly earns the money, and receiving a hefty tax-free dividend may perk up his interest in staying around here."

"Just to pursue that," said Clay, "your account of tax-paid earnings in KJ is in the millions now. You could actually pay out a $10 million tax-free dividend right now as a starting point for your tax fund."

"Ouch!" said Jim. "If we did that, we'd *surely* have to borrow for expansion. I just don't want to do that—I think."

"Well, give it some thought," said Clay. "Sooner or later the money will be used to pay taxes. Perhaps it would be better for KJ, over the long term, to learn to expand and prosper while at the same time paying a fair return on investment to its owners."

All Jim said in reply was "Hmmm."

"Clay," said Kate, "you said that taxes were due sooner or later," but you talked only about later. What happens if Jim and I die in a common disaster next week? We are flying to Ireland so Jim and I can fish, rest and shop. What if something happens to the plane? What if it's sooner, rather than later?"

"One answer to the 'later' is the tax-free dividends and investment fund," said Clay. "The best answer to the 'sooner' is really joint life insurance, as we have long discussed. If the corporation takes out the insurance, then, of course, 57 percent of it is in your estate because you own 57 percent of the stock. If your children, or trusts for your children, own the insurance, then the proceeds are available when needed tax free. I prefer trust ownership because of the mortality of your children if they are the owners.

"In terms of cost, a joint life policy would now cost you about $22,000 per year per million if all paid up in 10 or 12 years. Insurance that never becomes paid up would cost only $9,700 per million per year at age 60, assuming you are both in good health.

"In today's context, think of joint life insurance as being just one more way to have the tax funding on hand. With a constantly escalating demand, you run into the limitation of the cost of insurance as your age increases. Alone, it is not the solution. At some point, if you live long enough, the insurance companies will not issue more insurance. That, or its cost will get so prohibitive that buying it does not make sense. So, more joint life insurance is an important part of the tax funding plan, but not the whole of it from now on."

"Go on," said Jim. "I'm with you so far. We have this big tax bill at some time in the future—an unknown time. Perhaps next week. Perhaps in ten years. Perhaps more than thirty years. But we are talking about *succession* to the ownership of Kay Jim Electronic Devices. Taxes may be your life's work, but it isn't mine.

"But, before you speak, Clay, I'm going to answer my own question. I know my family can't succeed to the business if they don't pay the tax. But it sure burns my tail that such a huge proportion of presumed value has to be used to pay inheritance taxes." Jim's remarks dropped off to a mutter.

Clay resumed his discussion of the ways estate taxes can be paid. After twenty years of close friendship he understood Jim and his tirades.

"I told you," he continued, "that I want to spend this morning on how the taxes get paid. Later we'll talk about reducing or even eliminating taxes altogether.

"Let's say your estate owes $10 million in estate-taxes on the business. Let me sketch out some alternatives on how this gets paid.

Alternative 1: Pay the Tax Out of Your Own Assets. "Your first alternative is to pay the tax using your own assets. Assuming your estate has cash and securities, or insurance in trusts, or whatever, it can pay the $10 million when due, nine months after death.

Alternative 2: Redeem Nonvoting Stock. "A second alternative would be to redeem nonvoting stock. The estate sells back $10 million of stock at estate-tax value, free of income tax, and uses the proceeds to pay the tax. This assumes that KJ has $10 million handy to do this. It also assumes the consent of the other shareholders, which in your case should not be a problem.

Alternative 3: KJ Pays the Estate a Tax-Free Dividend. "Your third alternative: have KJ pay the estate a tax-free dividend. Remember, your undistributed Subchapter S income on which you have already paid a tax? This can be distributed to you or your estate free of income tax. So this is available to pay $10 million of estate-taxes. Again, this alternative assumes KJ has the cash to pay such a dividend. More than $10 million might be needed because such a dividend must be pro rata to all the shareholders.

Alternative 4: Corporation Borrows from the Bank. "If KJ doesn't have $10,000,000, it can go to the bank and borrow it. Then it can redeem your stock, as in alternative two, or pay a tax-free dividend, alternative three. KJ can deduct the loan interest at its 40 percent tax rate, so the effective interest rate is 6 percent, assuming the bank charges 10 percent.

Alternative 5. The Estate Pays Tax over Fourteen Years "You could choose a fifth alternative: Have your estate pay the tax over fourteen years. When a business interest comprises more than 35 percent of an estate, it may elect to pay the tax on that interest in installments. In the first four years interest only is paid; then, starting in the fifth year, principal is paid in ten equal installments plus interest on the unpaid balance.

"This presents an interesting wrinkle. The interest, itself, is deductible from the estate-tax. Then, when an interest payment is made, the tax is retroactively reduced and part of your 'interest' payment is credited as a payment on the tax. In effect, then, the interest is costing only fifty cents on the dollar because the estate deducts it. If the IRS rate is 10 percent, the effective after tax rate is 5 percent."

"What you are telling me," said Jim, "is that the estate can borrow from the IRS at a very favorable rate. Can the estate also redeem stock to make each annual payment when due?"

"Yes, that is where the two rules fit together. Each year on the due date the company redeems enough stock to pay the interest and tax due."

Kate leaned forward, most interested. "Clay, what if the stock goes up in value over the 15-year period? Is the stock still redeemed at date-of-death value?"

"Well, you can do it at the increased value, but you then have the problem of reporting gain in the sale and finding the cash to pay income tax. Economically, as long as the stock is all in one family, it does not matter.

However, the IRS would probably view a redemption at less than fair value as some kind of a gift. I think the thing to do is to leave things flexible now so the value matter can be handled at the time. If we gear things now to a specific value at time of redemption, we might create a problem if the value of the company declined over the deferred payment period."

"In any event, the redemption should be provided for in a shareholders' agreement so everyone understands that corporate funds must be used to pay your estate taxes.

Alternative 6: Pay Tax over Nine Years. "The sixth alternative is to pay part of the tax over a nine-year period. Where an estate can't qualify for the fourteen-year payment (yours can), it can elect to pay 90 percent of the tax over nine years if it shows the IRS it has reasonable cause to defer payment. Your estates would also have the option to pay over nine years.

Comparison of the Six Approaches to Paying the Estate Tax. "Here is what the different payment alternatives look like in millions of dollars per year. Assume that the business value is $20 million and that the tax due on that is $10 million. Of course, you can scale that up or down to any size estate you want." Clay handed copies of Table 22.2 to his friends.

After they'd studied Table 22.2, Clay continued: "Since you have payments at different time schedules, it's helpful to use present value as of the due date of the tax to compare them." They then studied Table 22.3

Conclusion: Solving the Tax Burden. "What do you conclude from all this?" asked Jim. "Seems to me that the company could, in fact, pay the debt service out of earnings, but that to do so could seriously impair its ability to continue to grow and prosper if the value continues to grow as we anticipate. I also conclude that *the 14-year payout is the most favorable because the present value of the future payments is lowest.*

"Another point: I have always used a 50 percent estate tax rate for illustration purposes. Actually, the top federal rate is 55 percent, more for a New York resident and those of other states with high tax rates."

"To summarize," said Clay. "KJ has always plowed back most of its earnings and run without any significant debt. If the tax burden we envision falls on KJ, it may survive but will not be the same. The $10 million burden I spoke of for illustration may be met by insurance and your liquid assets, but with your growth record it is more likely that such sources will be inadequate and KJ will have to furnish a major part of the tax. Its purpose for ten or fifteen years will be to work for the U.S. Treasury; a major part of its current earnings will go to taxes. It is almost inevitable that other things will slip, that the succession you wish to plan will not succeed."

He paused, and Kate and Jim remained silent, absorbed by their own thoughts. Clay switched tacks. "I smell bass frying for our lunch, so we'd better quit for now with the realization that expert use of payment options will certainly help, but they are not by any means a total solution. Something

Table 22.2. Approximate After-Tax Cash Outflow to Pay $10,000,000 of Deferred Estate Taxes
(Figures in millions of dollars)

Due Date Plus in Years	Alternatives 1, 2, 3: Pay Tax When Due	Alternative 4: Redeem Stock	Alternative 5: 14-Year Payment	Alternative 6: 10-Year Payment
0	10.0	1.3	0	1.0
1		1.3	1.0	1.9
2		1.2	0.9	1.7
3		1.2	0.9	1.5
4		1.1	0.8	1.3
5		1.1	1.6	1.2
6		1.1	1.4	1.0
7		1.0	1.3	0.9
8		1.0	1.1	0.7
9		0.9	1.0	0.6
10		0.9	0.9	0
11		0.9	0.8	0
12		0.8	0.7	0
13		0.8	0.6	0
14		0.8	0.5	0

Table 22.3

Alternative	Total Cash Paid Out*	Present Value at Due Date
1, 2, 3: Pay tax when due	$10.0 million	$10.0 million
4: Redeem stock	$14.5 million***	$ 8.1 million**
5: 14-year payment	$13.6 million	$ 8.2 million**
6: 9-year payment	$12.5 million	$ 8.5 million**

* Principal and interest.
** Present value is figured at 10%.
*** Corporation's debt service payments on loan to redeem stock.

must be done to reduce the tax drag, and *that* is what we are going to discuss this afternoon. Let's adjourn."

*   *   *   *

Planning the Future Ownership of the Business

"Well, Clay, let's hear more." Jim settled back into his armchair. "After lunch and a swim I can be more philosophic about all this."

Clay responded "That is all to the good, because philosophy is very important to what we are going to discuss today and tomorrow. I do not have any cookbook that furnishes magic recipes for your situation, for the colossus. The answers have to come from you both, from the way you think about the future. For the next hour or so, I'd like to talk about transferring all or part of KJ to outside interests as part of your succession philosophy. Later, and tomorrow morning, I'll get into transferring growth to your family. These broad concepts are not mutually exclusive but have to be presented separately." The Wolczks both looked puzzled but interested.

Clay pushed on. "What about bringing in nonfamily parties as owners? When we get this all sorted out, this may seem like a good idea. Jim, your focus is on preserving KJ as a viable entity, with traditions, friends, relationships, products, being invented—a personality by itself. Could we call it a soul?

"The philosophic question is really whether it must—or should—remain in your family, be controlled by your family, to achieve your personal goals for it.

"We have discussed before ways in which outsiders could participate, but let me go over them once again.

Give Charitable Gifts. First, there's the charitable bequest, which can be a great fail-safe device. Part of your stock can be bequeathed, at death of your survivor, to a friendly charity that you have established in advance as likely to be compatible shareholder for KJ."

"The point is that if the survivor of you two, planning his or her estate, can see available funding to pay, say $20 million in taxes, this means that another $20 million can go in gifts to your family (assuming, of course, a 50 percent tax rate). The balance can go to charity, which will be a long-term shareholder. Let me illustrate: Say Kate's estate is valued at $50 million because of the increase in value of KJ stock. It's reasonable to assume that the estate and KJ can come up with $20 million for taxes. This allows her to have a $40 million taxable estate. So she leaves the remaining $10 million in stock to charity, putting a limit on the size of her estate. *The issue is really whether to have the charity get it or have Uncle Sam get it.*"

"That is no choice at all," Jim retorted.

"Yes, but there are some drawbacks to a charitable gift. Let me list a few: First, KJ can no longer be a Subchapter S corporation if a charity is a shareholder. Second, dividends will have to be paid to some extent so that the charity can reasonably justify holding the stock indefinitely. Third, the charity may want representation of its interests in the board. Finally, the charity might eventually seek to sell the stock, but you could get some protection from that with a first-refusal agreement."

"If I have to make a philosophical judgment as to whether I like a charity as a partner or Uncle Sam as a creditor, you leave little choice," said Jim. "Go on with other options."

Establish an ESOP. A second option is an Employee Stock Option Plan. The concept is very similar, except that a company-controlled trust for part of the stock is the shareholder instead of the charity. The plan is very complex, and if you want to go that route, it would be better to set it up now, while you are around. An employees' stock bonus plan does provide certain benefits but is less regulated than an ESOP. A real cost of these options is the loss of the ability to continue under Subchapter S.

Consider an LBO. "The leveraged buyout is something to consider, a third option. Say Bob Lewis gets some investors together and buys *part* of your stock. You keep control, however. This puts cash (after capital gain tax) in your pockets and allows Subchapter S to continue, by agreement with the new shareholders. Here, you are trading part of your future growth for cash liquidity and hopefully management strength. If an LBO took place after the death of one of you, the capital gains tax on the estate's stock could be eliminated. I think the LBO fits very well as a device to use after one of you dies. It could be used as a device to assure continued management of KJ, but the cost is your independent family ownership.

Issue New Equity. In yet another option, the company can issue new stock with no gain. Say Bob Lewis' investors buy 20 percent of the company in new stock. For this they pay $10 million now and, by agreement with them, funds will be available in the future to redeem stock for your estate taxes. When your stock is redeemed to pay estate taxes, of course the investors will therefore own a larger percentage of the corporation, but your family can still remain in control if nonvoting stock is redeemed to pay taxes.

Consider a Public Offering. One way of solving the tax problem—at the cost of possibly creating worse ones—is taking your company public."

Jim's response to this option was quick. "Yes, we could have done that a dozen times in past years. Looking back, I'm glad we did not do it," he said.

"I know," said Clay. "But we have to lay out all alternatives here, and that is surely one of them. The offering can do these things for you: One, create a market for your stock so the estate can sell to pay taxes; two, inject cash into the company for your expansion plans; three, allow you to sell part of your stock in a secondary offering and thus provide cash for taxes.

"The drawbacks are manifest: The offering would probably have to be of voting stock, which might upset your control structure. Subchapter S would be lost because you would have more than 35 shareholders. Finally, as in the case of the merger proposals you've received, the company is just not yours anymore."

"That's enough!" said Kate. "Move on, Clay. There is no way Jim and I want to be part of a public company. KJ isn't geared up for that, and neither are Jim and I. If we ever did that, Jim's worries would really start. This one's *not* an option!"

Summary of Business Ownership Options. Clay had to smile. "Okay, Kate, I think I get the drift. No offering. I only brought it up to complete the picture."

"What picture?" asked Kate.

"The picture I am trying to show you is the various approaches that families with companies like KJ consider, and sometimes take, to counter the fact that it is the express policy of the United States of America to prevent the passage of large wealth from generation to generation. If the writers of the tax laws have their way, the colossus is doomed as a family company. We can debate that the cost of that policy to the general public is greater than any arguable benefit, but that is whistling in the wind. In short, Uncle Sam wants to break up KJ when you both die, and you want to preserve it. That is the picture."

"Well, I think I *see* that picture," said Kate. "Which approach, of those you've described, do you favor?

Clay thought a few moments before replying. "I would give different answers to different people, depending on their specific situation and what I know about them. For you and Jim, I can't imagine any outsider in the picture except Bob Lewis and other key employees, perhaps a future CEO." Jim's and Kate's expressions told Clay he was right on target. He continued.

"You want KJ kept in the family, and I would certainly expand the concept of stock for key employees, but only *key* employees who are really going to contribute measurably. The ESOP concept is fine in some cases, but too rule-ridden, too cumbersome for KJ.

"At this point," he went on, "the only outsiders I would permit to own stock would be a selected charity or several, and that only pursuant to the fail-safe concept I've described, only if the tax burden forces you to the choice of sharing with a charity instead of the IRS. In short, *pass KJ on to your descendants to the greatest extent possible.* If, and *only* if, your resources in liquid assets, insurance, and affordable redemptions from KJ are insufficient do you give non-voting stock to charity such as your respective alma maters. This leaves the question of how I can tell you how much to leave to charity. In answer to my own question, I can't." He paused, took a deep breath and summed up: "*At this point, the charitable gift of stock is only a possibility to mention: too many drawbacks. I think of it only as a last resort.*"

How to Transfer Business Value to the Family

Clay resumed. "Let us go back and take a new look at some concepts we have discussed over the years. The base of all of them was not to reduce your then current estate, but to transfer future growth so it won't be taxed. Here is what we have talked about:

Annual Gifts to Family. "You already know how well the first one works and certainly you should both continue your program of giving $20,000 worth of stock to each child and grandchild each year.

Use Balance of $600,000 Exempt Gift. "You also know that each of you can give $600,000 completely free of federal estate-taxes. Some of this you have used up in the past, but to the extent you have not, be sure to use up the balance in gifts of stock now.

Taxable Gifts. "Remember, years ago, I described the heresy of making gifts of stock to the extent of actually paying a gift tax? That still makes sense in the long term if the rate of growth of your estate-tax liability on the company exceeds the rate of growth of your invested cash. You can declare a tax free dividend from your S Corporation, KJ, to pay the gift tax.

"But," interjected Kate, "we have been over this before. Jim and I now own only 57 percent of KJ. If we declare a tax-free dividend to pay the gift tax, then the children and Bob Lewis get 43 percent of it."

"The answer to that is the same as my answer this morning. Let the children use their tax-free money to pay part of the gift tax, a 'net gift'. This payment by them has the additional effect of reducing the amount of the taxable gift."

"Clay, there is something about this that bothers me." Jim looked puzzled. "You say that KJ could pay out cash now so we can pay the gift tax on a gift of growth stock. Right?" Clay nodded. "But that money invested in

KJ will grow at the same 15 percent rate as KJ's value. So where is the cash saving?"

"Aha! Good question!" "If it were as mathematically simple as that, you would be right. But the other factor in the equation is that, the longer KJ's sales and earnings grow at a 15 percent compound rate, the higher a price:earnings ratio the IRS will assign to the stock. That is the other factor." Jim looked unconvinced, so Clay elaborated.

"When, years ago, we started talking about KJ, I valued it at 6 times earnings. Remember? Then, say ten years ago, I started to use 8 times. Now I'm using a 10 times earnings ratio for planning purposes. There is no assurance that the IRS would agree with that. Companies like KJ that are in the public domain are selling from 15 to 30 times earnings. I know it is difficult to compare a listed or publicly held company with KJ, but the IRS may try to do so."

"So what you are telling us," said Kate, "is to make hay while the sun shines. Give now while we can establish a reasonable value, because things may get worse later."

"Yes." Clay looked tired. "You've got it, Kate. And I am just plain beat. How about that swim now? Then dinner."

The Estate Freeze Revisited

The next meeting began next morning at ten-thirty. The day promised to be a hot one, an appropriate time to re-visit the freeze concept. Clay began with the observation that the best way to reduce estate taxes was not to own the property in the first place. This premise leads to the *concept of giving future growth to heirs now*, instead of waiting for Uncle Sam to tax it.

After reminding Kate and Jim of the general idea, he gave them a description of the various forms a "freeze" might take in their case. "Start with the preferred stock freeze. It does not work with a Subchapter S corporation, but it is a good example of the concept. Right now KJ has a weighted five-year average earnings of $3.8 million. Using a price:earnings ratio of ten to one, you come up with a value, conservatively, of $38 million and growing.

"Say you recapitalize and create an issue of $20 million of 10 percent preferred stock. This is paid out as a tax-free stock dividend, of which you own 57 percent. Before the transaction your common stock is worth about $38 per share, assuming 1,000,000 shares outstanding. Issuing the $20 million of preferred cuts the total value of the common from $38 million to $18 million, or $18 per share. You can give away more common stock, more growth, than before. You and the children would receive preferred dividends totaling $1.7 million before taxes. Bob Lewis would receive the remaining $300,000 of preferred dividends because of his 15 percent ownership. Your family would have about $1.2 million left of your dividends after income taxes.

"The $1.2 million would allow you and the children to pay gift tax on major gifts of the common, growth stock at $18 per share. The children would pay part of the tax under the net gift concept I explained previously."

"Are you suggesting that we actually *do* this, pay dividends of $2 million per year?" Jim asked.

"No, I would use preferred stock only if for some reason Subchapter S was not available and, even then, only in an unusual case. One such case might be a smaller corporation where the owners' compensation would just about be replaced by the preferred stock dividend. But not in your case."

"Okay, let's go on," said Clay. "You are already familiar with selling part of your stock to the children, which you did ten years ago. The mechanics of a sale of stock in a Subchapter S company are the same as then: Essentially you sell to the children payable over a period of ten to twenty years, and they pay you out of dividends. The sale price is established by expert appraisal and you receive secured promissory notes for the deferred part of the sale price. Your children have enough independent net worth to make this a realistic transaction. The notes are appraised too."

Clay summed up: "As long as the company's price:earnings ratio is in the area of eight to twelve times earnings, the dividend income will be enough to pay the debt service on the long-term note for the purchase price. This is the most effective freeze mechanism I can think of for an S Corporation."

"Clay," said Kate, "now we have heard all this, what in general do you think we should do?"

"I'll come up with detailed written suggestions later, but here is what it looks like as of now:

1. Get at least one expert appraisal of KJ, for the voting stock and for the nonvoting stock.

2. Continue your annual gifts of nonvoting stock to the children and grandchildren.

3. Call Joe Warren about more joint life insurance to be purchased in a tax-free trust. Don't get the kind that is paid up in 10 or 12 years. Get the kind where you pay until you both die. I'd think in terms of another $10 or $20 million if it's available.

4. Sell 150,000 to 200,000 shares of nonvoting stock to the children. This entails paying out an additional tax-free Subchapter S dividend, some of which you can loan back to the company if it needs cash at some future point.

5. In terms of management succession, I would expand stock ownership among key employees and get another two or three experienced busi-

ness persons on the board of directors. Pay them what they are worth. Give them deferred compensation if they would prefer that. Consider issuing some restricted stock to them and to the other directors to give them a long-term incentive."

He stopped momentarily, and then concluded. "I guess that is where I come out at this point. Sorry I don't have any magic potions for you."

Conclusion: Solving the Problem of Estate Planning for a Small Business "Colossus"

This chapter presents the most difficult of all Clay Hannon's efforts for the Wolczk family and KJ Electronic Devices, Inc.

Chapter 20 of this book deals with a relatively small business, whose owners are around forty years old, and the business has a fairly low tax value. Things are malleable, too, so the "tripod" approach of marital-deduction will, tax-free insurance trusts, and gifts to children yields a good solution to the limited problems then existing and reasonably foreseeable.

Chapter 21 presents problems that are more difficult, but they still susceptible to solution if Jim and Kate really act on Clay's advice. Continuing gifts, increased insurance, and either a preferred stock freeze for a C corporation or a sale of nonvoting stock for an S corporation would have enabled the Wolczks to eliminate much of the future growth from their estates. Insurance funding would easily handle the taxes on retained assets and the frozen value of the business.

If Jim and Kate did what Clay suggested at ages 40 and 50—i.e., adopt a gift program, then sell a major part of the balance of KJ stock to the children—there would really be no colossus stage from an estate-tax standpoint. But in the real world things rarely happen just as planned. Things go awry. People don't want to devote major time and resources to planning for a death that may be 30 or 40 years in the future. They refrain from making gifts because they don't want to enrich and perhaps spoil the children. People get divorced, or hang back in fear of divorce. Or they just do not believe in the long-term growth prospects that are projected at the earlier stages; most often, they are right. Perhaps only one in five hundred family businesses ever reaches the colossus stage—say $10 or $12 million of value and up, and still growing. But when you do wind up with a colossus and time is running out, the options are greatly reduced. The facile solution is not there.

So at the close of Sunday's meeting at his summer home, Clay said he would send them a specific written recommendation. He was admittedly stalling for time. Clay knew the Wolczks well, but he had to think through how their particular outlook on life would affect his answer. There are three general approaches to the colossus situation. In fact, you get three answers, depending on which philosophic approach you assume. These are the three possible approaches:

Approach 1: Keep it in the Family. The philosophy, or desire if you want to call it that, is to keep the Colossus closely within the family. In this case, Jim and Kate would have to prepare either to pay a major tax on the value at death of the survivor of them or do something drastic to eliminate growth from their estate.

Approach 2: Bring in Employees as the Family's Partners. The second approach is to broaden out ownership among employees. Bob Lewis and of course Molly Wolczk, will be key factors here, but other key people will have to be in on the deal, too. This broadens out ownership and thereby reduces the estate growth, but it can also provide a broad, stable management base to enable the colossus to pay the deferred estate taxes through redemption of stock.

Very likely the Wolczk family would here consider broad employee participation by way of an ESOP or a stock bonus plan, but the long-term economic effects of these plans must be carefully analyzed. They are not as rosy as they may seem at first blush.

Approach 3. Give Away Part of the Business as a Charitable Bequest. A third option, very desirable to some, is the charitable approach. The narrow family control of the first approach and the employee participation of the second do not appeal. Using Kay Jim Electronic Devices to do good works might be the answer. As Clay told his clients, a charitable gift or bequest of nonvoting stock can save taxes. "Would you rather Notre Dame had the money, or Uncle Sam?"

Mixing Approaches. Can Clay daub out a mix of the foregoing? Possibly. But mixing estate philosophies can lead to a quagmire because it is so difficult to forecast future events. In other words, you really cannot fine tune so complex a mixture.

As Clay thought about it, he could not see how the employee ownership approach or the charitable approach really fit in with Kate and Jim's real wishes. Be charitable? Yes. Give employees some interest in the company? Yes. But not the whole way. No. The Wolczks are family oriented and if possible they want to keep KJ in the family. Approach One is what Clay chose for his recommendation. A description follows.

Clay's Recommendation for the Wolczk Family

What do you do with a colossus, a large successful company with a promise of continued growth? Given the present state of America's economy vis-a-vis foreign competition, the United States should pin a medal on each of you and encourage you to keep on growing as fast as you can. Nay! Wrong! The formal policy of America is to break up aggregations of wealth, to keep it from being passed to future generation. This is the purpose of the gift tax, estate-tax, and generation skipping tax. Uncle Sam joined your firm as a senior partner because he does not want KJ to go on to future generations of your family.

If we could know the future at age 40, if we could be sure that a business would succeed and grow for years on end, we could take early steps to avoid or defer such taxes. But that time is long gone. When a business reaches a value of $12 to $15 million and up and is still growing, it is what I call a colossus. Kay Jim Electronic Devices, Inc. is just such a colossus. What do you do with it?

Sell? Merge? No. You don't want to do that. You want KJ to remain an independent entity.

Issue some stock to the public to create a market? You don't want to do that either. Selling stock is a very expensive way to get capital and funds for estate-taxes if all the costs are considered. Moreover, you don't want the estate-tax value of your remaining stock to be set by the whims of a fluctuating over-the-counter market. Going public may be nice for those who want to sugar off, get rich in a hurry, but not for the Wolczk family.

Create an ESOP and let the employees own most of the business? This is appropriate in some cases, but the regulations and red tape would stifle KJ. You have to move fast. If the regulators and lawyers are to take over and run your business, it's all over.

Give most of KJ to a charity? As in the case of an ESOP, independence and the ability to move quickly are hindered by the legitimate interests of the charitable owner.

We have discussed all these things, but none fit your case. You have told me you want KJ to remain in the family's control for the indefinite future. You are not averse to having part of the stock owned by valuable employees at all levels. Here is the specific program I recommend to you:

1. Distribute to the Shareholders Part of Your Accumulated Adjustment Account of Already-Taxed, Accumulated Subchapter S Earnings. You and the children should keep the funds in a special tax reserve account. This will reduce the net worth of the company.

2. After This, Have the Company Appraised. Make sure the appraisal is done by a professional appraisal company and by an investment banking firm, and that it includes values for the voting stock and nonvoting stock. This appraisal will be expensive, but worthwhile. My firm will retain the appraisers so that their work product will come under the attorney-client privilege.

3. Sell Stock to the Children. You now own 100,000 shares of voting common stock and 470,000 shares of nonvoting stock of KJ. On the basis of our recent appraisal, it is worth $37 per share, and earnings on an after-tax basis are $4.46 per share. I propose a leveraged buyout by the other shareholders (children and COO Bob Lewis) on these assumptions:

- Price: $37.00 per share (subject to additional appraisal).
- Terms: a secured note amortized over 20 years with interest at 10 percent; this results in an annual constant payment of 11.58 percent.
- Earnings coverage: three times. In other words, the purchasers' annual Subchapter S income, after providing for tax, must be at least three times the amortization they owe to you as sellers. This cushion provides safety including some leeway in the event the tax rules are changed again.
- Your after-tax cash income will increase, and you can, in an emergency, make cash available to KJ by way of interest-bearing loans; the cash you receive and invest will act as a fund to pay estate-taxes.
- The notes to you from the children and Bob are secured by a pledge of all their stock, including the stock they now own, until the notes are completely paid off. These notes must be appraised too, to make sure that they equal the value of the stock sold.

On this basis you can sell 223,800 shares (49,000 voting and 174,800 nonvoting) to the children and Bob Lewis. The deal would be summarized as follows:

Sell 228,500 shares at $37	$8,454,500 total price
Debt service over 20 years with interest at 10%, quarterly	$ 979,000 per year
Total shares then owned by purchasers (228,500 plus 430,000)	658,500 shares
Tax-free Subchapter S distributions per year to fund debt service	979,000 per year
After-tax Subchapter S income on KJ stock owned by purchasers (658,500 times $4.46)	2,937,000 per year
Coverage ratio	three to one

You will note that the purchasers' share of current corporate after-tax income is three times the debt-service requirement. This allows for a 67 percent decrease in dividends before the ability to pay the note is impaired. It also allows for the fact that the IRS may change the rules on deductibility of the interest the children and Bob will pay you, or make some other adverse change in the tax rules.

What does this transaction do? It freezes the value of the KJ stock sold and permits you to accumulate a fund of liquid assets to pay the estate-tax on the notes and your remaining stock and other assets. An installment sale note over $5 million may run into problems with the IRS and this must be addressed.

The effectiveness of such a transaction depends on the continuation of Subchapter S status, the continuing ability of the company's earnings to pay for the stock without a double tax. It also depends on no change in the tax laws regarding deductibility of the interest; we have to plan carefully for changes in the tax laws but the Company's rate of growth justifies some risk.

4. Keep the 51,000 Remaining Shares of Voting Common Stock to Provide You with a 51 Percent Controlling Vote as Long as You Want It. This stock should be in a revocable living trust so that it passes, without probate, to the person or persons you want to control KJ. For instance, if you want Molly and/or Bob to have control, the living trust would provide for immediate passage of the right to vote 51,000 shares of voting stock to them in the event both of you died. There would be no delay due to the requirement of probating a will.

5. Change Your Wills to Protect Your Voting Stock. Each of you will own 25,500 shares of voting stock, and your current wills leave such shares to the other. Change your wills now so that the trust referred to above transfers at your death such voting stock to the other in trust with income for life. This allows the surviving spouse to (a) elect to take the stock estate-tax-free (at the cost of having the whole 51,000 shares taxed in the survivor's estate), or (b) elect to pay the estate-tax on the 25,500 shares at the first death and so keep all this future value growth of those shares out of the survivor's estate. The beauty of the election is that the survivor of you has a "second look" at the situation then. It is difficult for us to now predict the facts and the needs of the future. In either event, the surviving spouse would be the trustee of the trust and vote the 51,000 shares as long as desired. In addition, the survivor of you can select the person or persons to have the 51 percent control in the future by giving or willing his or her 25,500 shares and by exercising the power to direct where the 25,500 shares in the trust are to go after the survivor's death.

6. Keep on Giving the Balance of Your Non-Voting Stock to the Children and Grandchildren at the Rate of $20,000 Worth per Year Each. Consider gifts to the children's spouses, too.

7. Finally, Set Up a Fall Back Charitable Gift. This is a different way to get a second look at the situation. Remember the survivor of you will own the proceeds of the sale paid up to that point, plus the balance of the $8,454,000 of notes. The notes are assets subject to estate-tax and to income tax as the payments are made to the estate of the survivor. If the facts at that time indicate a hardship in paying estate taxes, the *survivors' heirs* can disclaim part of the bequest of the notes and have them instead go to a charitable residuary gift. This saves estate-taxes if necessary. Having the notes go to a charity will not destroy the Subchapter S election, as would a charitable gift of stock. (Your own private foundation would not be a suitable recipient for such a charitable gift.)

8. Summary of Sale of Stock. In short, I am recommending to you a form of LBO where the other shareholders, not the corporation, purchase your stock at appraised value. This freezes the value of the stock by translating it into notes of fixed face value. Then the notes are taxed as part of your estates, but only at the current value. The future growth belongs to the children, grandchildren, and key employees who purchase from you. There is a cost to this. The cost is the income tax complexity of the transaction, accentuated by the risk of future tax law changes. Far overbalancing this income-tax cost is the liquidity saving resulting from the freeze of value of your interest in KJ.

Epilogue

How should you as the owner of a closely held business view the succession of that business wealth to another generation? The case study in Part 6 presented issues and ways of looking at the problems of succession. You should now have a feel for the effect of a flow of growth, and for the problems in your path.

Concepts such as the tripod and the freeze are presented for your consideration, but you should put them into effect only with professional advice.

The theme of our analysis is based on two facts of equal importance. First, succession to wealth and the continuation of a business depend on management. Management must be selected, trained, compensated, and given incentive to remain with the business.

Second, the compounding effect of growth over a generation, growth that ultimately may be subject to estate-taxes of 55 percent to 60 percent. This book examines the case of KJ and its long-term growth rate of 15 percent. We picked 15 percent because it brings KJ's value from $1 million to $38 million in one generation and allows us to discuss business of varying sizes. But even if 15 percent seems far-fetched for a given business now, consider the fact that mere historic inflation gives a dollar-value growth of around 5 percent a year. Add a point or two to account for real growth, and you have a rate that will compound greatly over a generation. A business worth $1 million when the owners are age 40 and that grows at only 7 percent for a 40-year life expectancy of the surviving spouse will be worth $15 million, and the tax on that will be over $7 million.

The growth fact is most important because, as the book repeatedly points out, Uncle Sam wants to be a senior partner in that growth at each generation. You can deal with this fact in two ways:

- Divert growth to the next generation by way of gifts, freezes, investment partnerships, and generation-skipping trusts.
- Provide liquidity for the ultimate tax growth that remains in the owners' names by use of insurance trusts, current distributions of income, and build-up of family wealth outside the business entity.

Only after you have done your best with these concepts do the redemptions to pay estate-taxes and long-term tax payment options become the prime focus. Of course, there are some tradeoffs: the cost of accumulating more liquid assets and insurance may exceed the cost and risk of a fourteen year deferred estate-tax payment.

Underlying this whole book is the importance of the Subchapter S election where a corporate business is involved. If the Wolczk family ever has to sell KJ, the cost of not being an S corporation will be enormous. But even if the business is never sold, the elimination of the double-tax via Subchapter S is crucial. When one gets to the colossus stage, a freeze using preferred stock would hardly ever make sense, whereas a freeze by selling S corporation stock to the family always remains viable.

It has been said before, but we'll say it again: this book is designed to be read by the business owner who wishes to develop ideas and gain information on succession planning. It is not a law book, nor is it intended to give legal or tax advice. If succession planning for your business is important enough to you that you would buy and read this book, it is also important enough for you to implement your plan correctly. Consult your professional advisors before taking specific actions. You will need their advice, for the tax and business laws contain many traps and fine points purposely not covered in this book of general ideas and philosophy.

One final word. If 39-years of estate planning has taught me anything, it is the value of involving your spouse in the whole process. Jim and Kate Wolczk are presented as a team in the estate planning process to illustrate my belief in the truth of this final word of advice.

                                        George C. Shattuck
                                        Cazenovia, New York

Glossary

C Corporation: A corporation which does not pass its income out to share-holders, but is taxed as a separate entity at tax rates up to 34 percent under Subchapter C of the Internal Revenue Code. Compare with S Corporation.

Closely-Held Business: A general term, here meant to describe a business owned by one owner or family, or by several unrelated persons or families.

Exclusion: This refers to the $10,000 one can give per person per year. You can just "exclude" this gift from consideration for tax purposes. It is referred to as "the $10,000 exclusion." The spouse can join and make it $20,000 per year per person.

Exemption: Our so called "exemption" is really a credit of $192,000 against the federal tax on the first $600,000 of taxable estate. Thus, it reduces tax at the lowest brackets, rather than the highest, which would be the case with a true exemption. Our word "exemption" is really a shorthand way of expressing the credit.

Family Business: Included in the concept of a closely held business (see above) but one basically owned or controlled by a single family.

Freeze: Transaction or series of transactions in which the owners receive the current value in a preferred interest and their beneficiaries own all or a major part of the future growth in value.

IRS: The IRS as used here, means the total body of laws, regulations, rulings, and agents' manuals which govern the enforcement and collective workings of the Internal Revenue Service.

Marital Deduction: A deduction for gift and estate tax purposes equal to the value of property transferred to a spouse or a trust for the spouse.

Rule of 72: A rule of thumb that a dollar invested at a given rate of interest will double in 72 ÷ the interest rate. Example: at 6 percent growth per year, an invested amount doubles in about 12 years. Try it on your calculator.

S Corporation: A corporation which has elected to have its income taxed directly to the shareholders, avoiding a corporate tax. See *Subchapter S* (below). Compare with a *C Corporation* which pays a tax on its income tax rates up to 34 percent.

Subchapter S: A provision of the Internal Revenue Code, and of many state laws, which permits shareholders of an electing corporation to report its income and losses on their returns, avoiding a tax at the corporate level.

$10,000 Exclusion: See *Exclusion.*

$600,000 Exemption: See *Exemption.*

Index

$10,000 annual exclusion
  as freeze device, 93, 96
  effect of inflation, 27
  explained, 6, 27
  gift to a trust, 45, 227
  illustrated, 22, 23, 25
  use of, 226, 227, 265, 275, 277
$600,000 exemption
  as freeze device, 89, 93
  effect of inflation, 27, 29
  explained, 4, 6, 222, 223
  illustrated, 7, 11, 23
  use of, 11, 14, 30, 227, 257

A

AAA account, 68, 243, 253, 280
Accumulated earnings tax
  liability potential, 43, 67
Appraisal
  contents, 73, 75, 77
  need for, 73, 86, 87, 147, 253, 277, 280
  stock in employee plan, 183, 185
Appraisal of value
  See Appraisal

B

Bequest to Spouse
  See Marital deduction
Bonus Out, 168, 169, 171
Book value
  shareholder agreement, 31, 33, 155, 195, 196
  valuation of business, 76, 78, 80, 84, 230
Buyout
  division among family, 39
  employee's stock, 162, 174–176, 184
  leveraged buyout, 194, 204, 205
  shareholders agreement, 193, 195, 200

Buy sell agreement
  See Redemption agreement
By law
  redemption of stock to pay taxes, 244
  restricting stock transfer, 33, 229
  sample form, 33
Bypass trust
  defined, 13, 14, 222, 241
  illustrated, 12, 13, 225
  sample form, 15, 17
  use of, 14, 222

C

C Corporation
  acquisition, interest deduction, 200
  distribution from, 65, 66, 274
  preferred stock freeze, 90, 98, 124, 144
  sale of assets, 205, 206
Charitable gift or bequest
  generally, 272, 275, 279, 282
  valuing stock, 86
Comparable Companies
  use in valuation, 79–81, 84, 155, 240
Control premium
  valuation, 82, 248
Coverage
  See Dividend Coverage
Creditors
  of corporation, 185, 197
  of donees, 30
  of estate, 56
Cross purchase agreement
  See Redemption Agreement
Crummy trust
  generally, 45, 47
  See taxes, funding for
Cumulative dividend
  use in freeze, 102, 103, 110, 127

D

Directors of corporation
  need for, 209, 211, 236, 237, 266
Disability
  management, 235, 236
  sale of stock, 155, 193, 246
Disclaimer
  general, 16
  marital deduction, 17
Disclaimers
  sample form, 17
  use of, 16
Discount, value
  environmental liability, 83
  investment companies, 85
  key person, 83
  lack of market, 81
  minority interest, 81
  purchase by employee, 157
  untaxed gain, 83
  value, 74, 81, 102
Dividend coverage
  explained, 105, 281
  illustrated 119, 146

E

Employee stock ownership plan
  See ESOP
Employee stock ownership trust
  See ESOP
Employees' incentive
  See Incentive for employees
Environmental liability
  See Discount, value
Equity Dilution
  employee plans, 171, 174, 184
ERISA
  employee stock plans, 163, 189
ESOP
  in general, 171, 174, 175, 179, 183–185,
    273
  sale by estate, 75, 264, 280
  valuing stock owned by, 75, 184
Estate tax
  as cost of business, 3, 21, 231
  tax rates, 3, 4, 57
Estate tax marital deduction
  See Marital deduction

F

Family partnership
  See Partnership, family

Freeze

Freeze
  described, 89, 97, 99, 247, 276
  dividends, 102
  expert counsel, 72, 110, 118, 144
  evaluation of, 123, 126, 133, 145
  gifts as form of, 90
  leverage, 103
  partnership interest, 117, 121
  preferred stock, use of, 100, 107
  qualified payment, 102
  sale of stock as, 111, 115, 252
  valuation, need for, 87, 98, 103, 110, 114

G

Gift splitting, 6
Gift Tax
  general, 6, 21, 93, 275
  marital deduction, 9
Gift to spouse
  See Marital deduction
Gifts
  See $10,000 annual exclusion
  See $600,000 exemption
Gross Estate
  defined, 4
Growth
  gift illustration, 25
  rate of 54, 107, 144
  removal from estate, 21, 71, 89, 276
  tax burden, 4

H

Health care proxy, 212, 237

I

Incentive for key employees
  general, 154, 168, 177, 246, 266
  incentive stock option, 161
  plans compared, 187
  sell stock to, 201
Inflation
  effect on exemptions and exclusions, 27,
    257
Insurance trust
  See Taxes, funding for
Interest on deferred estate taxes, 57
Interest on stock purchase notes, 115, 145

K

Key employees
  See Management

L

LBO, 38, 202, 273
Legal counsel
  Crummy trust, 51, 52
  insurance trust, *see* above
Leverage
  with ESOP, 183
  with life insurance, 38, 47, 48, 240
  with value freeze, 96, 103, 145
Leveraged buyout
  See LBO
Limited liability company
  general, 66, 117
  in freeze, 90, 118, 124
Living trust, 209, 210, 282
Living will, 212
LLC
  See Limited liability, company

M

Management
  continuance of business, 151, 202, 210,
    220, 235
  discount on value, 83
  incentive for, 153, 235, 236, 262, 263,
    266
  ownership, 35, 37, 38, 193
Married person
  See Marital deductions
  See Gift splitting
Marital deduction
  deferral of tax, 35, 50, 266
  disclaimer of
    See Disclaimer
  explained, 9–11, 14, 220, 241
  sample form, 14
  unlimited deduction, 4, 227, 264
Medicaid, 18

N

Non-voting stock
  charitable gift, 275
  employee plans, 188
  gift of, 30, 91, 95, 124, 277, 282
  transfer restricted, 30, 32, 193, 194

P

Partnership
  buy-sell agreement, 194, 200
  deferral of tax on, 60

Partnership (*cont'd.*)
  family, 44, 120, 257, 258
  freeze transaction, 90, 118, 144, 147, 257
  gift of, 285
  limited or general, 120
  management of, 210
  source of tax funding, 68
  value of, 75
Penalties
  See Tax penalties
Phantom stock, 162, 172, 187–192
Power of attorney, 212, 237, 238
Preferred stock
  earnings coverage, 105, 119, 145
  freeze, 90, 99, 125, 132, 247, 255
  issuance tax free, 110
  valuation, 101–103
Price earnings ratio, 77, 80, 264, 276
Public offering, 264, 274

Q

Qualified payment
  See freeze, id.

R

Redemption agreement
  control tax value, 201
  cross purchase agreement, 197
  problems created, 196
Redemption of stock, 66, 67, 197, 243, 269
Restricted stock
  incentive device, 153, 156, 164, 177,
    187–190
  succession plan, 202
  tax election, 157, 158

S

S Corporation
  benefits, 206, 227
  freeze by sale of, 90, 97, 111, 124, 252
  freeze, illustrated, 133
  funding of estate tax, 67, 243, 280
  qualified stock plan, 180
Shadow stock
  See Phantom stock
State estate taxes, 1, 53, 58, 260
Stock, restricted
  See Restricted stock
Stock bonus plan
  See ESOP
  generally, 171, 174, 179, 182, 187–190
  sale of stock to, 264, 273

Stock options, 154, 160–162, 187–190, 247
Stock redemption
  See Redemption of stock

T

Tax deferral
  See Tax payment
Tax expert
  use in freeze transaction, 72
Tax Payment
  deferral of, 55, 58, 59, 61, 197, 269–271
  due date, 5, 53
  funding for, 43, 55, 65
  See Taxes, funding for
Tax Penalties, 73, 86, 87, 162, 200

Taxes, funding for
  accumulation of funds, 43, 267
  last to die insurance, 50, 228, 242–245
  life insurance, 37, 44, 124, 220, 268
  limits of, 37
  trust, use of, 47, 50, 227, 230

V

Value
  defined, 74
  generally, *See* Appraisal
Voting stock
  ESOP, 188
  management ownership, 36, 207, 210
  retain control, 37, 90, 194, 274, 277, 282
  valuing stock, 82